W9-DGM-496

INTERPRETATION: MEDIEVAL AND MODERN

The essays in this volume, from the 1992 J.A.W. Bennett Symposium, explore varied aspects of interpretation of texts in Middle English literature, and, in one case, a modern interpretation of medieval material. A study of the dissenting hermeneutics of the Lollards as against scholastic synthesis and an analysis of the role of medieval figures in Caryl Churchill's play, *Top Girls*, open the volume. A section then illustrates the exploitation of the term *interpres* by Aldhelm and Bede, the problem of interpreting popular narrative poetry by taking into account the dynamics of performance, and the role of the translator as 'cross-cultural go-between'. A discussion of cases of authorial awareness *of* genres and *by* genres is followed by an examination of interpretative examples in the *Decameron* and by an analysis of the hermeneutical problems of mystical experience. The two final essays deal with the idea of *pictura ut poesis* in Alan of Lille and its interpretative consequences, and with the meaning of *fidus interpres* from Horace to Pandarus.

Piero Boitani / Anna Torti (eds.)

INTERPRETATION: MEDIEVAL AND MODERN

The J.A.W. Bennett Memorial Lectures
Eighth Series
Perugia, 1992

D. S. Brewer

First published 1993 by D. S. Brewer, Cambridge

D. S. Brewer is an imprint of Boydell & Brewer Ltd
PO Box 9, Woodbridge, Suffolk IP12 3DF, UK
and of Boydell & Brewer Inc.
PO Box 41026, Rochester, NY 14604, USA

ISBN 0 85991 382 1

British Library Cataloguing-in-Publication Data
Interpretation: Medieval and Modern. - (J.A.W. Bennett
Memorial Lectures)
I. Boitani, Piero II. Torti, Anna III. Series
820.109
ISBN 0-85991-382-1

Library of Congress Cataloging-in-Publication Data
Interpretation, medieval and modern / Piero Boitani, Anna Torti
(eds.).
p. cm.
"The J.A.W. Bennett Memorial lectures, eighth series,
Perugia, 1992."
Includes bibliographical references (p.) and index.
ISBN 0-85991-382-1 (acid-free paper)
1. Literature, Medieval - History and criticism. I. Boitani,
Piero. II. Torti, Anna.
PN671.I65 1993
809'.02 - dc20 93-21537

This publication is printed on acid-free paper

Printed in Great Britain by
St Edmundsbury Press Ltd, Bury St Edmunds, Suffolk

Contents

Contributors

Rita Copeland	University of Minnesota
Renate Haas	Pädagogische Hochschule Kiel
George H. Brown	Stanford University
Karl Reichl	University of Bonn
Juliette Dor	University of Liège
H. Ansgar Kelly	University of California, Los Angeles
Francesco Bruni	University of Venice
Vincent Gillespie	University of Oxford
James Simpson	University of Cambridge
John V. Fleming	Princeton University

Preface

The eighth Symposium dedicated to the memory of J.A.W. Bennett took place in Perugia, 6–8 April 1992, thanks to the continuing generosity of the City of Perugia and of the Regional Council of Umbria, and in particular to the warm support of President Francesco Ghirelli.

Ten scholars from various European countries and the United States gathered to discuss the problem of medieval theories of interpretation and of modern approaches to medieval texts, and the present volume contains the revised versions of the lectures delivered during the Symposium.

The collection opens with an essay by Rita Copeland, who suggests that scholastic efforts to legitimize the language of human rhetoric by containing it within the fixed domain of the literal sense represented an impossible solution to questions which were in fact raised again by the hermeneutics of the Lollards. The 'modern' counterpart to this is Renate Haas's analysis of Caryl Churchill's play *Top Girls* to throw light on the stories of Pope Joan and Griselda while challenging traditional male constructions of famous women figures.

With George Brown's essay on the *interpres* in Aldhelm and Bede the volume goes back to the historical foundations of medieval interpretation, while Karl Reichl warns modern readers of the dangers of approaching medieval popular narratives as if they were purely written texts, and Juliette Dor turns to the well-known topos of the *traduttore-traditore*, seeing the translator as cross-cultural go-between.

H.Ansgar Kelly examines some of the ways in which interpretation followed generic ideas of structure and content in the Middle Ages. Francesco Bruni picks up this theme by reading six tales from the *Decameron* and contrasting them to the theories expounded by Boccaccio in the *Genealogie*. Vincent Gillespie maintains that mystical writing can only be about thresholds of language, perception, and interpretation.

James Simpson discusses the aesthetic idea of *pictura ut poesis* in Alan of Lille's *De Planctu Naturae* and *Anticlaudianus* in order to question Robert Jordan's account of medieval and Chaucerian poetics. John Fleming closes the volume with a survey of the role of the *fidus interpres* from Horace through Boethius to Chaucer's *Troilus*, believing that the latter is an English 'interpretation' of the epic poem that the young Lollius would have written had he followed Horace's advice.

Interpretation is, as many theorists since Scotus Eriugena have maintained, infinite, but also – according to one of Umberto Eco's latest books – limited. We hope that this collection will fall somewhere between the two extremes of the pendulum's swing.

31 October 1992

Anna Torti
Piero Boitani

RHETORIC AND THE POLITICS OF THE LITERAL SENSE IN MEDIEVAL LITERARY THEORY: AQUINAS, WYCLIF, AND THE LOLLARDS

RITA COPELAND

It is well known that late medieval literary theory owes much to Aquinas's reconciliation of human rhetoric with the divine revelation of truth in the text of Scripture. Aquinas and those theorists who followed his method accomplished this *rapprochement* by redrawing the boundaries between the literal and the spiritual senses of Scripture and assimilating rhetorical language to the literal sense. Aquinas's critical move has been much studied for its impact on the exegetical theory and practice of the thirteenth and fourteenth centuries, especially for its new emphasis on the contributions of human authors to Scriptural discourse. But at what cost to rhetoric was this remarkable synthesis achieved? Medieval attempts to reconcile rhetorical figures and tropes with the literal sense left many conflicts about the status of rhetoric unresolved. In this essay I want to consider how the role of rhetoric was reconfigured as theories of the literal sense evolved from the relatively restricted context of clerical academic theory to the popular polemics of Wycliffite hermeneutics. I suggest here that scholastic efforts to legitimize the language of human rhetoric by containing it within the fixed domain of the literal sense represented an impossible solution to what was already an impossible problem: how can rhetorical language, the inherent nature of which is indirection and ambiguity, have a place in the truthful discourse of Scripture? The internal contradictions of the scholastic synthesis were re-opened and brought to the foreground in the dissenting hermeneutics of the Lollards, where the literal sense became a site of political contest. In the second part of this essay I will consider how Wycliffite critical theory drives a new wedge between rhetoric and the literal sense by representing rhetoric as a constraint from which the open, literal meaning of the text must be liberated.

The major assumptions of scholastic criticism on figurative language in the Bible emerge out of early medieval thought about figurative discourse. Bede's treatise *De schematibus et tropis* represents a mid-point, both chronologically and theoretically, between antique and high medieval articulations of the relationship between Scriptural symbolism and rhetorical language, what Bede calls *allegoria in factis* and *allegoria in verbis*.[1] As Armand Strubel shows, Bede advances on Augustine's semiotics by explicitly introducing and considering the place of rhetorical figuration in Scripture.[2] In *De doctrina Christiana* 2. 10. 15, in his discussion of the *signum proprium* and the *signum translatum*, Augustine certainly infers the existence of a level of rhetorical figuration in Scripture, but he does not pursue this question, and does not develop a theoretical explanation for a relationship between *signa translata* (things that symbolize other things, such as the ox that is understood to stand for the evangelist; see Deut. 25: 4 and I Cor. 9: 9), and the indirection or doubleness that characterizes rhetorical tropes. In *De Trinitate* 15. 9. 15 he seems to deny the trope allegory its rhetorical-linguistic claims, defining it instead as that which is found, not in words, but in historical events themselves.[3]

While drawing on Augustinian sign theory, Bede locates his whole discussion of figurative meaning under the aegis of rhetoric. His definition of the trope is consistent with ancient and early medieval rhetorical and grammatical treatments of the term: 'Tropus est dictio translata a propria significatione ad non propriam similitudinem ornatus necessitatisve causa' ('A trope is an expression which has been transferred from its proper meaning and understood in a sense which it does not have, either from necessity or for sake of ornamentation').[4] In this system allegory is the master trope, defined also in traditional rhetorical-grammatical terms as that 'which means something other than what it

[1] See Armand Strubel, ' "Allegoria in factis" et "allegoria in verbis" ', *Poétique* 23 (1975) 342–57.

[2] While Bede's *De schematibus* has been classified both as a rhetorical and as a grammatical treatise, his concern is with a body of figures traditionally associated with rhetoric. By late antiquity, however, the figures of speech could be treated under grammar, as in Donatus's *Barbarismus*, or under rhetoric, as in Martianus Capella's *De nuptiis Mercurii et Philologiae* 5, or under both, as in Isidore's *Etymologiae* I–II. See the discussions about classifying Bede's treatise in Martin Irvine, 'Bede the Grammarian and the Scope of Grammatical Studies in Eighth-Century Northumbria', *Anglo-Saxon England* 15 (1986), p. 36, and James J. Murphy, *Rhetoric in the Middle Ages* (Berkeley and Los Angeles, 1974), p. 77. See also the excellent study of Bede's indebtedness to late classical rhetoric by Roger Ray, 'Bede and Cicero', *Anglo-Saxon England* 16 (1987) 1–15. Ray suggests that Bede may have known Cicero's *De inventione*.

[3] 'Sed ubi allegoriam nominauit apostolus non in uerbis eam reperit sed in facto cum ex duobus filiis Abrahae, uno de ancilla, altero de libera, quod non dictum sed etiam factum fuit duo testamenta intellegenda monstrauit'. *De Trinitate* (15. 9. 5), ed. W. J. Mountain, *CCSL* 50 (Turnhout, 1968).

[4] Text and translation from Calvin Kendall, ed. and trans., *Libri II De arte Metrica et De schematibus et tropis; The Art of Poetry and Rhetoric*, Bibliotheca Germanica, ser. nova, vol. 2 (Saarbrücken, 1991), pp. 168, 169. Cf. Isidore, *Etymologiae* I. 37. 1; *Ad Herennium* 4. 31. 42; Quintilian, *Institutio oratoria* 8. 6. 1.

says' ('quo aliut significatur quam dicitur').[5] But under the influence of Origen and Augustine, Bede introduces a dialectical doubling of the levels of allegorical operation: 'Notandum sane quod allegoria aliquando factis, aliquando verbis tantum modo fit' ('It is important to observe that allegory is sometimes historical and sometimes purely verbal').[6] According to Bede at this point in his exposition, purely verbal allegory, or *allegoria in verbis*, is distinguished from historical or factual allegory, *allegoria in factis*, on the basis of one important principle: figuration may function at several levels and in several modes in the text of Scripture, but allegory in its purely rhetorical form has no 'proper' or 'literal' sense of its own. In the example given from Isaiah 11: 1, 'There shall come forth a rod out of the root of Jesse, and a flower shall rise up out of his root', the root, rod, and flower may be likened, for the purpose of interpretation, to the house of David, the Virgin, and Christ, but they have no literal, and in this sense, historical meaning, since the enunciation has no necessary referent in reality. The verbal images bear only a contingent poetic (what we can loosely call metaphorical) resemblance to spiritual truths. Unlike *allegoria in factis*, in which a historical event in Scripture (such as Abraham's two sons) can also point beyond itself in typological fashion to another meaning (in this case to symbolize the Old and New Testaments), *allegoria in verbis* has no facticity of its own, but exists purely as a rhetorical figure to point beyond itself.[7] As Calvin Kendall puts it, verbal allegory is not bivalent in the way that factual allegory is, since the meanings of verbal allegory are to be found only in the interpretations placed on it.[8] The human imagination constructs a contingent relationship of resemblance or similitude between the verbal image and historical-theological realities.

But Bede also seems to lose the force of the distinction that he makes between verbal and historical allegory by allowing verbal allegory (and in this sense, rhetorical tropes in general) a place among the various spiritual levels of Scripture. In the following portion of his exposition, where he offers a version of the traditional four senses of Scriptural interpretation (historical and typological prefiguration, and the moral and anagogical senses), he permits *allegoria in verbis* to perform the same function as historical allegory by asserting that it can express figuratively the moral and anagogical senses of Scripture. Here he confuses the very

5 Kendall, pp. 192, 199; and see Kendall's introduction, p. 24.

6 Kendall, pp. 196, 201.

7 See Strubel, ' "Allegoria in factis" et "Allegoria in verbis" ', p. 351; and Johan Chydenius, 'La théorie du symbolisme médiéval', *Poétique* 23 (1975), p. 329. Irvine's account of this problem assumes a greater similarity between Bede and Augustine's *De doctrina Christiana* than does Strubel's; see 'Bede the Grammarian', p. 37.

8 Kendall, introduction, p. 27.

issue that he had earlier set out to clarify, for he has inserted human rhetoric (*allegoria in verbis*, with its uni-dimensional and merely contingent value) into the polyvalency of facts, the multiple theological referents that can only be produced and designated within the sacred economy of salvation.[9] Thus Bede actually makes it difficult to differentiate, along absolute lines, the valences of human rhetoric and of events that have spiritual meanings (what Augustine calls *signa translata*, things used as signs of other things).

One way to describe the ambiguities that arise in Bede's influential account is that he is struggling to establish a rapport or even point of contact between two entirely different terminological and theoretical systems, on the one hand the classical rhetorical program of tropes and figures, and on the other hand the Alexandrian hermeneutical system of the three or four levels of Scriptural meaning and interpretation. He attempts to achieve this rapport by doubling one rhetorical category, the master trope allegory, into the pair *allegoria in verbis* and *allegoria in factis*. Verbal allegory, one half of this new pair, he retains under the category of rhetoric; the other new entity, factual or historical allegory, he transfers over to the Alexandrian hermeneutical system, in which the historical sense gives way allegorically to the tropological and anagogical senses.

But the legacy of Bede's attempt to define the function of rhetoric and reconcile the two systems is some confusion among later exegetes rather than a sense of progress towards clarity. The best known example of this is the attempt by Peter of Poitiers (fl.1167–1205), in his *Allegoriae super tabernaculum Moysi*, to accommodate Bede's terminology to contemporary thinking about the importance of the literal sense which was stressed by the Victorine masters Hugh and Andrew. Exegetes continually faced the question of whether thay would include metaphor in the historical-literal sense, and whether prophecy could refer literally to Christ or should be understood as belonging among the mystical senses of Scripture.[10] Peter distinguishes between two classes of signification. In the first, words signify things, either immediately or indirectly through metaphor, the equivalent of Bede's *allegoria quae verbis fit*. In the second class, things signify things, which corresponds with *allegoria in factis*. But in discussing this second class, historical symbolism, he

[9] Strubel, ' "Allegoria in factis" et "Allegoria in verbis" ', p. 352: 'Bède reprend ici, à l'intérieur des distinctions qu'elle fait naître, l'opposition *allegoria in factis* et *in verbis*. Or l'étagement des sens n'est possible qu'à l'intérieur de *l'allegoria in factis*. Si on y introduit l'*allegoria in verbis*, comme le fait Bède, on la place du côté du sens spirituel'.

[10] Beryl Smalley, *The Study of the Bible in the Middle Ages* (Oxford, 1952; reprint Notre Dame, Indiana, 1978), p. 232; on Hugh and Andrew of St Victor see pp. 83–263.

recurs to Bede's definition of *allegoria in verbis* and the example of the root, rod, and flower as allegories of Jesse's race, the Virgin, and Christ. Here he adds an uncomfortable note: 'quidam tamen dicunt hoc esse historiam per metaphorice transsumpta verba narratam' (others, however, consider this to be a metaphorical representation of history).[11] Peter wants to include this example under historical prophecy: and unlike Bede, he seems to think that the presence of verbal allegory does not by itself bar a text from operating through the primary literal sense. Whereas Bede cannot allow verbal allegory any literal referent, Peter of Poitiers, along with his Victorine predecessors as well as later figures such as Stephen Langton, thinks of prophetic metaphor as part of the literal sense, which is the foundation of the text.[12]

The struggles that we see in Bede and among twelfth-century exegetes to define the place of poetic metaphor and other tropes underscore the problems that the claims of rhetoric posed as soon as there was any attempt to account theoretically for its contribution to the construction of meaning in sacred language. Augustine's influential semiotics in the *De doctrina Christiana* skirts the issue. Bede broaches it directly; but his basic assumption that rhetorical figuration serves chiefly an ornamental rather than instrumental function in discourse, that it is a 'clothing' and 'adornment' rather than the substance of speech, impairs his analysis, for on this assumption he is forced to dissociate rhetorical language from any realm of truth, historical or theological.[13] In *The Friar as Critic*, Judson Allen reviews twelfth-century debates about the literal sense and their implications for thirteenth- and fourteenth-century literary criticism. His explanation of the literal sense, that it 'consists of the things to which words refer', summarizes the arguments of theorists like Hugh of St Victor who seek a way to resolve the problems that arise from Augustine's silence and Bede's ambiguity and to reinstate the referential

[11] P. S. Moore and J. A. Corbett, eds., *Allegoriae super tabernaculum Moysi* (Notre Dame, Indiana, 1938), pp. 100–2. See also the editors' discussion of this crux in their introduction, pp. xix–xxiii, where they find the distinction between allegory and history recounted metaphorically to be ambiguous. See also Smalley, *Study of the Bible*, p. 232; and Chydenius, 'La théorie du symbolisme médiéval', pp. 329–30.

[12] See Smalley, *Study of the Bible*, pp. 233–4; and Beryl Smalley, 'Stephen Langton and the Four Senses of Scripture', *Speculum* 6 (1931) 60–76.

[13] 'Quod grammatici Grece "schema" vocant, nos habitum vel formam vel figuram recte nominamus, quia per hoc quodam modo vestitur et ornatur oratio' ('Scholars call an artificial arrangement of words a *schema* in Greek; speakers of Latin properly call such an arrangement a 'habit', or an 'adornment', or a 'figure', because in this way language is so to speak clothed and adorned'), Kendall, pp. 168, 169. On the debasement of rhetoric to a merely ornamental function, see the account of the crisis of oratory that led to the Second Sophistic and rhetoric's later decline in Tzvetan Todorov, *Theories of the Symbol*, trans. Catherine Porter (Ithaca, N.Y., 1982), pp. 60–83.

value of figurative discourse.[14] Hugh intimates this problem when he criticizes those who read only the spiritual sense, for 'then the metaphors and similes, which educate us spiritually, would have been included in the Scriptures by the Holy Spirit in vain'.[15] Allen proposes that in these contexts involving both sacred texts and secular poetry, the 'literal' sense means, in effect, the 'literary' sense, the poetic surface which has an almost integumental exteriority, and which constitutes the most reductionist form of meaning.[16] But Allen's explanation, elegant and powerful as it is, does not address the difficulties that arise out of the theoretical desire to locate and confine rhetoric within the literal sense, especially the critical conflicts that this produces in late medieval polemic about the role of the literal sense as the purveyor of true meaning.

Aquinas's positive contribution to this long debate consists not in the introduction of new ideas, but in the careful attention that he gives to achieving some theoretical consistency among many competing ideas. In his discussions in the *Summa theologiae* and the *Quaestiones quodlibetales* 7 he seeks to clarify the difference between metaphor (including the difficult category of prophetic metaphor) and the various spiritual senses of Scripture. He accomplishes this by articulating principles that had been grasped by earlier writers, notably Hugh of St Victor, but which were not before so precisely expressed.

Aquinas explains the relationship between *allegoria in verbis* and *allegoria in factis* by making a strict demarcation between the domain of words, which are instituted by humans, and things or events of history, which God alone creates and to which he assigns meaning. Scripture can thus have multiple senses, because words constitute the literal sense, and the things to which words refer can give way to a multiplicity of spiritual senses.

> Manifestatio autem vel expressio alicujus veritatis potest fieri de aliquo rebus et verbis; inquantum scilicet verba significant res, et una res potest esse figuras alterius. Auctor autem rerum non solum potest verba accommodare ad aliquid significandum, sed etiam res potest disponere in figuram alterius: et secundum hoc in sacra Scriptura manifestatur veritas duplicitur. Uno modo secundum quod res significantur per verba: et in hoc consistit sensus litteralis. Alio modo secundum quod res sunt figurae aliarum rerum; et in hoc consistit sensus spiritualis, et sic sacrae Scripturae plures sensus competunt.[17]

[14] Judson Boyce Allen, *The Friar as Critic* (Nashville, 1971), p. 11.

[15] *De scripturis* 5. 13, *P.L.* 175. Translation quoted from Smalley, *Study of the Bible*, pp. 93–4.

[16] *The Friar as Critic*, pp. 26–7.

[17] *Questiones Quodlibetales* 7. 6. 14. Text from the Parma edition, vol. 9 (Fiaccadori, 1859); reprint New York, 1949). On this passage, see P. Synave, 'La doctrine de Saint

(The manifestation or expression of these truths can be accomplished either through words or things; that is to say, words signify things, and one thing can be a figure of another thing. Now the author of all things has the power not only to use words to designate things, but to order things in such a way that they serve as figures of other realities; and in this way sacred Scripture manifests truth in a double fashion. At one level, things are signified through words: and this is what constitutes the literal sense. At the second level, things serve as figures of other things; and this constitutes the spiritual sense. And so sacred Scripture can produce multiple senses.)

This effectively clears away the ambiguity of Bede's formulation, for the valences of words are entirely distinguished from the valences of facts. Words themselves cannot supply the spiritual senses of Scripture: only the facts, the historical events ordained by God and 'subject to his providence' are endowed with spiritual and mystical significances beyond themselves.[18] Moreover – and this is Aquinas's definitive answer to the difficulties encountered by earlier generations of exegetes – there are really only two senses of Scripture, the literal and the spiritual (the spiritual can be multiplied according to the Alexandrian divisions of moral, allegorical, and anagogical). The distinctions are clear: the words of Scripture pertain, always and entirely, to the literal sense. There is no slippage, such as Bede allows, of *allegoria in factis* into the domain of linguistic phenomena:

Manifestatio autem quae est per verba, facit sensum historicum sive litteralem; unde totum id ad sensum litteralem pertinet quod ex ipsa verborum significatione recte accipitur.

(*Quaestiones quodlibetales* 7. 16. 15)

(The manifestation [of truth in Scripture] which is accomplished through words produces the historical or literal sense; thus all that is properly understood from the signification of words pertains to the literal sense.)

Words point to things literally, and those things – events, objects, and facts – are ordained to yield up higher truths. This recalls Hugh of St Victor's effort, especially in the *Didascalicon*, to save the literal sense.[19] As Aquinas puts it, everything is grounded in the literal sense, which is

Thomas d'Aquin sur le sense littéral des Écritures', *Revue biblique* 25 (1926), p. 41. Compare also *Summa Theologiae* 1. 1. 10 resp.

[18] 'Sicut enim homo potest adhibere ad aliquid significandum aliquas voces vel aliquas similtudines fictas, ita Deus adhibet ad significationem aliquorum ipsum cursum rerum suae providentiae subjectarum'. *Questiones quodlibetales* 7. 6. 16. See Mark D. Jordan, *Ordering Wisdom: the Hierarchy of Philosophical Discourses in Aquinas* (Notre Dame, Indiana, 1986), pp. 29–30.

[19] *Didascalicon*, ed. C. H. Buttimer (Washington D.C., 1939), book 6, chs. 1–4.

the necessary vehicle of our perception of things and their higher meanings:

> Illa vero significatio qua res significatae per voces, iterum res alias significant, dicitur sensus spiritualis, qui super litteralem fundatur, et eum supponit.
>
> (That meaning, however, whereby the things signified by the words in their turn also signify other things is called the spiritual sense; it is based on and presupposes the literal sense.)[20]

But there is a further dimension to this reasoning: words pertain only to the literal sense, and all that is comprised in linguistic use is part of the literal sense. Thus even rhetorical figures – metaphor, fictive similitude, and parable or rhetorical allegory – as linguistic phenomena, are assimilated to the literal sense:

> Significare autem aliquid per verba vel per similitudines fictas ad significandum tantum ordinatas, non facit nisi sensum litteralem. . . (*Quaestiones quodlibetales* 7. 6. 16)
>
> (Signifying something through words or through fictive similitudes whose purpose is to signify something, produces nothing but the literal sense.)

This of course provides an important solution to Bede's inference that rhetorical allegory, *allegoria in verbis*, has no literal application, a position that later exegetes found difficult to accept, especialy in the case of prophetic metaphor. Aquinas reverses Bede on this: Aquinas's view is that *allegoria in verbis* is a linguistic phenomenon, and thus must have a literal reference. The *Summa* offers a supplemental explanation of this:

> Sensus parabolicus sub litterali continetur, nam per voces significatur aliquid proprie et aliquid figurative. Nec est litteralis sensus ipsa figura, sed id quod est figuratum. (*Summa theologiae* 1. 1. 10 ad 3.)
>
> (The parabolical sense is contained in the literal sense, for words can signify something properly and something figuratively; in the last case the literal sense is not the figure of speech itself, but the *object it figures* [emphasis mine].)

Thus in a metaphorical expression, the immediate sense is not the figure itself, but what the figure represents.[21] As Umberto Eco puts it,

[20] *Summa theologiae* 1. 1. 10. Text from Parma edition vol. 1 (1852; reprint New York, 1948); translation from Blackfriars edition, ed. and trans. Thomas Gilby (New York, London, 1964), vol. 1.

[21] See Albert Blanche, 'Le sens littéral des Écritures d'après Saint Thomas d'Aquin', *Revue Thomiste* 14 (1906), p. 194; cf. Strubel, ' "Allegoria in factis" et "Allegoria in verbis" ', p. 355.

'Parabolic sense. . .is the meaning of a verbal or pictorial image which is so appropriate and so well proportioned to its sense that it proclaims itself to be at one with it'.[22] Aquinas's example is that when Scripture speaks of God's 'arm', the literal sense of this figure of speech is not that God has a physical limb, but that God has the power that is typically ascribed to an arm, that of doing and making (*Summa theologiae* 1. 1. 10 ad 3).

It is this argument and its consequences, the assimilation of rhetorical figuration to the literal sense, that raises profound and, I think, irresolvable problems for the status of rhetoric in Aquinas's system. Aquinas offers a very clear picture of the function of rhetorical figuration in the domain of the literal sense: rhetoric is reduced to a system of signs the only purpose of which is to yield up meaning:

> . . .fictiones poeticae non sunt ad aliud ordinatae nisi ad significandum; unde talis significatio non supergreditur modum litteralis sensus.
>
> (*Quaestiones quodlibetales* 7. 6. 16)
>
> (Poetic fictions have no purpose except to signify; and such signification does not go beyond the literal sense.)

On this view we must enlarge our definition of the literal sense: by the literal sense Aquinas understood every signification which has its immediate origin in words or poetic fictions of which the only *raison d'être* is to serve as signs.[23]

This is a purely mechanical view of rhetorical language. It is strikingly close to Goethe's view of allegory as a rhetorical convention, in counterdistinction to the symbol, which represents the premiere expression of Romanticism's organic aesthetic. For Goethe, allegory (as the master trope of rhetoric) works by signifying directly; its only purpose, as Todorov puts it, is 'to transmit a meaning'. It offers 'an instantaneous passage through the signifying face of the sign toward knowledge of what is signified'.[24] According to Goethe,

> . . .there are. . .works of art that sparkle by virtue of reason, wit, gallantry, and we include in this category all allegorical works as well; of these latter we expect the least, because they destroy our interest in representation itself, and shove the spirit back upon itself, so to speak, and remove from its field of vision all that is truly represented. The allegorical differs from the symbolic in that what the latter designates indirectly, the former designates directly.[25]

22 Umberto Eco, *The Aesthetics of Thomas Aquinas*, trans. Hugh Bredin (Cambridge, Mass., 1988), p. 153.

23 Blanche, 'Le sens littéral des Écritures', p. 194.

24 Todorov, *Theories of the Symbol*, p. 201.

25 Goethe, 'On the Objects of the Plastic Arts', quoted in Todorov, *Theories of the Symbol*, p. 199.

Unlike the symbol, which Goethe describes as exceeding and defying any rational attempt to articulate and exhaust its organic potential for creating meanings, allegory as a rhetorical trope is finite in its meanings and reducible to a simple code to which we need only the interpretive key:

> In [allegory] there is more of accident and caprice, inasmuch as the meaning of the sign must be first communicated to us before we know what it is to signify; what idea, for instance, is attached to the green colour, which has been appropriated to hope?[26]

We see this principle in Aquinas's understanding of rhetorical figuration or the parabolic sense. Scriptural parable, including prophetic metaphor, is an established and conventional code, a system of poetic usages that can be unlocked by any trained reader. Thus the goat of Daniel 8 can be understood immediately as a poetic similitude standing for Christ; it is part of a stock of poetic conventions that can be decoded once we know what significance to attach to them.[27] For Aquinas, as for Goethe nearly five hundred years later, rhetoric is reducible to a purely mechanical and conventional function. We should not decontextualize the positions of these two important theorists, as if their similarities with one another were a mere coincidence or curiosity; on the contrary, the scholastic theologian and the Romantic aesthetician represent points on a historical continuum of rhetoric's gradual but perceptible debasement to a merely conventional and arbitrary function, the dynamics of which were set in motion in the early Christian era, and various expressions of which are to be found up through the early modern period.[28] But my interest in this comparison is more specific, for I use it to point up a very important difference between the two that returns us to the particular problematic of Aquinas's system. Whereas for Goethe the instrumentalizing of rhetoric serves as grounds for a virtual rejection of it as too mechanical an operation, for Aquinas the instrumentalization of rhetoric represents the only way of saving and preserving it. Aquinas's assimilation of rhetorical figuration to the literal sense is a way of ensuring a legitimate place for rhetoric by containing its threat of proliferating and unstable reference.

In a classic essay, 'The Resistance to Theory', Paul de Man argues that the contested status of literary theory in the modern academy, what he calls the 'resistance to theory', is 'a resistance to the use of language

[26] Goethe, *Theory of Colours*, quoted in Todorov, *Theories of the Symbol*, p. 202.

[27] *Quaestiones quodlibetales* 7. 6. 15 ad 1; see Eco, *The Aesthetics of Thomas Aquinas*, p. 154; cf. Strubel, ' "Allegoria in factis" et "Allegoria in verbis" ', p. 355.

[28] In addition to the classic study by Todorov, *Theories of the Symbol*, see also the essay by Gérard Genette, 'Rhetoric Restrained', in Genette, *Figures of Literary Discourse*, trans. Alan Sheridan (New York, 1982), pp. 103–26; and more recently, C. Jan Swearingen, *Rhetoric and Irony* (New York, 1991).

about language', a resistance, in effect, to reading rhetorically.[29] As a rhetorical inquiry, theory is concerned, not with the meaning or the value of texts, but with 'the modalities of production and of reception of meaning' (7); it is more interested in 'language as a system of signs and of signification. . .than as an established pattern of meanings' (9). De Man argues that literary theory in the modern academy has the same contested role that rhetoric had in the late classical and medieval trivium. The trivium as a whole constitutes one of the most traditional and general linguistic models, for each of its sciences, grammar, rhetoric, and dialectic, deals with the operations of language from different epistemological perspectives (13–15). What de Man brilliantly articulates here is the historically uncertain status of rhetoric as a scientific language that deals with the unfixing of linguistic reference: rhetoric deals with devices of persuasion, the most visible and characteristic of which are tropes and figures, which operate by 'turning' or 'transferring' words from their proper significance. The threat that rhetoric always poses is to unfix the stable referentiality that the other trivium sciences, grammar and dialectic, promise. Its relationship with grammar, with which it shares the study of figures of speech, is particularly strained, for where grammar offers a prescriptive and determinate knowledge of linguistic codes, rhetoric's interest in the tropological dimension of speech undoes or destabilizes grammar's claim to making language a transparent medium (15–17).

De Man's articulation of the kind of threat that rhetoric poses to ideal claims of fixed referentiality can help us to discover what is at stake in Aquinas's placement of rhetorical language within the strictly delimited realm of the literal sense. It illuminates the conflict between the determinacy of grammatical knowledge and the slipperiness of rhetorical usage. For Aquinas to locate rhetorical figures and tropes in the literal sense is effectively to incorporate rhetoric within the secure boundaries of grammar since grammar, or grammatical exposition, is associated with the literal sense, the letter and the surface meaning, as we find in Hugh of St Victor's *Didascalicon* (6. ch. 8). The purpose of Aquinas's move is to save rhetoric as a component of Scriptural discourse by taming it, confining it within the fixed boundaries of literal, grammatical exposition. The power of rhetorical doubleness, its inherent capacity to turn language away from its proper signification, can be contained if it is incorporated into the literal sense, which is, by definition, always manageable and open. If rhetorical language can be identified with the literal sense, its meaning should become plain. In this way, rhetoric is returned to the ordered control of a stable, authoritarian system of exposition.

It is necessary for Aquinas to preserve rhetorical figuration and

[29] Paul de Man, 'The Resistance to Theory', *Yale French Studies* 63 (1982), p. 13.

validate its place in Scriptural discourse. Earlier exegetes such as Bede had of course demonstrated the presence of figures and tropes in Scripture; but for Aquinas's theological system as a whole it is also important to offer a substantive explanation as to why Scripture uses rhetorical language. At the very beginning of the *Summa theologiae* he takes up the question of whether Scripture uses metaphors, similitudes, and other forms of poetic representation, explaining and validating their place in Scripture according to the terms of the larger Aristotelian principles of sensory cognition that inform his doctrine. Human knowledge begins in corporeal sense, and poetic metaphors constitute sensory modes of representation which give us access to the higher 'world of intelligence through the world of sense' (1. 1. art. 9, resp.). But while the presence of rhetorical figures in Scripture may be justified on these grounds, it is still necessary to explain how they work in sacred writing, and to address the difficulties that had challenged earlier exegetes as to how tropes are to be understood in Scripture. It is important here to note that Aquinas admits the opaque nature of rhetorical language. In describing metaphorical usage he invokes a language of bodily disguise, veils, or wrappings, descended from ancient rhetorical and philosophical discourse about the integumental character of figures and tropes:

> [C]onveniens est sacrae Scripturae divina et spiritualia sub similitudine corporalium tradere. . . . Unde convenienter in sacra Scriptura traduntur nobis spiritualia sub metaphoris corporalium; et hoc est quod dicit Dionysius. . . *Impossibile est nobis aliter lucere divinum radium, nisi varietate sacrorum velaminum circumvelatum*. . . . [R]adius divinae revelationis non destruitur propter figuras sensibiles, quibus circumvelatur, ut dicit Dionysius.
>
> (*Summa theologiae* 1. 1. 9 resp.–ad. 2)

> Holy Scripture fittingly delivers divine and spiritual realities under bodily guises. . . . Congenially, then, holy Scripture delivers spiritual things to us beneath metaphors taken from bodily things. Dionysius agrees, *The divine rays cannot enlighten us except wrapped up in many sacred veils*. . . . Dionysius teaches in the same place that the beam of divine revelation is not extinguished by the sense imagery that veils it. . . .

With the acknowledgement of rhetoric's opacity, its ambiguity or doubleness, comes a method of stabilizing it and restricting its multiple valences. To save rhetoric, Aquinas deforms it: he suppresses the basic capacity of metaphor to mean two things at once. In the example of the arm of God, cited above from 1. 1. art. 10 of the *Summa*, Aquinas explains that the literal sense is not the figure, but what is figured, so that the literal sense of the metaphor is not that God has an arm, but that he has the power of doing and making commonly ascribed to a human arm.

On this reading, we move immediately, in a reductive and mechanical way, to the paraphrasable content of the metaphor. In New Critical terminology we would say that this reading moves immediately to the tenor, leaving the vehicle behind. Of course this makes rhetorical language a transparent passage to meaning. Thus the threat of rhetorical doubleness and unstable ambiguity is dehorned: rhetoric becomes a manageable linguistic system whose only purpose is to yield up meanings, after which its value is spent. The literal sense, as Aquinas tells us, contains nothing false (*Summa theologia* 1. 1. 10 ad. 3). With the literal sense thus elevated, rhetoric is tamed and redeemed.

An important corollary of these arguments is that the literal sense represents the intention of the author (*Summa theologiae* 1. 1. 10 resp.). Aquinas's exegetical successors, notably Nicholas of Lyre, also develop this premise.[30] It is necessary, on theological and philosophical grounds, for Aquinas to assign the literal sense, with its metaphorical significations, to the intention of the human author, for this maintains a strict hierarchical separation between the verbal realm of the human author and the symbolic realm of the divine author.[31] Authorial intention is the link between rhetoric and the literal sense. It is the principle for authenticating the meaning or meanings of the literal sense, since it is possible, according to this rule, for the literal sense to have multiple meanings, insofar as the human author understood and intended such a multiplicity (*Summa theologiae* 1. 1. 10 ad 1; *Quaestiones quodlibetales* 7. 6. 14 ad 5).[32] Aquinas is very careful to establish the validity of the literal sense as the ground of all arguments to be drawn from Scripture, and to this end uses intention to rule out the possibility of doubleness or ambiguity of meaning, for the things signified by words, according to the intention of the human author, may in turn reveal further significances (*Summa theologiae* 1. 1. 10 ad 1). It is in the spirit of such a concern to suppress any hint of ambiguity in the literal sense that later exegetes, among them Nicholas of Lyre and Richard Fitzralph, introduce the notion of a double literal sense (*duplex sensus litteralis*), of which one part is a 'proper' sense, and the other part a metaphorical one: both kinds of signification represent the author's intention.[33]

30 See A. J. Minnis, ' "Authorial Intention" and "Literal Sense" in the Exegetical Theories of Richard Fitzralph and John Wyclif', *Proceedings of the Royal Irish Academy* 75 (1975), 1–31.

31 See Jordan, *Ordering Wisdom*, p. 30.

32 See Synave, 'La doctrine de Saint Thomas d'Aquin', pp. 58–9. On the further implications of this principle of intention, see C. Spicq, *Esquisse d'une histoire de l'exégèse latine au moyen âge*, Bibliothèque Thomiste 26 (Paris, 1944), p. 251.

33 Minnis, ' "Authorial Intention" and "Literal Sense" ', pp. 4–10; A. J. Minnis, A. B. Scott, eds., with the assistance of David Wallace, *Medieval Literary Theory and Criticism c.1100–c.1375: The Commentary Tradition* (Oxford, 1988), pp. 205–6; G.

But while the theological and exegetical rationales may be coherent, the system strains against the very nature of rhetoric. At its root, rhetoric and its tropological dimension is about the impossiblity of there being a manifest, plain truth. The attempt to anchor the verity of the literal sense in the principle of intention is especially telling in the deformation of rhetoric that it involves. Intention is the most flexible and expedient of rhetorical concepts, adaptable and attributable in any circumstances. What we see here is the conflict between the desire to acknowledge the human-produced rhetoricity of Scripture and the need to suppress the doubleness, ambiguity, and referential instability that rhetoric always implies.

This is the contradiction that Wyclif and his followers expose and challenge. What is often seen as their return to a stern and severe realism is also the basis of their acute recognition of the impossibility of assimilating rhetoric to the openness of the literal sense. Wyclif confronts the real pressures that rhetoric exerts on meaning, and I would suggest that he understands far better than Aquinas the force of rhetoric as discursive interference and indirection. It is because he recognizes the destabilizing power of rhetoric that he resists it. He does not open his system to accommodate the claims of rhetoric, nor does he seek to relieve rhetoric of the danger that it bears by trying to make peace between rhetoric and the literal sense. He assesses rhetoric for what it is, and on these grounds rejects it utterly as an element in the language of Scripture. Unlike Aquinas who wants to save rhetoric by changing its character, Wyclif has no investment in the preservation of rhetoric as a necessary corporeal approach to the *invisibilia* of divine truth; but in denying the role of rhetoric in Scripture he negatively affirms the true nature of rhetoric.

Wyclif's polemics on the nature of Scriptural language, as set forth in his treatise *De veritate sacrae scripturae*, are not directed against Aquinas or Thomistic theorists such as Lyre and Fitzralph: the objects of his attack are the 'logic choppers' and 'geomancers' of the fourteenth-century schools, Nominalist thinkers such as Ockham and Holkot. More generally, he is derisive of the quick fashion changes of academic theory.[34] But in terms of the role of rhetoric, Wyclif's position is strongly differentiated from that of Aquinas. Wyclif seeks to reconcile the undeniable presence of figurative language in Scripture with the necessary assumption of Scripture's literal truth. He does so by declaring

R. Evans, *The Language and Logic of the Bible: The Road to Reformation* (Cambridge, 1985), pp. 43–7.

[34] Minnis, ' "Authorial Intention" and "Literal Sense" ', pp. 13–17; on 'geomancers' and the 'modern generation', see *De veritate sacrae scripturae*, ed. Rudolf Buddensieg

the language of Scripture to be a singular system, governed by its own particular linguistic logic, which he calls the *vis* (or *virtus*) *sermonis*. Aquinas had also declared Scripture to be unique in having both a literal and a spiritual sense, but on Aquinas's view, human rhetoric still has a place in sacred language. For Wyclif, however, human eloquence, or rhetoric, is outside the domain of Scripture. Nothing that we recognize as figurative or rhetorical in ordinary speech has any claim on the linguistic functions of Scriptural eloquence:

> quod ista est vera de virtute sermonis secundum quamlibet eius partem et quod professores scripture sacre debent sequi eam in modo loquendi quoad eloquenciam et logicam plus quam aliquam alienam scripturam gentilium. (1: 2 / 7–10)
>
> (On account of the *virtus sermonis* Scripture is true in each and all of its parts, and the exponents of sacred Scripture ought to follow its particular mode of speaking, insofar as eloquence and logic are concerned, more than any other worldly writing.)

On these grounds alone can the true meaning of Scripture be said to be contained in the literal sense. If Scripture uses figurative language, those figures are not to be judged 'improper' by the standards applied to ordinary rhetoric, for such rhetoric is now outside the parameters of Scriptural usage. The literalism of Scripture can only be absolute by virtue of the categorical exclusion of human rhetoric:

> et hinc ecclesia et sancti doctores post exposicionem sensus scripture concedunt verissime de virtute sermonis, quod Cristus est 'agnus, ovis, vitulus, aries, serpens, leo, vermis', sed ad sensum misticum, qui est ut plurimum literalis. nec moveat dictum Augustini capitulo sexto quarti libri De Doctrina cristiana, quo dicitur quod 'nec ipsos autores decet alia eloquencia nec alios ipsa'. hoc enim est verum ad verba, cum quilibet rethor habet propriam eloquenciam, sed sensus est, quod illa eloquencia non decet alios autentice, sed imitatorie. . . . (1: 5 / 1–11)
>
> (For this reason the Church and the sacred doctors concede most reasonably, after the exposition of the sense of Scripture, by *virtus sermonis*, that Christ is lamb, egg, calf, ram, serpent, lion, worm, but according to the mystical sense, which is the most literal sense. The dictum of Augustine should stand, where he says in chapter 6, book 4 of *De doctrina christiana*, that 'no other eloquence befits these authors, nor this eloquence any other authors'. The words of this are true, for any speaker has his own eloquence; but the sense is that this eloquence befits no other authors naturally, but only by imitation.)

(London, 1905), 1: 114/20–5; on the modishness of Oxford debate, see 1: 54/6ff. For an overview of Wyclif's scriptural theories, see Michael Hurley, S. J., ' "Scriptura sola": Wyclif and his Critics', *Traditio* 16 (1960) 275–352; on *De veritate sacrae scripturae*, pp. 293–8.

Ordinary eloquence, the medium of 'other authors', has no purchase on Scriptural discourse, the realm in which 'these authors' operate. Just as human rhetoric is inappropriate to God, so divine eloquence is not fitting to human usage. The very question of 'proper' as opposed to 'improper', as applied to figures of speech, is dialectically doubled here: the 'impropriety' of figurative language, in which an attribute that is not 'proper' to an entity is linked with it rhetorically through the indirectness of allegory or metaphor, becomes, in Wyclif's system, an inappropriate or 'improper' understanding of Scriptural language. Scriptural language is always 'proper' or literal, and its very nature or 'property' is for the literal to be identical with the mystical sense, as governed by the 'propriety' of the *vis sermonis*. The *vis sermonis* is to be understood as the authorial intention of Scriptural speech, and hence as God's intention as author of Scripture (see *De veritate sacrae scripturae*, 1: 43 / 17 ff.).[35] The distortive effect of rhetoric is now utterly banished from the domain of Scripture, not because Scripture uses no figures, but because God uses a language that defies human rules, a language in which the 'improper' is always 'proper' or literally true by virtue of his intention.[36] On the terms of the *vis sermonis*, figurative usages are both stylistically 'fitting' and ontologically 'proper'. The author of Scripture uses a fitting rhetoric, not the common rhetoric of pagan usage.[37]

Rhetoric is now completely external to the body of Scripture. The necessary and absolute literalism of Scripture cannot accommodate rhetoric in any form, not even a rhetoric, as Aquinas would have it, stabilized and purged of its indirectness. Wyclif seeks to work no changes on rhetoric: he simply excludes it from the picture. The domain of the literal sense, governed by the *vis sermonis*, is enlarged to occupy and encompass the territory vacated by a now irrelevant, mundane rhetoric. Always immanent in the literal sense is the divine authorial intention, which confers a comprehensive wisdom on the literal so that it can never be mistaken for the false or commonplace. Indeed, any misreading of the literal sense is the result of false intention on the part of the reader, who may use the interpretation of

35 G. R. Evans, 'Wyclif on Literal and Metaphorical', in Anne Hudson and Michael Wilks, eds., *From Ockham to Wyclif*, Studies in Church History, Subsidia 5 (Oxford, 1987), pp. 259–66, esp. pp. 263–5.

36 Evans, 'Wyclif on Literal and Metaphorical', p. 263; David Lyle Jeffrey, 'Chaucer and Wyclif: Biblical Hermeneutic and Literary Theory in the XIVth Century', in Jeffrey, ed., *Chaucer and Scriptural Tradition* (Ottawa, 1984), pp. 109–40, esp. pp. 115–23.

37 See Gustav Adolf Benrath, *Wyclifs Bibelkommentar*, Arbeiten zur Kirchengeschichte 36 (Berlin, 1966), p. 64.

Scripture to advance vain or selfish interests.[38] Here we can see how the mechanism of distortion, indirection, and ambiguity has been relegated to a place outside the text: the capacity for rhetorical equivocation now resides entirely in the bad intentions of certain readers who wilfully and cynically impose indeterminate readings upon the text and purvey such equivocations as authentic (see *De veritate sacrae scripturae* 1: 36/ 20–22; 111/2–5, 12–19).

In Lollard polemic on Scriptural interpretation, we see the radical effects of Wyclif's removal of rhetoric from the literal sense. Lollard theory wants to liberate reading along political lines, first by postulating the integrity and hence translatability of the literal sense, and second by directing attention to the accessibility of meaning itself. A treatise on biblical translation presents a realist case for theorizing meaning as outside the possession of language:

> Sithen that the trouthe of God stondith not in oo langage more than in another, but who so lyueth best and techith best plesith moost God, of what langage that euere it be, therfore the lawe of God writen and tauȝt in Englisch may edifie the commen pepel, as it doith clerkis in Latyn, sithen it is the sustynance to soulis that schulden be saued. And Crist comaundid the gospel to be prechid, for the pepel schulde lerne, kunne it and worche therafter. Whi may we not thanne writ in Englische the gospel and al holy scripture to edificacioun of cristen soulis, as the prechour schewith it truly to the pepel? For, if it schulde not be writen, it schulde not be prechid.[39]

This realist position, that the particulars of language are not constitutive of meaning, is written into Lollard justifications of their linguistic medium. As a tractate on secular rulers puts it, 'witte stondis not in langage but in groundynge of treuthe, for tho same witte is in Laten that is in Grew or Ebrew, and trouthe schuld be openly knowen to alle manere of folke'.[40] In Scripture, the 'truth of God' that stands outside the domain of linguistic particulars is the literal sense which the divine author intended.

The opposing argument, that meaning is bound by language, is of course what Archbishop Arundel employs in the Oxford *Constitutiones* of 1407, where he determines that 'it is dangerous, as St Jerome declares, to translate the text of Holy Scripture out of one idiom into another, since it is not easy in translations to preserve the same meaning

38 Jeffrey, 'Chaucer and Wyclif', p. 122; see the text of Wyclif's *postilla* on Luke 9 printed in Benrath, *Wyclifs Bibelkommentar*, p. 364.

39 Text in Anne Hudson, ed., *Selections from English Wycliffite Writings* (Cambridge, 1978), p. 107 (hereafter cited as *SEWW*). Here and throughout, 'th' is substituted for the character 'thorn'.

40 Hudson, ed., *SEWW*, p. 127.

in all particulars'.[41] Arundel's reductive appropriation of Jerome's views on translation makes an opportunistic case for a rhetorical idea of the text, in which the particularity of idiom contains and defines the meaning. As Jerome says, rhetorical figuration presents one of the greatest obstacles to idiomatic translation in general.[42] The orthodox construction of the problem of translation, as represented by Arundel, forces Lollard theory into its most radical, but also most productive, extreme. If the literal sense, which is what the author intended, includes the idiomatic particulars of rhetorical language, then it would be impossible to translate from one language to another without losing the literal sense. Thus the Lollards must theorize rhetoric as not of the literal sense, for otherwise the literal sense, and hence the sacred text as a whole, would be untranslatable. This places the Lollards in the interesting position of affirming classical (especially Ciceronian) views of the discursive power of rhetoric to shape meaning and indeed to distort it. But rather than attempting to accommodate rhetoric by denaturalizing and disempowering it, as scholastic criticism had done, the Lollards refuse rhetoric any place in the language of Scripture. In this of course they reproduce Wyclif's arguments on the *vis sermonis*. A Lollard sermon dealing with the Eucharist draws its explanation of linguistic signification from *De veritate sacrae scripturae*: 'And so ȝiue we God leue to speke as him likith, al if we speken not ay so bi this same autorite. These wordis that God spekith schulde we algatis graunte, and declare hem to trewe vndirstonding'.[43] Where Lollard writing does give attention to the nature of figurative speech in Scripture, as in chapter 12 of the *Prologue* to the Wycliffite Bible, the governing assumption is still this Augustinian dictum of the special character of divine eloquence.[44]

But Wyclif's distinction between the terms of human and divine discourse assumes another dimension in Lollard polemic about vernacular translation. For the Lollards, rhetoric is not simply theoretically incommensurate with the idea of a divine intention that

[41] Text in D. Wilkins, ed., *Concilia Magnae Britanniae et Hiberniae* (London, 1737) 3, p. 317; trans. quoted from Herbert B. Workman, *John Wyclif: A Study of the English Medieval Church* (Oxford, 1926; reprint Hamden, Ct., 1966), 2, p. 194.

[42] See Jerome's preface to his translation of Eusebius's *Chronicle* in J. K. Fotheringham, ed., *Eusibii Pamphili chronici canones latini* (London, 1923), p. 1/ 12a–25b. For Jerome's views on Biblical translation, see Epistle 57 to Pammachius in I. Hilberg, ed., *S. Eusebii Hieronymi opera, epistularum pars 1, CSEL* 54 (Vienna, 1910), pp. 508–10. Interestingly, Jerome says that the Bible demands close literal translation rather than idiomatic rendering.

[43] Hudson, ed., *SEWW*, p. 114 and notes, p. 194; cf. *De veritate sacrae scripturae* 1: 5/ 10–11.

[44] See Josiah Forshall and Frederic Madden, eds., *The Holy Bible, made from the Latin Vulgate by John Wycliffe and his Followers* (Oxford, 1850), pp. 43–8.

manifests itself in a coherent literal sense. It also represents for them a very real threat of linguistic disempowerment. If rhetoric, with all of its idiomatic particularity, is constitutive of the literal sense, it would confine the sacred text within the Latin of the Vulgate. Rhetoric would become a linguistic prison, an insurmountable barrier to the Lollard objective of opening the text to the linguistic accessibility of the vernacular. One of the most important theoretical projects of the Lollards is to challenge the fiction of the immanent and hence universal authority of Latin, the fiction that underwrites the hegemony of the Vulgate. Wyclif's arguments about the *vis sermonis* serve the Lollards' purpose here: truth is constructed outside the terms of human language, and human language is at best a conveyor, never a repository, of truth. Indeed, the stability of meaning cannot depend on particularities of language which would unfix meaning. This is the theoretical claim that entitles diverse languages to a singular truth and that grounds the Lollard project of a vernacular Scripture. For the Lollards, to disempower rhetoric by excluding it from the literal sense is to empower the vernacular as an authoritative linguistic medium. It is no less than a liberation of the literal sense from the false bonds of a particular language, and thereby the liberation of reading itself.

In this context, then, rhetoric becomes a constraint from which both the text and the act of reading must be freed. Lollard theoretical writing creates a nexus of meanings around the idea of 'openness'.[45] 'Open' is applied to the scriptural text itself, denoting clarity of meaning and of grammar in the translation. The *Prologue* to the Wycliffite Bible, customarily ascribed to John Purvey, asserts that the best kind of translation is

> aftir the sentence and not oneli aftir the wordis, so that the sentence be as opin either openere in English as in Latyn, and go not fer fro the lettre; and if the lettre mai not be suid in the translating, let the sentence euere be hool and open, for the wordis owen to serue to the entent and sentence, and ellis the wordis ben superflue either false.[46]

Translating only according to the words risks fragmenting and distorting the 'open sentence' which has an innate integrity. On these lines 'open' is identified with truthfulness, as in the translator's declaration that 'I purposide with Goddis helpe to make the sentence as trewe and open in

[45] I owe the idea of considering the multiple connotations of the word 'open' to Ralph Hanna, 'The Difficulty of Ricardian Prose Translation: the Case of the Lollards', *Modern Language Quarterly* 51 (1990) 319–40.

[46] *Prologue*, ch. 15; Forshall and Madden, eds., *The Holy Bible*, p. 57. Cf. the discussion immediately following on making the 'sentence open' through grammatical equivalences between Latin and English.

English as it is in Latyn, either more trewe and more open than it is in Latyn'.[47] By extension, the text is also 'open' to future translators who may better express 'the trewe sentence and opin of holi writ', for 'where oon seid e derkli, oon either mo seiden openli'.[48] In this sense of an unfinished and ongoing collective project, neither one version of the text nor one translator has a monopoly on the open truth of Scripture. Even the Augustinian principle of charity, which is invoked as the rule for reading what is both 'hidden' and 'open' in Scripture, constitutes an exegetical economy of openness, for 'he that hooldith charite in vertues, either in goode condiscouns, hooldith bothe that that is opyn and that that is hid in goddis wordis'.[49] Charity is both of the text and metatextual, common to all readers but possessed by no one reader. This metaphysic of 'openness' is thus linked to the idea of an 'open' text as a communal and collective social practice which admits a multiplicity of languages and readers. By this logic, 'open' also takes on its political inflection of public rights and common accessibility. Implicit in the idea of 'openness' is anti-elitism, as in Purvey's endorsement of Nicholas Lyre's *Postilla*: 'Heere Lire rehersith the sentence of seint Austyn, and of Isidre in these reulis, and declarith hem opinly by holy scripture and resoun, and countrith not Austin, but declareth him ful mychel to symple mennis witt'.[50] 'Simple men's wit' becomes the abiding standard, the 'open' measure, for who should be allowed to read Scripture.

The literal sense is the site of openness in every sense, grammatical, hermeneutical, and political. The text itself is 'open' in the sense that it is not 'possessed' from within by the conflicting and potentially disruptive force of rhetoric. An 'open' text does not require elaborate clerical mediation and explanation. Conversely, the 'closing' of the text is something that is done to it against its nature. The idea of 'closed' also has both a hermeneutical and political inflection. As the *Prologue* declares, the Bible is withheld and monopolized by 'covetous clerks' fearful of losing the textual privilege of their class:

> for thouȝ couetouse clerkis ben woode by simonie, eresie, and manye othere synnes, and dispisen and stoppen holi writ, as myche as thei moun,

[47] *Prologue*, ch. 15; Forshall and Madden, eds., *The Holy Bible*, p. 57.
[48] Ibid., pp. 57, 59.
[49] Ibid., p. 46. Cf. the invocation in the *Prologue* of the traditional scholastic principle that the literal sense is the foundation and standard of all meaning in Scripture: 'and worschipfully and heelfully the Holy Goost mesuride so holy scripturis, that in opyn placis he settide remedie to oure hungir, and in derk placis he wipte awey anoies; for almest no thing is seyn in tho derknessis, which thing is not founden seid ful pleynly in other placis' (Ibid., p. 50).
[50] Ibid., p. 55.

ȝit the lewid puple crieth aftir holi writ, to kunne it, and kepe it, with greet cost and peril of here lif.[51]

Such covetous possession of Scripture also takes the form of hermeneutical dominion and obstruction: clerks 'prechen sumwhat of the gospel, and gloson it as hem liketh'.[52] Most importantly, the wilful closing or mystification of the text through false exegesis is represented in terms of rhetorical obfuscation: according to the English version of the *Vae octuplex* sermon, 'summe prechen fablis and summe veyne storyes, somme dockon hooly wryt and somme feynon lesyngus; and so lore of Godis lawe is al put obac'.[53] This veiling of meaning through ambiguity or indirection ('fables', 'vain stories', 'lies') is a distortion imposed from outside the text, almost like an integument externally manufactured by false intentions and laid over the true literal sense. A Lollard tract known as 'The holi prophet David saith' attacks the elaborate systems of exposition associated with the friars in terms that clearly mark a distinction between literal truth and external mechanisms of rhetorical 'colours': 'Thei takyn the nakid vndirstondynge bi presumcion of mannes witt, and bryngen forgt pride veynglorie and boost, to coloure here synnes and desceiue sutilli here negebours'.[54] The false readers of Scripture seek to 'colour' or veil their own sins with subtle deception; but there is also an echo here of the false work of rhetorical figuration which 'colours' the naked or literal text with subtle ambiguities (the *colores* of rhetoric). Rhetoric is now outside the text: rhetoric hides the open (naked) text, and it is the tool of unscrupulous readers. The naked text has its own internal coherence, and rhetoric is something that is belatedly done to Scripture. Thus for the Lollards, the linking of intention to rhetoric is a sign of false hermeneutical intention. The divine author of Scripture does not intend rhetorical ambiguity.

Lollard polemic succeeds so well in externalizing rhetoric from Scripture, banishing it to a secondary domain of false intention outside the true text, that the paradigm can be taken up by Lollard adversaries, who in their turn characterize the literal exposition of the Lollards as a false rhetoric imposed on the text. What the Lollard opponents object to, of course, is the supposed Lollard preference for literal over mystical

51 *Prologue*, ch. 15; Forshall and Madden, eds., *The Holy Bible*, p. 57. On the question of 'covetous clerks' and closed access to books, see Richard H. and Mary A. Rouse, 'The Franciscans and Books: Lollard Accusations and the Franciscan Response', in Hudson and Wilks, eds., *From Ockham to Wyclif*, pp. 369–84.

52 Hudson, ed., *SEWW*, p. 107.

53 Pamela Gradon, ed., *English Wycliffite Sermons* vol. 2 (Oxford, 1988), pp. 366–7. Text also in Hudson, ed., *SEWW*, p. 75.

54 Text in Margaret Deanesly, *The Lollard Bible* (Cambridge, 1920; reprint 1966), p. 447.

exposition (an inaccurate charge, as any glance at Lollard Biblical exposition shows). But in the polemical discourse of orthodox prosecutors, literalism occupies the same structural position as rhetorical indirection does in Lollard polemic. In 1397 John Croft, a Herefordshire squire, had to take an oath foreswearing any contact with the Lollard heresy, including 'English books extracted wickedly (*sinistre*) from sacred Scripture according to the naked text (*nudum textum*) by those commonly known as Lollards', who 'try not only to beguile our simplicity, but even more, cause perverse people to deviate stubbornly from the sound and true understanding of sacred Scripture and revealed truth and the orthodox faith'.[55] We see how the naked text itself has become somehow the false coloring belatedly imposed on Scriptural truth, the vehicle of perverse hermeneutical intention. In the trial proceedings against William Swynderby, who was tried as a heretic in 1389 before John Trefnant, Bishop of Hereford, the Lollards are condemned for expounding sacred Scripture to the people

> ad litteram more moderno aliter quam spiritus sanctus flagitat, ubi vocabula a propriis significacionibus peregrinantur et novas divinari videntur, ubi non sunt iudicanda verba ex sensu quem faciunt sed ex sensu ex quo fiunt. . . .
>
> (according to the letter in the new way, otherwise than as the Holy Spirit commands, where the words stray from their proper signification and seem to be newly divined, where the words are judged, not from the sense that they make, but from the sense out of which they are made (i.e., from the sense they are made to make).[56]

Here the language of censure directed against literal exposition exactly mirrors Lollard condemnation of rhetorical distortion, the vain fables that estrange words from their proper meaning. It hardly matters that rhetoric means an entirely different thing to each camp, that the Lollards see it as an obstruction of the literal sense and that their adversaries see it as an obstructive and perverse literalism. For both, rhetoric is perceived to be outside the text, where it becomes the attribute of the enemies of Scriptural truth, the appeal used by false and wayward intentions.

If rhetoric is always a destabilizing force, it can never be comfortable in its relationship with the literal sense. In the critical debates I have traced here, from the scholastic attempt at a synthesis to the Wycliffite confutation of any such accord, the status of rhetoric undergoes radical change: from something to be contained and

[55] W. W. Capes, ed., *Registrum Johannis Trefnant, Episcopi Herefordensis*, Canterbury and York Series 20 (London, 1916), p. 48.

[56] Capes, ed., *Reg. Johannis Trefnant*, p. 232.

delimited, its role in scholastic theory, to something that contains or imprisons and must be resisted, its avatar in Wycliffite polemic. Moreover, once rhetoric is divorced from the literal sense, it no longer needs to be justified by any linkage with authorial intention; in this dissociated state, it acquires a new value, linked now with false and belated hermeneutical intention. At the root of this, of course, is that medieval criticism distrusts rhetoric for its power to undo the truth claims of any discourse, and theories of the literal sense must either denature or demonize rhetoric in order to maintain their claims to coherence. To read this phase of medieval critical theory from the perspective of rhetoric's fortunes is to read a history of unresolved and contradictory relations. But there is one powerful conclusion that can be drawn from this history of rich contradiction: rhetoric is precisely what is political about the literal sense. If the literal sense is always the site of contest over control of the text, rhetoric is the means of that control; and it is the regulation of rhetoric, whether through accommodation or resistance, that determines what is literal about the literal sense.

POPE JOAN AND PATIENT GRISELDA AS 'TOP GIRLS': LATE MEDIEVAL LITERATURE VIA POETIC DECONSTRUCTION

RENATE HAAS

Introduction

Over the times, the distance one has seen between artistic and academic interpretation has varied greatly, as have the distances between the academic variants, not least between literary and philosophical interpretation. In recent years, diverse forms of deconstruction have again brought academic re-reading rather close to poetic procedures, while, on the other hand, a number of contemporary fictional works have been taken as deconstructionist. Among them is Caryl Churchill's famous play *Top Girls* from 1982.[1] Elaborating Jacques Derrida's critique of representation, usually in decidedly feminist directions, most of these scholars have treated Churchill's theatrical innovations and analysed their effects more globally,[2] but several have also suggested that the play deconstructs the concept of its title or the ideology underlying it.[3] Nevertheless, the concept of 'top girls', past or present, has more been taken for granted than scrutinized or related to the traditions from which it derives. This is rather astonishing as the brilliant first scene presents five notable women, 'top girls', from the past. They come together in an exquisite restaurant - appropriately named Prima Donna in the first production - in order to celebrate the success of the contemporary 'top girl' Marlene, who has been promoted to managing director of an elegant employment agency. Two of these figures, Pope Joan and Patient Griselda, are late-medieval creations, and two more are closer to our

[1] All references are to the post-production edition (London, 1984).

[2] See particularly Elin Diamond, '(In)Visible Bodies in Churchill's Theater', in *Making a Spectacle: Feminist Essays on Contemporary Women's Theater*, ed. Lynda Hart (Ann Arbor, 1989), pp. 259–81; Janelle Reinelt, 'Feminist Theory and the Problem of Performance', *Modern Drama* 32 (1989) 48–57; and Amelia Howe Kritzer, *The Plays of Caryl Churchill* (London, 1991).

[3] Joseph Marohl, 'De-realised Women: Performance and Identity in Top Girls', *Modern Drama* 30 (1987) 376–388, esp. p. 387; and Beate Neumeier, 'Past Lives in Present Drama: Feminist Theatre and Intertextuality', *anglistik & englischunterricht* 41 (1991) 63–76, esp. pp. 73–74.

European Middle Ages than to the present. Lady Nijo lived in thirteenth-century Japan, whose economic, social, and religious system shows a number of parallels to medieval Europe, and Dulle Griet is the central figure of a painting by Pieter Brueghel from the middle of the sixteenth century. The only guest from a clearly modern period is Isabella Bird, the famous Victorian traveller and writer.

Therefore, since Churchill in her first scene lays special emphasis on medieval figures, her poetic deconstruction may also be worth the attention of medievalists.

Eliciting the aporias of the plots

Joan and Griselda's life-stories are built into the party conversations, in which the ladies try to get to know one another and chat about everything under the sun. They are told by the protagonists themselves in retrospect, but come in bits and pieces. At the same time, they are the only ones to be presented in chronological order and in such units that the decisive features of their plots remain intact – an achievement Churchill facilitates by making Joan arrive late and Griselda even later and thereby creating a greater or lesser need for a compact introduction.

In the case of Joan, for instance, all the constitutive elements as they have been established most influentially by Martinus Polonus's chronicle,[4] Boccaccio's *De casibus virorum illustrium* (IX,6)[5] and *De mulieribus claris* (CI)[6] are preserved.

At an early age, dressed in male clothes, Joan steals away from home with her boy-friend in order to study in Athens or, according to the other principal variant, in England. After her friend's death, she continues her studies and turns to Rome, where her lectures win her fame. She is elected Pope and, after a while, takes a chamberlain for her new lover. She gets pregnant and, not knowing when her child is due, is overcome by labour during a procession. Between the Colosseum and St Clement's she gives birth in public and is killed (or simply dies or is driven away). In consequence, the procession is rerouted and the *sella stercoraria* is introduced.[7]

4 The passage about Joan, which may be a slightly later interpolation, is reprinted and discussed in *Päpstin Johanna: Ein Lesebuch vom Mittelalter bis heute*, ed. Klaus Völker (Berlin, 1977), pp. 12–14.

5 Eds. P. G. Ricci and V. Zaccaria in *Tutte le Opere di Giovanni Boccaccio*, general ed. V. Branca, IX (Milan, 1983), pp. 772–74.

6 Ed. V. Zaccaria in *Tutte le Opere di Giovanni Boccaccio*, general ed. V. Branca, X (Milan, 1970[2]), pp. 414–18.

7 The *sella* is not mentioned in Martinus's chronicle or by Boccaccio, but is related to the female Pope by other late-medieval sources, e.g. the Greek writer Laonicus Chalcocondylis. *Päpstin Johanna*, pp. 17–18.

In both cases, Churchill first lets her characters act for a while on the present-day level of the party and, in so doing, unobtrusively suggests concepts which are central to their well-known life-stories and which she is going to probe in her critical retelling of them. For Joan, the key-word is 'heresy' (p. 6), and this self-assessment of hers does indeed point to the factual *conditio sine qua non* of the literary plot: the teaching of the Church that a woman cannot become Pope. If a woman manages none the less to sneak in, she is a heretic (in a broad understanding of the term).

The principal means Churchill uses for testing out the traditional story of Joan as of Griselda is realism, in particular, psychological realism. Concerning Joan's story, this means above all that Churchill emphasizes her brilliance of mind. Already by Joan's very first utterance, which refers to the time prior to the well-known story, she establishes her as a child prodigy. Starting the elaboration of the story proper, she lets Joan mention that even at the age of twelve, when she stole away from home with her sixteen-year-old friend, she was convinced that she knew more science than he did and almost as much philosophy (p. 8). Shortly afterwards, she substantiates this claim of Joan by making her quote some of her sophisticated arguments in the quarrel she had with her friend about the teachings of John the Scot, immediately before her friend died. After the friend's death, Churchill not only stresses Joan's love of learning but also hints at her awkward isolation. Highly plausibly, she makes this another incentive for Joan to absorb herself completely in her studies: 'There was nothing in my life except my studies. I was obsessed with pursuit of the truth' (p. 12). No wonder that the combination of exceptional talent and the hardest work leads to excellence and fame and that the superb philosopher-theologian and teacher is finally elected Pope.

All this, of course, intensifies the question of Joan's guilt, her 'heresy'. Where does it precisely lie, where does it start? With finesse, Churchill plays down Joan's sexual relations with her first friend very much and accentuates the circumstance that, after his death, Joan has been living in perfect chastity and has reached the apex of her learning under these conditions. She has been leading a sexless life like a priest and, in all other respects, has excellently fulfilled her male role, which has become her second nature.

In order to heighten her treatment further, Churchill adds an intermediate stage: Joan's election to cardinal and her reaction to it. Joan falls ill and lies 'two weeks without speaking, full of terror and regret' (p. 12). This clearly represents a guilt reaction; the guilt, however, is not named or explained. After the two weeks, the author lets Joan get up, 'determined to go on', 'seized again with a desperate longing for the absolute'. The status of Pope is linked for her with the hope for final insight. Churchill thus gives Joan a noble motivation. Her love of wisdom may be extreme, but it is not viewed negatively as hubris. Rather it appears natural in a person of such gifts and also has something religious about it.

After Churchill has questioned the pivotal assumption of the plot most poignantly and has done so by staying within traditional views, she continues with decidedly modern accents and open irony. A central motive for Joan's further behaviour is her disappointment at the fact that the status of Pope has not brought her the insight she had been longing for. In the sarcastic formulation of retrospect from the twentieth century, which links up the gender-question: 'I thought God would speak to me directly. But of course he knew I was a woman' (p. 14). The truth this Joan discovers is that whatever she says is true because it is accepted as true. In consequence, she begins to enjoy her power and the luxury, and finally chooses a lover from the great number of male attendants surrounding her.

With supreme irony and as a highly appropriate answer to tradition, Churchill develops Joan's fall into the narrative climax of her version (pp. 16–17). Activating the visual potential of the *casus*, she makes us first imagine the protagonist in her robes, high up on horseback, leading a huge crowd of clergy and common people in the procession. 'Total Pope', in Marlene's words. But then the birth-pangs gradually increase until Joan has to descend from her superior position to squat down on the ground for a respite. As great waves of pressure go through her body, she loses control of herself. Sounds like a cow lowing strike her ears and she realizes that they have escaped her own mouth. At last, the baby just slides out onto the road.

This 'tragedy' is, however, received as a 'comedy' by its immediate audience, the five women listening to Joan. The initial agitation of the crowd, 'The Pope is ill, the Pope is dying', which Joan has mentioned, evidently strikes them as funny. Since four of them are mothers themselves, such misinterpretations of a process as natural as childbirth may seem to them absurd, and they picture to themselves the confusion and embarrassment, particularly of the clergy. Churchill further adds to their amusement by letting Joan report that one of the cardinals exclaimed, 'The Antichrist', and fell over in a faint. In so doing, she gives the devil motif a comic turn, whereas in the tradition it has been primarily used to brand either Joan's intellectual aspirations or her sexual misconduct.[8]

Yet the 'comedy' does not last long, as Churchill retains the traditional ending, and its starkest variant at that. Joan is seized by her feet, dragged

[8] See Elisabeth Frenzel, *Stoffe der Weltliteratur* (Stuttgart, 1983^{6}), pp. 584–86.

out of town and stoned to death, and the author leaves it open by whom in the crowd, the clergy or the masses or both. Still, tragedy is not the final note. According to the fiction of Scene 1, Joan is obviously alive and the events are so much a thing of the past that she remembers some details no longer. Therefore, after some talk about other topics, Churchill can finish Joan's story as a 'comedy'. The subject matter here is the rerouting of the procession and the introduction of the *sella stercoraria*, especially the prosaic folk explanation of the mysterious papal inauguration ceremonies surrounding this pierced chair at the Chapel of the Saviour. In a carnivalesque mood, the ladies, who by then have had enough alcohol, amuse themselves at the thought that under great pomp nothing else is checked but the right sex of the future Pope and that although he must by no means be a woman he is wearing womanlike clothes.[9]

In the brief introduction of Griselda, which starts while the women are still giggling over the end of Joan's narration, Churchill nevertheless provides more than a keyword for the reception of her story. First Marlene presents her to the others in the following way: 'Griselda's in Boccaccio and Petrarch and Chaucer because of her extraordinary marriage' (p. 20). Unobtrusively, the characterization 'extraordinary marriage' goes straight to the core and, like 'heresy' in the case of Joan, suggests the simplistic traditional evaluation which will again be questioned by the fresh telling of the tale. Here, however, the questioning is also done highly directly. It is two cutting criticisms by Marlene which start off the recapitulation. The first aims at the pattern: 'Yes, Griselda's life is like a fairy-story, except it starts with marrying the prince'. The second – her answer to Griselda's modest objection that Walter is only a marquis – specifies the assumption which centrally underlies the pattern and the social system with which both are intimately linked:

> Well everyone for miles around is his liege and he's absolute lord of life and death and you were the poor but beautiful peasant girl and he whisked you off. Near enough a prince. (p. 20)

Accordingly, the retelling of the story, which is much shorter than in Joan's case, dismantles the fairy-tale glamour and romanticism, again by probing pivotal points of the plot. One of them is – already signalled by Marlene's comment – the concept of happy ending and its common equation with marriage. As highlighted by Marlene, Griselda's story proper begins with the wedding, and the elaboration brings out that this means no happy ending in even two respects. First, there is no real love story which it might conclude, because Churchill makes clear that before

[9] See 'someone looked up his skirts', 'pull up his robe', and the parallel association of 'kilt' (p. 19).

Walter turns up on the wedding day, the two have only seen each other from a distance and not exchanged a single word. No tender feelings are mentioned for either, only the general surprise. The bride is the last thing Walter needs for his wedding, and his marriage condition appears the harsher. Secondly, the marriage means the beginning of Griselda's tribulations, and the happy ending does not come at the other traditional points either: neither after Griselda has given birth to her first child nor after she has born the son, who can carry on the line. At both stages, Churchill accentuates that they are commonly considered turning points towards happiness: once, by letting Nijo express the hope that then 'it all ended happily'; before, by highlighting the inversion of the traditional expectation in making Griselda stress the happiness of the marriage *after* her sacrifice (p. 23). Long delayed, the happy ending comes only with the second employment of the wedding motif, Walter's marriage with the young girl from France, which – with a kind of magic trick – is turned into a big family reunion. After all that has preceded it in this critical retelling, the ending does, however, no longer appear particularly happy. Very appropriately, Churchill, among other things, raises the question whether Griselda can feel anything for the children she obediently sacrificed when she gets them back as near-adults (p. 25).

The late-medieval comedy thus remains no more a comedy than Joan's late-medieval tragedy remains a tragedy.[10] Instead, Churchill's version reveals in what highly problematic way the Griselda plot brings together older elements and how questionable these are in themselves, too. Basically, the Griselda figure is a saint-prototype – the patient sufferer – secularized. In older or more traditional variants blending legend and folklore, the constancy of the long-suffering wife is tried through the taking away of her children, wicked intrigues leading to her repudiation, and her humiliation to a servant in the place where she formerly functioned as mistress. Usually these sufferings are inflicted by heathens or other evil persons such as malignant mothers-in-law, mostly in the absence of the husband. Yet in the pointed, still more secularized conjointure of the Griselda plot, whose author may well have been Boccaccio, it is the husband himself who wilfully tests and tortures his patient wife. The secularization of the ideal Christian wife is thus carried to absurd extremes. Since the original legitimization is only loosely connected, Griselda appears a mere object of her husband. Moreover, by preceding the story of Griselda with her version of Pope Joan's, Churchill has also eroded this possibility of legitimization.

[10] In 'Caryl Churchills *Top Girls* und die Möglichkeit oder Unmöglichkeit einer feministischen Komödie', *anglistik & englischunterricht* 45 (1992) 139–54, I study in greater detail how Churchill sounds the traditional patterns of comedy.

Like Marlene has stated, in the private as in the public sphere, Walter is lord over life and death, and Churchill accentuates to what inhumanity Griselda goes in her unquestioning obedience. Her first baby is taken away from her breast and although she fears that the stranger is going to kill it even before he is out of the room, she offers not the least resistance. She merely asks him humbly to allow her to give the child a last kiss and to bury it where no animals can dig it up (p. 23) – touches of the traditional story that, in this critical retelling, can only strike us as naïve sentimentality. Griselda's obedience does not come out more humanely either when, in the context of her sacrifice of the son, Churchill alludes to the question whether she saw through Walter's pretext and was prepared to let the child be killed only because he wanted to see if she loved him enough. To the author, Griselda's behaviour seems to contain, at least from a certain stage, a self-imposed ban on thinking and feeling, and it certainly is not by chance that her Griselda has very little initiative and hardly expresses thoughts and feelings of her own. In a context where we at last might see the events from Griselda's own perspective, it is still Walter's arguments and views plus, occasionally, common opinion that we get. Griselda seems to have no personality of her own, her language is clichéic and impersonal.

The fundamental question, which Churchill has raised with Marlene's very first introduction of Griselda and to which she alludes repeatedly during the recapitulation, is that of normality. In what sense is Griselda's marriage 'extraordinary'? Is it a rare exception or is it the heightened realization of an ideal basically still valid? Among the women present onstage, Nijo, whose own life closely parallels Griselda's, is the one to receive her story in accordance with its centrally implied values and norms. Marlene and Joan, in contrast, are the ones to express the most criticism and lack of understanding.

Critique of the Western metaphysical tradition

Joan, the most intellectual of the group, allows Churchill to extend her explorations into philosophy and theology. Her critique operates on various levels and, among other things, again exploits the tensions between the medieval and the contemporary, as may be seen from Joan's first philosophico-theological comment: 'Because angels are without matter they are not individuals. Every angel is a species' (p. 4). This represents a standard distinction of medieval metaphysics, along Aristotelian lines, and aptly serves to stamp the ten-year-old girl as a child prodigy. In the context of a late-twentieth-century party, it nevertheless sounds rather strange, as the statement is completely isolated from its larger system of thought with its definitions and specific procedures. Understandably, the other women take such a demonstration of learning with nothing else but laughter. To (non-medievalist) readers, however, the statement in its oddity may also hold some fascination, especially as it seems to associate the individual and individuality with matter, with the body and thus appears to run counter to the main current of our cultural tradition with its privileging of the mind.

Beyond such basic effects, Churchill develops her critique by providing a larger, coherent argumentation and indicating its theoretical context. In addition, two comments preceding the longer discussion may be seen as deriving from the same specific system of thought and thus preparing it. P. 4:

> [1] Death is the return of all creatures to God.
>
> [2] Damnation only means ignorance of the truth. I was always attracted by the teachings of John the Scot, though he was inclined to confuse God and the world.

The argument itself (pp. 10–11):

> [3] I'd quarrelled with him over the teachings of John the Scot, who held that our ignorance of God is the same as his ignorance of himself. He only knows what he creates because he creates everything he knows but he himself is above being – [. . .]
>
> [4] St Augustine maintained that the Neo-Platonic Ideas are indivisible from God, but I agreed with John that the created world is essences derived from Ideas which derived from God. As Denys the Areopagite said – the pseudo-Denys – first we give God a name, then deny it, then reconcile the contradiction by looking beyond those terms – [. . .]
>
> [5] [. . .] all the time I was nursing him I kept going over the arguments in my mind. Matter is not a means of knowing the essence. The source of the species is the Idea. But then I realised he'd never understand my arguments again, and that night he died. John the Scot held that the individual disintegrates and there is no personal immortality.

Very aptly, Churchill makes her ninth-century Pope fascinated by the theories of the greatest thinker of the age, John Scot Eriugena. Partly diluted by their transfer into the vernacular, partly more pointed, most of the arguments can indeed be taken as derived from Eriugena,[11] and his

[11] This is the easier as Eriugena's marked ambiguities and inconsistencies can and, in fact, have been interpreted highly divergently. Statement [1] may be seen as an allusion to Eriugena's adaptation of the Neoplatonic *progressus* and *regressus* of all being from Itself as Origin to Itself as End. For a critical interpretation of Eriugena's eschatology, to which Joan's statements [2] and [5] come close, see Ulrich Rudnick, *Das System des Johannes Scottus Eriugena: eine theologisch-philosophische Studie zu seinem Werk* (Frankfurt, 1990), pp. 314–18 and 327. Regarding the charge of

system, in which he tried to enrich the Neoplatonism of the West with the neglected Greek variants, is at least alluded to. Churchill has even focused on some of Eriugena's most characteristic teaching. Parallel to him and in accordance with her character, Joan shows a special interest in the nature of the mind and of knowing. However, what foundation is there for knowledge if God is said not to know himself and if the highest concept is not being, but – not mentioned here explicitly – non-being, *hyperousia*, *superessentia*? In such a train of argument Western metaphysics seems to collapse. Its definitions with their oppositions give way, knowledge seems to blend with ignorance, finite with infinite, being with non-being.

At the same time, Churchill has also heightened the tensions between Eriugena's teachings and the official ones into blatant contradictions. Twice, both in his own century and at the beginning of the thirteenth, writings of Eriugena were suppressed by the Church, whereas today they attract much attention from Catholic theologians, too. Although Joan is conscious of questionable tendencies in Eriugena ('inclined to confuse God and the world'), her rewordings succumb to the same danger and seem to deny God's omniscience and the immortality of the human soul emphatically.

Joan's philosophizing gets still more frustrating when read without background knowledge or when merely heard in the theatre. Although some of the statements sound quite modern (for instance, the pseudo-Dionysian *modus procedendi*), her reasoning appears ridden with contradictions, as the contemporary senses of various terms no more effect a reassuring chain of thought than do the medieval ones. In their frustration, readers may perhaps become conscious of how much the meanings of most terms have changed since the Middle Ages – some, like 'individual', nearly to the opposite –, while the dichotomy between matter and mind, body and soul, basic to Western philosophy, still exerts a pervading influence.

This fundamental critique of Western philosophy and Western thought in general is subtly continued in the elaboration of Joan's story. Her growing disillusionment and split attitude towards learning have already been mentioned, but several moves of particular relevance still remain to be highlighted. One is Churchill's handling of the traditional cause of

pantheism, see Dermot Moran, *The Philosophy of John Scottus Eriugena: A Study of Idealism in the Middle Ages* (Cambridge, 1989), pp. 84f. For an interpretation of Eriugena's *nousology* as a deconstruction of the ontological tradition of Augustine and his followers, see Moran, *passim*, e.g., pp. 99–102 and 152; for a more traditional reading, see John J. O'Meara, *Eriugena* (Oxford, 1988). Concerning Eriugena's adaptation of Pseudo-Dionysian negative theology, see Moran, pp. 92f. and Rudnick, pp. 321f.

Joan's fall: her ignorance about birth. Among the most influential late-medieval authorities, Martinus Polonus (or an interpolator) adduced this explanation factually,[12] whereas Boccaccio, in *De mulieribus claris*, gloatingly dwelled upon the irony that the woman who for a long time had managed to deceive people lacked the *ingenium* ('genius', 'cleverness', 'tricks') to hide the unchaste birth.[13] While even in Martinus's neutral formulation Joan's ignorance reflects negatively upon her, Churchill makes it reflect on the Western intellectual tradition: its absurd privileging of the mind over the body and its gender-bias. Joan, the acknowledged paragon of learning, does not know how to interpret the signs of her own body and to take the simple precautions of which women of far less education are capable. Accordingly, the public humiliation of this highest spiritual authority to a suffering animal comes as a natural consequence.

Even beyond the traditional story, the implicit criticism continues. Towards the end of the party, all the other women from the past protest openly against the limitations imposed on them by their respective societies – including Griselda, who begins hesitatingly to question Walter's behaviour (p. 27). In this mood of self-assertion, Joan starts to quote Latin lines about the sublime tranquillity of the philosopher from Lucretius's *De rerum natura* Book II. As if she cannot communicate with the others on her own level, she recites the strange-sounding verses to herself until she is stopped by Marlene. A little later, Joan is unable to pick up the thread of Lucretius's philosophical poetry. After several attempts, she helplessly ends with 'terrorem' and is sick in a corner, which means that she is the one who is presented as the most miserable at the close of the scene. Her body, it seems, has had to teach her another lesson about her nature, community and the value of learning. Her body speaks its own language whereas the philosophico-theological discourse is not really hers.[14] Ironically, Joan's last intact lines have concerned the philosopher's insight 'that nature vehemently demands nothing else for itself but that pain be separated from the body and absent and that it [i.e. nature] may delight in the mind'.[15]

[12] 'Tempus partus ignorans': *Päpstin Johanna*, p. 13.

[13] Ed. Zaccaria, p. 418.

[14] Studying Churchill's critical experimenting with theatrical illusionism, Elin Diamond (p. 266) sees in Joan's vomiting (the representation of her vomiting) a reminder 'of the unseeable, unknowable female body wrapped in a male costume, a metonymy for cultural as well as theatrical invisibility.'

[15] 'nonne videre / nil aliud sibi naturam latrare, nisi utqui / corpore seiunctus dolor absit, mente fruatur / [. . .]'

Critique of the 'top girls' tradition

Since Churchill does not limit herself to bringing Joan's and Griselda's stories into an implicit dialogue through their juxtaposition but intensifies the social character of the telling to the utmost by inserting numerous reactions of the other women and quite often even uses their speculative or critical questions for parts of the reconstructions, she effects great complexity. Thus, despite the brevity, she manages more or less to cover the history of the reception of Joan's story, as she alludes to its most important variants and the most frequent uses to which it has been put over the centuries. Her play with *casus*, *exemplum*, tragedy, comedy and the pact with the devil has already been mentioned, also how she extends the critique of the Church into a critique of the Western philosophical tradition. Further, by presenting Joan as a 'real' person, she approaches history,[16] and the (homo)erotic ambiguities, which the eighteenth century loved to exploit, come in particularly via comments by Marlene.[17] What is more, through diverse reactions of her women, Churchill also goes beyond the traditional variants of reception, which have been predominantly male.

With the Griselda story, such comprehensiveness is more difficult, because the majority of later authors brought in much additional matter in order to achieve new effects. The most frequent changes have concerned Walter's motivations, which were either extenuated or worsened,[18] and Churchill integrates both possibilities through Griselda's defence and the criticism of the others. Yet the effect which is still more important here is that Nijo's uncritical understanding brings out the substantial congruences between their two lives despite the enormous geographical distance. Though the circumstances and superficial details vary, both Griselda and Nijo are the property of their husbands (official or semi-official), both have to sacrifice their children and to take new women to their husbands, both, at a later stage, suffer repudiation. Since Nijo has brought up these details in earlier phases of the conversation, Griselda's story, to some degree, appears as a variation on hers.

[16] Churchill leaves it to the audience what status they attribute to Scene 1 within the fiction of the whole play, which through its representation on the stage pretends to reality. It has been interpreted as Marlene's dream, but realistic consistency is far less a concern of Churchill than imaginative experiment which refuses to be limited by simple either/or logic. Therefore, Churchill has compared her earlier play *Traps* to an impossible object, or a painting by Escher, where objects can exist like that on paper, but would be impossible in life. *Plays: One* (London, 1985), p. [71].

[17] Cf. *Päpstin Johanna* and Frenzel, pp. 584–86.

[18] Frenzel, pp. 261–65.

Indeed, the overall effect of the first scene is very much that of a *tema* – 'top girls' – *con variazioni*, or a 'sym-phony', in which no voice really dominates like a soloist's. Again and again the other women associate details from their own lives, be they contrasts or parallels, and especially into Joan's story so many foreign elements are inserted that one realizes only through special focus on it that its course nevertheless helps Churchill to give some basic structure to her variations on the 'enterprising top girl'. This is the type to which all the women belong, except Griselda whose career of passivity provides the underlying structure for the next section. The subthemes Churchill varies go far beyond set pieces, in fact, they are numerous and both of greater and lesser importance. While Joan and Griselda already mark opposites, the other women represent further periods or cultures. Views, therefore, are as multi-faceted and change as quickly as in a kaleidoscope. No woman agrees with another in every point, but through minute reactions and direct comments they continuously affirm and question each other. Often affirmation and rejection come simultaneously. Some of this is very funny, as Churchill uses these smaller juxtapositions with superb irony. Just one example: while Joan gets on the audience's nerves with her Eriugena dispute, Isabella gives vent to the Western prejudice that 'Buddhism is really most uncomfortable'(p. 10).

As can be seen from this instance, an important effect of such a composition is that clichés are broken up. These include 'lady', 'love', etc., and the audience may realize how some of them determine its own ways of thinking; for example, when Nijo automatically interprets Joan's stealing away with her boyfriend as a romantic elopement, while Joan herself stresses the intellectual basis of the relationship and her spirit of competition (p. 8).

The most important concept, however, which is broken up is the comprehensive one of the 'top girl' or the *mulier clara*. The overwhelming majority of recycled elements from the lives of the 'top girls' are rather prosaic and typical of most women's existence. Moreover, all the celebrities of the scene have had to pay a very high price for their rise. None of them has been able to combine it with a peaceful rearing of children; on the contrary, most of them have had to give their children away or even suffer their being killed. On the other hand, their courage, changing of their lives and extraordinary achievements, which Marlene celebrates in her toast (p. 13), have still remained within the limitations imposed on them by their patriarchal societies, or just on their margins. They have only brought the individual to the top but otherwise were isolated phenomena which did nothing to improve the fate of their 'sisters'. And even during the festivity, the mutely serving waitress brings out that the corollary of 'top' is 'bottom'. Correspondingly, the language of the chatting of the women lacks originality, and as the philosophico-theological discourse only works within its closed system and, to an undazzled eye, is rather clichéic, not even the most learned of them strikes us as truly individual. Thus, the women of the first scene seem quite close to Boccaccio's *mulieres clarae*, which in *De casibus* he found no difficulty in subsuming under the *viri illustres*.[19]

In the later scenes, the actresses of the 'top girls' from the past and of the waitress play the roles of various contemporary women and girls, mostly from lower ranks or, at least, below Marlene. By such double or triple casting, Churchill subtly signals historic continuity and once more questions our cherished concept of individuality and individual greatness. The same effect is produced by the sole exception, the stability of the player/role dyad in the case of Marlene. Whereas in the first scene her negative traits do not yet appear fully, the rest of the play serves to radically dismantle the contemporary 'top girl' and her egoistic individualism. While she praises Maggie Thatcher and is looking forward to 'stupendous' years, the audience realizes that through such modern 'top girls', as through their predecessors, nothing is going to improve for women in general, and not even for Marlene's own daughter. Like the celebrities, Marlene had to sacrifice her daughter, Angie, to her career and now, in spite of lip-service, she does not stir a finger to help the naïve and somewhat retarded girl to an acceptable future.

Counterimages

In the end, audiences are dismissed with 'shots' and images that linger on and haunt their sensibilities. It is hard to forget the final impression of Joan, especially as the play closes with a similar, even more touching expression of helplessness when all that Angie can say is 'frightening'.

Another haunting image, almost a leitmotif of the first scene, is the father killing his own child. This is elaborated most by Nijo in her descriptions of how her illegitimate second and third babies had to be put out of the way by her lovers. Purposefully, Nijo's descriptions are set into Joan's story (pp. 16–18), where they frame the death of her new-born child and underscore an aspect of her story which has been utterly neglected in the course of its tradition. Nijo's images are, of course, revitalized and varied in the context of Griselda's sacrifices. There, Churchill also accentuates another variant of the motif, already present in

[19] Already leading classical poets, such as Virgil and Ovid, had extended the meaning of 'viri' and subsumed the less important second sex. See also the condescending sexism of the title, which Churchill uses ironically.

Nijo's report: the mother in her dumb obedience to the father and patriarchy letting her infant be killed and, thus, indirectly killing it herself. Again the ultimate perversion – the mother actually killing her child under the constraints of patriarchy – has indeed been suggested by Nijo concerning the fate of her fourth baby (p. 18). Finally, towards the end of the scene, the motif is given a more general form when Griet recalls how a soldier ran her baby daughter through with a sword (p. 28). The image of the man, and especially the father, killing the helpless child to Churchill, it seems, crystallizes the inhumanity of patriarchy,[20] and the negative phallic associations of the last instance appear intended as a counterbalance to the dominating imagery of our culture.

Similarly, but with comic effect, the *sella stercoraria* serves Churchill to literally hollow out the central symbol of (male) authority in Western tradition, the *cathedra* (p. 19). Though made out of solid marble, the *sella* has a hole in its seat like the 'throne' of colloquial speech, the toilet, and Michael Selmon has shown how Churchill develops the surrounding ritual into the 'satiric portrait of a shrine where priests kneel beneath the phallus'.[21]

Poetic deconstruction and scholarship

Churchill's procedures and effects come quite close to recent deconstructionist readings of literary scholars. Her poetic deconstruction even seems to have preceded the spread of the practice in academia by several years[22] and to be distinguished by a still higher degree of finesse and complexity (as further analysis might show). Therefore, it appears worthwhile for scholars to include her deconstruction, as well as similar ones by other contemporary writers, into their considerations. Like secondary literature, it may help us to see new aspects and to recognize more of the subtle differences between Boccaccio's two versions of the Joan story or between his version of Griselda and those by Petrarch, Chaucer and others. Quite often Churchill's modernity, which refuses to take medieval phenomena for granted, may prove illuminating. Moreover, on the wider, theoretical level, a comparison of her deconstruction

[20] For the importance of the motif in Western literary tradition and its often uncritical use, see, e.g., Horst S. and Ingrid Daemmrich, *Themen und Motive in der Literatur: Ein Handbuch* (Tübingen, 1987), pp. 198–99.

[21] Michael Selmon, 'Reshuffling the Deck: Iconoclastic Dealings in Caryl Churchill's Early Plays', in *Caryl Churchill: A Casebook*, ed. Phyllis R. Randall (New York, 1988), pp. 49–69, here p. 54.

[22] See, e.g., the research on the *Clerk's Tale* in the annual bibliographies of *Studies in the Age of Chaucer*.

with current academic practices might yield deeper insights for both sides.

Here, however, I would like to broach some more specific questions, to which Churchill's *Top Girls* returns us with increased poignancy. The fact that it has been primarily late-medieval life-stories the dramatist chose, in her first scene, for deconstructing the ideology of the 'top girl' may give us an impulse to work out still better the characteristics of the *mulier-clara* tradition and the specific contributions made to its establishment by Boccaccio, Petrarch, and Chaucer.

This, to me, seems to imply intensified attempts at understanding how the literary endeavours concerning the *mulier clara* of the poets just named, and of others, related both to the changing social conditions and to their aesthetics: e.g., how they envisaged new roles for (male) poets in a world where secular intellectuals, allowed to found a family, managed more and more to assert their authority beside the traditional one of the clerics; how they experimented with new forms and functions of literature and, to this purpose, sought to change, manipulate or control meaning; how this was reflected in their epistemological concern; and, last but not least, how their ambitions bore upon the situation of women and women's efforts towards (re-)gaining interpretive authority.

In the case of the Griselda figure, we may try to specify more clearly what Boccaccio, Petrarch and Chaucer contributed so that it could become, in the formulation of the nineteenth-century German feminist Hedwig Dohm, 'diese Idiotin an Gefühl und Verstand' ('this idiot of feeling and judgement'), whom so many women over the centuries were expected to emulate[23] – the marital example being the predominant use in tradition. For such inquiries, the following aspects particularly suggest themselves: (a) the possible causes of the extraordinary fascination the figure exerted from the start and across the times – in the same century, the story was recast repeatedly and in various languages, namely Italian, Latin, French and English; in the next, it was five times translated or adapted by Germans. . . (b) to what degree and why individual authors ignored or played down the critique contained in the earliest literary version of the story extant, Boccaccio's. Petrarch's role seems to have been paramount and, into our days, he has also been followed (or paralleled) by numerous literary critics, mostly male, who likewise preferred to consider the last *novella* as 'longe dissimilis'[24] to most others

[23] Berta Rahm ed., 'Artikel und Auszüge aus Schriften von und über Hedwig Dohm', in Hedwig Dohm, *Emanzipation* (Zurich, 1982^2), p. 210.

[24] All quotations of *Seniles* XVII, 3 are from the recent edition by Ursula Hess (a revision of J. Burke Severs's) in her *Heinrich Steinhöwels 'Griseldis': Studien zur Text- und Überlieferungsgeschichte einer frühhumanistischen Prosanovelle* (Munich, 1975), pp. 173–238, here p. 173.

in the *Decameron*. Accordingly, until quite recently, Boccaccio's *novella* has been praised as the 'apoteosi della nuova Maria' (Vittore Branca) or criticized as a step backward and defence of the feudal system.[25]

Despite, or rather because of, Petrarch's enormous influence, we should perhaps approach with less awe his fascination with the Griselda story and the way he used his own version of it as a touchstone for the appropriate reception of the new secular literature. We might, for once, scrutinize them under the aspect of wishful male thinking, intensified by senile sentimentality. Quite a number of features point in this direction: the emotionality of Petrarch's reactions to Boccaccio's *novella*, while the moral he later assigns to his own version is not mentioned once;[26] the context of his adaptation – the ailing near-septuagenarian recast the 'dulcis ystoria' among other things in order to reject a suggestion of Boccaccio which he found abhorrent, namely that, in view of his bad health, he should retire from his literary labours and leave the field to younger men;[27] his characterization of his *Griselda* as a work of old age, which he would not have undertaken in youth, and his (wholly serious?) self-criticism concerning senile *loquacitas*;[28] his ambivalence about the direction of the story's exemplary teaching – before his ambiguous final disclaimer,[29] he did much to present Griselda as a model for wives, starting with his programmatic announcement to the recipient of the letter that it was going to be 'de Insigni Obedientia et Fide Uxoris'; his intensification of Griselda's submission and corresponding elevation of

25 See Christa Bertelsmeier-Kierst, *'Griseldis' in Deutschland: Studien zu Steinhöwel und Arigo* (Heidelberg, 1988), pp. 116–17.

26 Hess, pp. 173–74, on the one hand, and p. 238, on the other. See also Anne Middleton, 'The Clerk and His Tale: Some Literary Contexts', *Studies in the Age of Chaucer* 2 (1980) 121–50, here: p. 126; and Kathryn L. Lynch, 'Despoiling Griselda: Chaucer's Walter and the Problem of Knowledge in the *Clerk's Tale*', *Studies in the Age of Chaucer* 10 (1988) 41–70, here: p. 66. Note also the great care Petrarch took with his version and its revisions. The circumstance that the sentence where he avoids personal judgement on Walter's 'cupiditas retentandi' seems to have been muddled as early as in the archetypes of the two lines of transmission may point to illegibility due to repeated corrections. See Hess, p. 200, and Franz Josef Worstbrock, 'Petrarcas "Griseldis" und ihre Poetik', in *Geistliche Denkformen des Mittelalters*, eds. Klaus Grubmüller et al. (Munich, 1984), pp. 245–56, esp. p. 252.

27 See *Seniles* XVII, 2 in Francesco Petrarca, *Prose*, eds. Guido Martellotti et al. (Milan, 1955), pp. 1134–59, esp. pp. 1140–44 and 1152–56. See also Middleton, p. 131.

28 See the beginning and ending of *Seniles* XVII, 4 in Elie Golenistcheff-Koutouzoff, *L'Histoire de Griseldis en France au XIVe et au XVe Siècle* (Paris, 1933; reprint Geneva, 1975), pp. 266–70.

29 'Hanc historiam stilo nunc alio retexere visum fuit, non tam ideo, ut matronas nostri temporis ad imitandam huius uxoris pacienciam, que michi vix imitabilis videtur, quam ut legentes ad imitandam saltem femine constanciam excitarem[. . .]'. (Hess, p. 238) In this often-quoted statement from *Seniles* XVII, 3, the negation of 'non tam ideo, ut. . ., quam ut' is not clearly exclusive. The most frequent, simplifying use

husband Walter to a Godlike role;[30] his appreciation of his first reader's highly emotional response as proof of his *humanitas*[31] (is it not a little too easy for a man to indulge in the sentiments of his 'mollissimum cor' when he can be absolutely certain that he will never be reduced to such an extreme female role?);[32] and, finally, his criticism of the Veronese friend who refused to be captured by the story, and in whose refusal we may now see also an opposition to the absurdly exaggerated female role and a different view of what is possible, plausible or extraordinary.[33] To deconstructionists, at least, such re-readings should not be too iconoclastic.

('not in order to. . ., but to. . .') does not completely cancel the literal meaning, which distinguishes different degrees: 'not so much in order to. . ., as to. . .' Thus, *Le Livre de Griseldis* makes only a small shift in translating Petrarch's formulation by 'non pas tant seulement que. . ., mais aussy'. See Middleton, p. 146 and Charlotte C. Morse, 'The Exemplary Griselda', *Studies in the Age of Chaucer* 7 (1985) pp. 51–86, esp. pp. 74–75.

30 See especially the frequent use of diminutives in reference to Griselda, her emphasis on her continuing status of *ancilla*, and her renunciation of thoughts and feelings of her own. See, e.g., Worstbrock, pp. 250–52.

31 See Golenistcheff-Koutouzoff, p. 267, and Middleton, p. 134.

32 If this friend burst into tears at Griselda's sacrifice of the baby daughter, as Petrarch's report seems to suggest ('cum epistole medium vix transisset'), his emotionality may have contained a considerable amount of male self-pity.

33 Worstbrock (p. 250) has praised Petrarch's originality in emphasizing the extra-ordinary – instead of the merely possible or plausible – as a medium for poetic truth. But it should be noted that in his criticism of the Veronese, Petrarch absolutizes his own standards while associating his friend for the same fault with the *vulgus*. He imputes to this friend the lack of imagination characteristic of the masses, who believe what is impossible to themselves must be so to all. See also Morse, p. 61.

THE MEANINGS OF *INTERPRES* IN ALDHELM AND BEDE

GEORGE H. BROWN

Aldhelm, the first English man of letters, and Bede, the father of English history and the most learned man of his age, were interpreters all their professional lives, interpreters of school texts, of literature in prose and poetry, of historical sources, of Scripture, of Latin and Anglo-Saxon culture. They not only used the term *interpres* in manifold ways; they themselves demonstrate the function and are even the embodiment of the word. As educators and authors, they saw themselves as interpreters and transmitters of the great treasures of Western Christianity.[1]

Before discussing Aldhelm and Bede, I shall, in appropriately medieval order proceed *de nomine*, expounding the basic meanings of *interpres* that inform their consciousness and their writings. After treating the topic as a word-study, I will look at the works of Aldhelm and Bede not only for their treatment of the word but also for their own functions as *interpretes* in their cultural *milieu* and for their attitudes toward *interpres* as translator (in the sense of *Dolmetscher*, *cicerone*, *dragoman*). I wish at least to call attention to the ideological construction of the newly converted society of which Aldhelm and Bede were such a notable part. After selectively sampling their hermeneutic uses of *interpres* and exploring its meanings in their *conversatio* (way of life), I want to show how Aldhelm and Bede, while sharing a common early medieval grounding in monastic education, differ markedly in their conception, use, and method of interpretation.

The Latin word, *interpres*, began its long and varied career in a suitably Roman fashion, as a legal and business term. From a variety of early and classical Latin texts, its first meaning is patent: 'a broker', 'agent', 'negotiator', 'go-between', 'middleman', 'intermediary' (synonymous with [*inter*]*nuntius*). However, the etymology of *interpres* is

[1] I wish to thank my colleague, Seth Lerer, for suggesting this topic to me. His recent book, *Literacy and Power in Anglo-Saxon Literature* (Lincoln, NE, and London, 1991) deals with a number of important issues in Aldhelm and Bede's writings that I take up and develop here. As my citations in the sections on Aldhelm and Bede show, I have profited much from this skilful *interpres*.

obscure.[2] Although the derivation of the first element of the word, *inter-*, is obvious, the second part, *-pres*, is not at all clear. Modern philologians can be as capricious in their etymological surmises as were the late Latin and medieval grammarians. A number of authorities in the nineteenth century conjectured that the *-pres* of *interpres* derives from *pret* as in *pretium*; and *The Oxford Latin Dictionary*, while registering dubiety, opines that this is perhaps so. Postulating a related Indo-European root, Calvert Watkins, following Pokorny, declares *-pres* a suffixed zero-grade form of *per*, 'to traffic in'. This seems likely. The same root in suffixed form, *per-n-e*, results in Greek πέρνημι. 'I sell', whence πόρνη, 'prostitute'. The verbal root *per* derives from the base *per* of prepositions and preverbs.[3] Other philologists, however, have argued that *-pres* is related to Indo-European **prat* and Gothic *fraþi*, meaning 'thought', 'understanding', so that *interpres* = 'between mindsets'. On the other hand, *The Oxford English Dictionary* concurs with Lewis and Short's *Latin Dictionary* that the root corresponds to Sanskrit *prath*, 'to spread abroad'. Bergk, Usener, and Niedermann had earlier adopted Isidore of Seville's interpretation that *interpres* comes from *inter partes*, with the added explanation that *interpres* thus represents a metathesis of **inter-pers*, and therefore indicates 'he who stands between the parties'.[4] Rejecting most of these and other conjectures, Walde and Hofmann simply conclude, 'Etymologie unsicher'. They note, however, that *interpres* is an 'altes Word der Handels- und Rechtssprache wie *arbiter* und *sequester*, neben denen es mehrfach begegnet'.[5] In law, *arbiter* denoted a person appointed or chosen to settle a dispute, then came to mean an overseer, and an executor; Livy refers to Agrippa Menenius as 'interpreti arbitroque concordiae ciuium' ('this mediator and executor of civil harmony').[6] A *sequester* first designated a third party to whom disputed property was entrusted pending a decision, then, in Roman organized bribery, an agent with whom the promised sum was deposited,

2 The following discussion of etymology is indebted to *Thesaurus Linguae Latinae* (*TLL*); Charlton T. Lewis and Charles Short, eds., *A Latin Dictionary* (L&S); P. G. W. Glare, ed., *Oxford Latin Dictionary* (*OLD*); R. E. Latham *et al.*, eds., *Dictionary of Medieval Latin from British Sources*, in progress (*MLBS*); A. Walde and J. B. Hofmann, eds., *Lateinisches Etymologisches Wörterbuch* (Heidelberg, 1938) (*LEW*); *Oxford English Dictionary*, 2nd ed. (*OED*); *Webster's Third New International Dictionary of the English Language, Unabridged*, ed. Philip Babcock Gove (Springfield, MA, 1976).

3 *The American Heritage Dictionary of the American Language* (New York, 1969), Appendix: Indo-European Roots, *per*[1] and *per*[7].

4 Isidore of Seville, *Etymologiarum siue Originum libri XX*, ed. W.M. Lindsay (Oxford, 1911, reprint 1966), book X, letter I, 123.

5 *LEW*, I.710.

6 Titus Livius, *Ab urbe condita*, II.xxiii, 11, cited in *OLD*, s.v.

as Cicero remarks in his oration against Verres: 'qui sequestres aut interpretes corrumpendi iudicii solent esse' ('those who are accustomed to act as agents or go-betweens for the corruption of judges').[7] The pseudasconian scholion on this text distinguishes thus: 'sequestres sunt apud quos pecunia deponitur, interpretes per quos indicitur pactio' ('sequesters are those among whom money is deposited, interpreters are those among whom an agreement is proclaimed').[8] So *interpres* finds itself in the company of business 'wheelers and dealers'.

Thus, no matter what its true etymon may be, ancient and modern philologians have all attempted to link the word's etymology with a primary meaning of (1) a 'go-between', 'intermediary'. From this were derived in both classical and medieval Latin a number of extended meanings, which are duly recorded in several columns of the *Thesaurus Linguae Latinae*.[9] Here it will suffice to list some of the main derived meanings. From 'middleman' and 'broker' it ameliorated to (2) 'spokesman', 'ambassador', and (especially of priests) 'messenger' of a god: Virgil calls Mercury 'interpres diuum Ioue missus ab ipso'.[10] (3) A third signification is 'explainer', 'expounder', 'interpreter' of a fact or text: for instance, Cicero says that 'interpretes . . . grammatici poetarum' ('grammarians are the interpreters of the poets'), and Pliny describes astronomers as 'caeli interpretes' ('expounders of heaven').[11] (3a) More specifically, the interpreter can be an explainer of omens, oracles, dreams: of this type Cicero has Quintus remark in *De divinatione*, 'somnis uaticinationibus oraclis, quod erant multa ambigua, explanationes adhibitae sunt interpretum' ('For dreams, prophecies, and oracles, since many of them were obscure, resort was made to the skill of professional interpreters').[12] (3b) Or the interpreter can be an expositor of laws: so Juvenal as well as Livy and Cicero refer to 'interpres legum'.[13] Finally, (4), an *interpres* can be a translator of a foreign language: for instance, Varro, speaking of Delphi, explains that 'nostri

[7] Cicero, *In Verrem*, I.36, cited in *OLD*, s.v.

[8] Pseudasconii Scholia, in *Ciceronis orationum scholiastae*, ed. Th. Stangl, (Vienna and Leipzig, 1912), 218.26, cited in *LEW*, I.711. Apuleius uses *sequestra* for a sexual go-between, bawd: 'anus quaedam stuprorum sequestra et adulterorum internuntia', *Metamorphoses*, 9.15, cited in *OLD*, s.v.

[9] *TLL*, pp. 2250–53; see also *OLD*, p. 947, from which a number of my examples are taken.

[10] Virgil, *Aeneid*, 4.356.

[11] Cicero, *De divinatione*, 1.18. 34; C. Plinius Secundus, *Naturalis historia*, 2.55; also Cicero, *De divinatione*, 2.44.92 (= astrologers).

[12] Cicero, *De divinatione*, 1.51.116. Note that in the same section Cicero speaks of 'explanatores omnium horum, ut grammatici poetarum'.

[13] Juvenal, 4.79; Livy, *Ab urbe condita*, 3.55.8; Cicero, *De natura deorum*, 1.39; cf. 2.11.

interpretes ὀμφαλόν umbilicum dixerunt' ('our translators have rendered omphalon as navel').[14] Cicero, in speaking of his translations of Attic orators, makes a distinction between the accurate, slavish word-for-word translator, *interpres*, and the *orator*, who translates the sense of the passage, bearing in mind the idiom of the target language.

> Converti enim ex Atticis duorum eloquentissimorum nobilissimas orationes inter se contrarias, Aeschinis et Demosthenis; nec converti ut interpres, sed ut orator, sententiis isdem et earum formis tamquam figuris, verbis ad nostram consuetudinem aptis. In quibus non verbum pro verbo necesse habui reddere, sed genus omne verborum vimque servavi.
>
> (I translated the most famous orations of the two most eloquent Attic orators, Aeschines and Demosthenes, orations which they delivered against each other. And I did not translate them as an interpreter, but as an orator, keeping the same ideas and the forms, or as one might say, the figures of thought, but in language which conforms to our usage.)[15]

Cicero's distinction demonstrates a classical consciousness of the relative fidelity of translation and of the close association of translation and interpretation, and Cicero opts for the interpretative mode. Horace concurs in his pithy admonition: 'Nec uerbum uerbo curabis reddere fidus / interpres' ('Nor should you attempt to render word for word as a faithful translator').[16] In his famous apologetic letter, *Ad Pammachium de optimo genere interpretandi*, St Jerome quotes these passages and uses them to defend his own method of translating Christian sources: 'Ego enim non solum fateor, sed libera uoce profiteor me in interpretatione Graecorum absque scripturis sanctis, ubi et uerborum ordo mysterium est, non uerbum e uerbo sed sensum exprimere de sensu' ('For I do not only admit but I profess with free voice that in translation of the Greeks [except for the holy Scriptures, where there is mystery even in the order of the words] I do not express word for word but sense for sense').[17] In translating Porphyry's *Eisagoge*, Boethius deliberately runs counter to the tradition of Horace, Cicero, and Jerome by insisting on giving an

[14] Varro, *De lingua latina*, 7.17.

[15] Cicero, *De optimo genere oratorum*, trans. H. M. Hubbel, Loeb edition (Cambridge, MA, 1949), 5.14.

[16] Horace, *Ars poetica*, ed. H. Rushton Fairclough, Loeb edition (Cambridge, MA, 1955), 133–4.

[17] Jerome, *Sancti Eusebii Hieronymi epistulae*, ed. Isidor Hilberg, CSEL 54 (Vienna and Leipzig, 1910), 57.5 (I.508); also in Saint Jérôme, *Lettres*, ed. Jérôme Labourt (Paris, 1953), III.59, and in Hieronymus, *Liber de optimo genere interpretandi (Epistula 57): ein Kommentar*, ed. G.J.M. Bartelink, Mnemosyne 61 (Leiden, 1980), p. 13. For the later medieval development of the topic, the *fidus interpres*, see John V. Fleming's essay in this volume. I wish to acknowledge and thank Prof. Fleming for information and bibliography on this important subject, and for allowing me to summarize the pertinent elements of its early usage here.

exact word-for-word translation of the Greek philosophic treatise; he disregards stylistic elegance for literal accuracy, incurring the 'fidi interpretis culpam' ('the fault of a faithful interpreter').[18] In the many glosses and translations that were the standard staple of the Middle Ages, Boethius's method generally held sway.

The function of *interpres* as a translator from one language to another was well known to Bede. Indeed, he frequently refers to the 'septuaginta interpretes' (the Greek translators of the Septuagint Bible) in his commentaries. He himself worked from the Greek text in order to interpret the Acts of the Apostles.[19] Bede's disciple Cuthbert claims that Bede had turned to translating the Gospel of John in his last days, and reports that during his last days Bede continually recited the grim little Old English poem now known as 'Bede's Death Song'. However, Aldhelm and Bede did not translate Latin sources or their own works into the vernacular. This was to be done in a later Anglo-Saxon epoch, most notably by King Alfred at the end the ninth century and by abbot Ælfric of the Benedictine Reform at the end of the tenth century.[20]

All of the interrelated meanings of *interpres* from classical and late antique sources reappear in early medieval texts. The augmented noun *interpretator*, 'explainer', 'interpreter', first appears in Tertullian, who employs it three times. The only Father to use the coinage is Augustine, who also uses *interpretator* three times. Then it is not found again until Sedulius Scottus in the ninth century, who uses it but once.[21] Anglo-Saxon scholars like Aldhelm and Bede, well versed in classical and patristic texts, use *interpres* in its complete semantic range and add their own nuances.[22] In all the meanings of *interpres* I think it important to note

[18] Boethius, *In Isagogen Porphyrii, Editio secunda*, ed. Samuel Brandt, CSEL 48 (Vienna and Leipzig, 1906), p. 148, cited in the essential article by W. Schwarz, 'The Meaning of *Fidus Interpres* in Medieval Translation', *JTS* 45, 73–78.

[19] Beda, *Retractatio in Actus Apostolorum*, ed. M. L. W. Laistner, in *Bedae venerabilis opera*, CCSL 121 (Turnhout, 1983), p. 105: 'quaedam quae in Graeco siue aliter seu plus aut minus posita uidimus, breuiter commemorare curauimus; quae, utrum neglegentia interpretis omissa uel aliter dicta an incuria librariorum sint depreuata siue relicta, nondum scire potuimus'.

[20] I shall discuss in another essay the important question of why vernacular glosses and translations were favoured in the later Anglo-Saxon period but practically non-existent in the earlier period.

[21] Data from CLCLT. See, for example, Tertullian, *De monogamia*, ed. E. Dekkers, in *Tertulliani opera omnia*, II, CCSL 2 (Turnhout, 1954), ch. 6, line 34.

[22] For Aldhelm's knowledge of classical sources, see Michael Lapidge and Michael Herren, eds., *Aldhelm: The Prose Works* (Cambridge, 1979), p. 8 and note 18, and Rudolf Ehwald, ed., *Aldhelmi Opera*, MGH auct. antiqu. XV (Berlin, 1919), pp. 544–546. For Bede's acquaintance and use of classical works, see my *Bede the Venerable* (Boston, 1986), pp. 24–31, and notes 1 and 2 (pp. 112–13) and 15 (p. 114), M. L. W. Laistner, 'The Library of Venerable Bede', in A. Hamilton Thompson, ed., *Bede: His Life, Times and Writings* (Oxford, 1935, reprint 1969), pp. 237–66.

that the *inter-* is always a solid factor: the medium is never not there. Every message, every discourse is transmitted by way of a person who gives a structure, order, and limit to the source. Every *interpres*, true or false, modifies, colours, arranges, forms his matter. Aldhelm and Bede show themselves to be very aware of that.

In the east-west traffic of classical literature and of the Bible, *interpres* usually serves as the Latin equivalent of the Greek ἑρμηνεύς or διερμενευτής. Indeed, ἑρμηνεύς shares much the same range of meanings, from pragmatic 'broker' through professional 'interpreter', divine and human, of a fact or text, to 'translator' of a language.[23] Its etymology is not so simple as most of us, including my colleague, Kurt Mueller-Vollmer, have been led to believe. Prof. Mueller-Vollmer introduces his handbook, *The Hermeneutics Reader,* with the statement that 'the etymology of the term hermeneutics carries an obvious relation to Hermes, the messenger god of the Greeks, and suggests a multiplicity of meanings'.[24] In this, Mueller-Volmer is only agreeing with a long tradition, attested to by Augustine in *De civitate Dei*, and Isidore's *Etymologiae*.[25] However, the foremost recent etymologists of the Greek language, Emile Boisacq, Pierre Chantraine, and Hjalmar Frisk, all insist that ἑρμηνεύς is a technical term without an etymology: Frisk adds that it is 'wahrscheinlich kleinasiatischen Ursprungs'.[26]

Interpres is our concern here; I have only spoken of ἑρμηνεύς because of its relevance to our term and to our hermeneutic investigation. I should mention other words that might be linked to *interpres* in this context, such as *commentator*, *exegetica, expositor, glossator*, and *tractator*. Cumulatively they demonstrate the scope and magnitude of the interpretational vocabulary and suggest the extent of the hermeneutic enterprise. Doing a survey on the CETEDOC data-base CLCLT,[27] I found that Bede, who uses some form of *interpres* about 600 times, also employs frequently (about 480 times) some form of the verb *exponere*,

23 See Liddell and Scott, *Greek-English Lexicon*; William F. Arndt and F. Wilbur Gingrich, eds., *A Greek-English Lexicon of the New Testament and Other Early Christian Literature* (Chicago, 1957); G. Kittel, ed., *Theological Dictionary of the New Testament* (Grand Rapids, 1964), s.v.

24 Kurt Mueller-Vollmer, ed., *The Hermeneutics Reader* (New York, 1989).

25 Augustine, *De civitate Dei*, CCSL 47, book 7, ch. 14, line 13; Isidore, *Etymologiae*, book VIII, ch. 11, par. 45 and 49.

26 Emile Boisacq, ed., *Dictionnaire étymologique de la langue grecque*, 4th ed., (Heidelberg, 1950); Pierre Chantraine, *Dictionnaire étymologique de la lange grecque* (Paris, 1983); Hjalmar Frisk, ed., *Griechisches Etymologisches Wörterbuch* (Heidelberg, 1960), s.v.

27 Supplemented by Putnam Fennell Jones, *A Concordance to the Historia Ecclesiastica of Bede* (Cambridge, MA, 1929). Bede's *HE* and his commentary on the Book of Revelation are not available on CLCLT.

'to expound', 'set forth', 'explain' (in this he is following classical writers and the Fathers, especially Jerome and Gregory the Great). Although he uses the noun *expositio*, he never employs in the singular the noun *expositor*, common in later exegesis, as in the *Glossa ordinaria;* even in the plural Bede uses it only nine times (certainly not with classical meaning of 'one who exposes a child'!). Bede also follows the Fathers' example in sometimes using the verb *tractare*, 'to handle', 'treat', 'investigate' in a hermeneutic sense (some seventy times), and he speaks of *tractatores* seven times, as in the phrase characteristic of his perceived role as an allegorist: 'sequens magnorum uestigia tractatorum' ('I, following the steps of the great tractators').[28] Some forms of these words common in later medieval authors are unusual or even nonexistent in early Anglo-Latin texts. For example, again surveying Bede's writings, we find he never uses *commentator* and employs some form of *commentar-* only nine times; *exegetica* is never found, and a form of the Greek root ἐξηγητ- appears only twice ('exegete' and 'exegesis' did not catch on in the West until after the Renaissance). Various forms of *glossa* show up forty-five times in Bede's treatises, but *glossator* never. The verb *pando,* in its senses of 'to render visible', 'disclose', 'uncover', 'make known', 'reveal', was taken over from classical sources by Christian exegetes, and both Aldhelm and Bede use the term for 'to interpret'.[29] There are a number of verbs used by classical writers for 'translate', such as *verto*, *converto*, *transfero*, *reddo*, and *exprimo* without a matching agent-noun; *interpres* is the noun of choice, and this is usual in medieval Latin as well.

The wealth of synonyms for *interpres* in the patristic and medieval thesaurus causes no surprise. The Fathers all thought of themselves as interpreters and spent most of their professional lives interpreting Scripture and one another, and they developed an extensive professional language of exegesis. Similarly, Bede proclaims himself as an interpreter 'sequens vestigia patrum' and uses their vocabulary for traditional and original exegesis.

Turning to the Bible text, we see that ἑρμηνεύς in the Septuagint Old Testament and the Greek New Testament and the Latin *interpres* in St Jerome's Latin Bible appear a number of times in various nominal and verbal forms, and so do other interpretative words, such as *explano,*

[28] *De templo* prolog., CCSL 119A, p. 144, line 55.

[29] Aldhelm also uses *pandesco.* I know of only one occurrence of the agent-noun *panditor* in the entire history of Latin. Guido Aretinus (d. c. 1050) calls Boethius 'Panditor huius artis' [sc. musicae]; see *Novum Glossarium Mediae Latinitatis*, ed. Yves Lefèvre, fascicule P-Panis (1985), s.v.

explico, expono, indico.[30] It is important to note that the Bible distinguishes between the *interpretes* of the pagans and the *interpretes* of God's chosen people, insisting that the true interpreter must be divinely imbued and inspired. Particularly noteworthy are the episodes of the patriarch Joseph as the interpreter of the butler's and baker's dreams in chapter 40 of Genesis and of the pharaoh's dream in chapter 41. In chapter 40, verse 8 (see also 41: 16), the text stresses that interpretation must come from God through the instrument of his gifted interpreter, Joseph: 'Dixitque ad eos Ioseph / numquid non Dei est interpretatio / referte mihi quid videritis' ('Joseph said to them, does not interpretation belong to God? Tell me what you have dreamed'). Similarly, in the Book of Daniel, 2: 27–28, Daniel asserts that 'no wise men, enchanters, magicians, or astrologers can show to the king the mystery which the king has asked, but there is a God in heaven who reveals mysteries' ('sed est Deus in caelo revelans mysteria'). Jerome's commentary on this text was known to Aldhelm and Bede.[31]

In the New Testament, not only are the apostles, Paul, and members of the *ecclesia* (as in I Corinthians 12: 10, 14: 28) the interpreters of Jesus's message, but the gospels themselves are interpreters of the Old Testament. Ultimately Jesus himself is, as St Ambrose says, the 'verus interpres Christus'.[32] Not only does Christ in Luke 4: 18 interpret the text of Isaiah in the synagogue but presents himself there as the interpretation and fulfilment of the message: the medium is indeed the message. He reveals the meaning of the Scriptures to the disciples during his life, and as the risen Christ in Luke 24: 27 he expounds the Old Testament prophecies to the two disciples on the road to Emmaus. In Christological discourse through the following centuries his essential position as *interpres*, mediator, between God and man as God-man, is explored by the Fathers and dogmatized in the credal Symbola.

To interpret the meaning of the Scriptures and of Christ, fathers and monks learned their hermeneutic principles and techniques from the schools, from grammarians of the late antique world, from the literary classics, from the Bible and its ardent exegetes, like Philo and Origen, who established hermeneutic procedures of literal and allegorical interpretation.

[30] For Greek, see Kittel and Arndt; for the Latin Bible, consult *Novae Concordantiae Sacrorum Iuxta Vulgatam Versionem Critice Editam*, ed. Bonifatius Fischer (Stuttgart, 1977), 5 vols.

[31] Hieronymus, *Commentariorum in Danielem Libri III* {*IV*}, ed. F. Glorie, CCSL 75A (Turnhout, 1974); see Lerer, *Literacy and Power*, p. 128.

[32] Ambrosius Mediolanensis, *Expositio euangelii secundum Lucam*, CCSL 14, book 7, line 496.

Isidore of Seville's *Etymologiae* known throughout Europe and especially popular in the British Isles, was plundered by Aldhelm and used by Bede (even though Bede had reservations about Isidore's reliability). It served as a universal encyclopedia and general lexicon of the Latin language in the early Middle Ages. Isidore has three entries on *interpres*. First in Book II, *De rhetorica et dialectica*, while cursorily summarizing Aristotle's *De perihermeniis* (*On Interpretations*), a work he judges 'subtilissimus nimis', Isidore gives a curiously modern and for our larger theme an apt definition: 'Omnis enim elocutio conceptae rei mentis interpres est' ('Every expression of a conceived thing is the mind's interpreter'. In Book VI, *De libris et officiis ecclesiasticis*, as soon as he has described the Bible and libraries (that is, from Biblis to Bibliothecis), he considers *De interpretibus*. First he deals with the seventy *interpretes* of the Septuagint Bible; then he lists the other famous editors and translators of the Biblical text, namely, Aquila, Symmachus, Theodotion, Origen, and Jerome, whose version Isidore especially commends. Finally, in Book X, *De vocabulis*, Isidore gives two main definitions of *interpres* that express the roles of interpreter as translator and exegete: 'Interpres, quod inter partes medius sit duarum linguarum, dum transferet. Sed et qui [quem] interpretatur et hominum quibus divina indicat mysteria, interpres vocatur [quia inter eam quam transferet]' ('Interpreter, [so called] because he is the medium between two languages while he translates. And also he is called interpreter who interprets and explains the divine mysteries to men').[33]

The missionaries who brought Christianity to Anglo-Saxon England had to serve as interpreters in both senses, transferring a foreign language and bringing literacy to a West Germanic people of principally oral tradition, and introducing the mysteries of the Christian religion in its Latin cultural matrix. In selecting the major events of English history, Bede was certainly right in placing in high relief the coming of Christianity to England in the Augustinian mission of 597.[34] The recent exhibition of the British Museum and the British Library, called 'The Making of England: Anglo-Saxon Art and Culture AD 600–900', graphically displayed to the eye the enormous ideological and cultural importance of the eventual adoption of Christianity in Anglo-Saxon England. In the stunning catalogue of the exhibition the art historian, Susan Youngs points out:

> The acceptance of the Christian religion was of far-reaching importance because it involved the introduction of literacy and the written record, the

[33] Isidore, *Etymologiae*, II.27; VI.4; X. lit. I, 123.

[34] Bede's *Ecclesiastical History of the English People* (*HE*), ed. Bertram Colgrave and R. A. B. Mynors (Oxford, 1969), I.25–33.

> introduction of Latin as a vehicle for the transmission of knowledge and because, implicitly, it involved the acceptance of an authority beyond the boundaries of the kingdom, acceptance of the servants of the Church as a source of local authority, and as consumers of precious resources.[35]

For the mission, Pope Gregory had ordered Augustine to take along Frankish interpreters ('de gente Francorum interpretes') to 'bring the best of news' to the powerful King Æthelberht and the Kentish people; but of course the real intermediaries (interpreters) between the Roman Church and its Scriptures and the Germanic pagan Anglo-Saxons were the somewhat reluctant Augustine and his forty companions. They were aided greatly in their mission by the mediation of Queen Bertha, Æthelberht's Christian wife of the Frankish royal family.[36] The 'proselytizers of the new religion had behind them the fortifying knowledge that this was indeed the *old* religion, the faith of emperors, of the Roman world. . . .'[37] Most of the information we have about the conversion process comes through the interpretative filter of Bede, who describes the gradual extension of Christianity, with some setbacks, until it achieved the conversion of all the Anglo-Saxon nations in less than a century (by the 680s).

Christianity, like its disaffected parent Judaism and its hostile sibling Islam, was and is a religion of the book. In all three religions the scribe held an important position, not just as an amanuensis but also as a conveyor and interpreter of the book.[38] The Bible was interpreted by books – commentaries, homilies, liturgical manuals, laws, monastic and ecclesiastical rules, penitentials, papal and episcopal correspondence, apologetics, chronicles and histories. Those books, to be read and understood, depended upon other books: grammars, glossaries, educational treatises, literature. The Augustinian missionaries therefore were obliged to establish an educational program to train a native clergy as writers and interpreters of the book to the people. Within a generation there was a functioning school system. After the first native archbishop of Canterbury, Deusdedit, died and then his designated English successor, Wigheard, also died in miasmic Rome before receiving the pallium, Pope Vitalian appointed the aged Greek monk living in Rome,

[35] Susan M. Youngs, 'Pagan and Christian', in *The Making of England: Anglo-Saxon Art and Culture AD 600–900*, ed. Leslie Webster and Janet Backhouse (London, 1991), p. 15.

[36] *HE* I.25.

[37] Youngs, 'Pagan and Christian', p. 15.

[38] As one indication of the major role of the scribe in the Christian tradition, note that the portraits of the Evangelists in the early medieval Gospels are regularly depicted as scribes, after the model of Ezra.

Theodore.[39] This the pope did in 668, on the advice of the Neapolitan abbot, Hadrian, who with the Northumbrian Benedict Biscop was sent along with Theodore as a companion.[40] The consequences of the mission for education in England were momentous. The Greek Theodore and the African Hadrian established in Canterbury a prestigious school that served as a model for major monasteries throughout Anglo-Saxon England and for zealous literati like Aldhelm and Bede. Full of admiration, Bede says of Theodore and Hadrian:

> Because both of them were extremely learned in sacred and secular literature, they attracted a crowd of students into whose minds they daily poured the streams of wholesome learning. They gave their hearers instruction not only in books of holy Scripture but also in the art of metre, astronomy, and ecclesiastical computation. As evidence of this, some of their students still survive who know Latin and Greek as well as their native tongue.[41]

'The nature and results of their teaching', adds Michael Lapidge, 'can be seen in the recently discovered commentaries on the Pentateuch and the Gospels, which are a record of their classroom exposition of the biblical text as it was copied down by their English students. These commentaries draw on an extraordinary range of patristic authorities, mostly Greek, including Basil, John Chrysostom, Clement of Alexandria, Ephrem the Syrian, Epiphanius, Gregory of Nazianzen and others'.[42]

Foremost among Theodore and Hadrian's students was Aldhelm, who became abbot of Malmesbury and ended his career as bishop of Sherbourne (d.709). Well versed in classical, biblical, and patristic texts, he displayed his learning with verve in all his writings. He fostered a prose style once thought to derive from Irish clerical training but now shown to have continental origins.[43] This style has been described as 'hermeneutic', which, although the adjective gets its name from glossaries of abstruse words called 'Hermeneutica', aptly indicates

39 On Theodore's interesting and complex background see Michael Lapidge, 'The New Learning' in *Making of England*, pp. 71–72; see also his 'The Anglo-Latin Background', in *A New Critical History of Old English Literature*, ed. Stanley B. Greenfield and Daniel G. Calder (New York, 1986), pp. 1–10, with references in note 13 to articles by Nicholas Brooks, Allen Frantzen, and Bernhard Bischoff.

40 'The Pope, fearing that [Theodore's] orthodoxy might be corrupted by his Greek upbringing, arranged for Benedict Biscop and Hadrian to accompany him to Britain', *The Oxford Dictionary of the Christian Church*, ed. F. L. Cross and E. A. Livingstone, 2nd ed. (Oxford, 1983), p. 1360.

41 *HE* IV.2, pp. 332–35. See my commentary in *Bede the Venerable*, pp. 6–8.

42 Lapidge, 'New Learning', p. 71.

43 See Michael Winterbottom, 'Aldhelm's Prose Style and its Origins', *ASE* 6(1977), 39–76; Lapidge, 'Anglo-Latin Background', p. 11.

something about Aldhelm's purpose in writing such a turgid, ostentatious, arcane, florid, alliterative prose. For it glosses the topic by means of bookish allusion and pedantic exposition. A good example of his hermeneutic mode is the ponderous *Epistola ad Acircium*, to King Aldfrith of Northumbria. The preface includes the longest disquisition on the allegorical meanings of the number seven that I know in early medieval Latin (taking more than a dozen pages in Ehwald's edition).[44] Explicating the allegorical significance of seven by exhaustively ransacking every biblical and classical Latin instance housed in his library and memory is indubitably a form of interpretation, even if couched in the purplest of prose.

The main part of the epistle contains two tracts on metrics. After the first, *De metris*, Aldhelm enters his collection of one hundred *Enigmata*, ostensibly as illustrations of the properties of the hexameter. In the preface to the *Enigmata*, which is in the form of an acrostic, Aldhelm calls upon the eternal *Arbiter* to grant him 'to reveal by your decree the hidden mysteries of things through my verse' ('Munera nunc largire, rudis quo pandere rerum/ Versibus enigmata queam clandestina fatu').[45] Aldhelm says God will be able to inspire him, 'freely breathing his holy gifts into my obtuse mind' ('Inspirans stolidae pia gratis munera menti' – line 15). He concludes: 'But if these (present) Enigmata in verse, after all blemishes and awkwardness have been completely expunged, are to come off well at an hexametrical pace, and if no delusion seduces my mental efforts with empty deception, I shall begin (to sing of) even mightier (themes), if God – who once strengthened his warrior Job – shall refresh the parched inwards of His servant with a draught of everlasting dew' (lines 25–31). Clearly, in this serio-comic book of riddles Aldhelm as a revealer of nature and the mysterious qualities of things has elevated his revelatory role by comparing himself with Moses, David, and Job. The *enigmata* that follow are the expression of an Anglo-Saxon scholar writing in the literate Latin culture newly housed in the southwestern Anglo-Saxon monastery. The *enigmata* reveal their bookish Latin pedigree. Nicholas Howe has shown that many of the enigmata are based on descriptions of objects in Isidore's *Etymologiae*, and 'at least forty of the *Enigmata* depend directly on linguistic puzzles and clues'.[46]

[44] Ehwald, *Aldhelmi opera*, pp. 62-74. Translation by Michael Herren in *Aldhelm: The Prose Works* (Cambridge: D. S.Brewer, 1979), pp. 34–44.

[45] Lapidge and Rosier, *Aldhelm: The Poetic Works* (Cambridge, 1985) 70; *Enigmata*, praefatio, 7–8.

[46] Nicholas Howe, 'Aldhelm's *Enigmata* and Isidoran Etymology', *ASE* (1985) 14, 37–59, at p. 57.

In his recent book, *Literacy and Power in Anglo-Saxon Literature*, Seth Lerer has called attention to the fact that 'Aldhelm frames the whole collection [of *Enigmata*] in two treatments of the scope and enigmatic power of Creation', with the first four riddles recapitulating 'the designs of the preface, as earth, wind, cloud, and nature come together to present a microcosm of the ninety-odd poems that follow', and the series is enveloped at the end with a long climactic riddle, *De Creatura*. The riddles deal with nature and artifacts, but textually in game.

> If. . . the phenomenon of learned riddling is to place the world of experience on the page, then the engagement with that riddling is also to take place on the page. The proper understanding of the *aenigmata* is to be attained through the accepted methods of grammatical explication. The dialogue between the student and the teacher, the reader and the text, occurs not through the mouth, but on the folio.[47]

As further evidence of this textuality, Lerer cites the heavily glossed tenth and eleventh-century manuscripts of Aldhelm's *Enigmata.*

'Incipiam potiora', Aldhelm had pledged in his Letter to Acircium, but the *potiora* turned out to be not commentaries on Scripture, as Bede would do, but an aureate treatise on virginity, first in prose, then, following the tradition of the *opus geminatum*, in poetry.[48] For writing these works on virginity Aldhelm had long literary precedence. Nearly every major Church Father had written such a treatise: 'Tertullian, Cyprian, Jerome, Ambrose and Augustine in prose, and Alcimus Avitus and Venantius Fortunatus in verse'.[49] However, although Aldhelm was following tradition, as an interpreter he had enough independence to change on account of Anglo-Saxon and specifically the Barking Convent's social structure the traditional ecclesiastical distinction between virginity, widowhood, and marriage to virginity (*virginitas*), chastity (*castitas*), and marriage (*iugalitas*) (chapter 19).[50]

Sections of the dedicatory preface to Abbess Hildelith, 'teacher of the regular discipline and the monastic way of life', and the other noble nuns of Barking, will demonstrate well the kind of magisterial *interpres* Aldhelm personifies. Note how literacy is for Aldhelm the principal means of communicating Christian ascetic discourse, and how the whole monastic curriculum forms an interpretative program in the religious life. He says in section II that he is responding to Hildelith's letters, in which

47 *Literacy and Power*, pp. 106, 107.

48 On the genre of the *opus geminatum*, see the bibliography I cite in my *Bede the Venerable*, p.123 n. 9, especially the essays by Michael Lapidge, Gernot Wieland, and Peter Godman.

49 Lapidge, *Aldhelm: Prose Works*, p. 52.

50 See Lapidge, *Aldhelm: Prose Works*, pp. 53–56.

he admired her extremely rich verbal eloquence and sophistication. He rejoices in these daughters of the Word, spiritual athletes striving for the crown, who, 'traversing the spacious race-courses of the Scriptures, are known to exercise the most subtle industry of their minds and the quality of their lively intelligence through assiduous perseverance in reading'.[51] Exuberantly expanding the old literary topos of the bee drawing nectar, he continues:

> In the same way your remarkable mental disposition, roaming widely through the flowering field of scripture, traverses them with thirsty curiosity. . ., scrutinizing with careful application the hidden mysteries of the ancient [Mosaic] laws. . ., and now exploring wisely the fourfold [Gospel] text of the evangelical story, expounded through the mystical commentaries of the catholic fathers and laid open spiritually to the very core and divided up by the rules of the fourfold ecclesiastical tradition according to *historia, allegoria, tropologia*, and *anagoge*; now duly rummaging through the old stories of the historians and the entries of the chroniclers, who by their writing have delivered to lasting memory the chance vicissitudes of times gone by; now, sagaciously inquiring into the rules of the grammarians and the teachings of experts on spelling and the rules of metrics (as they are) measured out into accents (and) times, fitted into poetic feet, broken up into cola and commata – that is, into pentimemeres and eptimemeres – and, indeed, divided individually into a hundred kinds of metre.[52]

The recondite Aldhelm in his admittedly 'verbose garrulity and garrulous verbosity' is himself a plucker 'of crimson flowers or purity from the meadow of holy books',[53] and he approvingly defines the abbess and her literate nuns as anthologizers, as well as adepts of the monastic curriculum, whose studies bring them as dedicated virginal witnesses to full service of the Word. As he scrolls through the famous figures of the Old Testament, Elijah, Elisha, Jeremiah, and Daniel, he presents them as loyal messengers of God and chaste channels of God's mysteries. Daniel is the ideal *interpres*: 'To him above other mortals, as a reward in exchange for his chastity, hidden things lie open and things closed in the mystical coverings of the sacraments are divinely unlocked'.[54] For Jerome and for Isidore, Daniel is 'an interpreter of dreams and visions, symbols and *aenigmata*', who accurately explains Nebuchadnezzar's dream and also predicts the coming of Christ; for

[51] Lapidge, *Aldhelm: Prose Works*, pp. 60–62.

[52] Translated by Lapidge, *Aldhelm: Prose Works*, pp. 61–62, with some omissions.

[53] *De virginitate prosa*, c. 19; quoted in Lapidge and Herren, *Aldhelm: Prose Works*, p. 58.

[54] On the presentation of Daniel as interpreter in Aldhelm and in the Old English Daniel, see the astute analysis by Lerer, who also cites these lines, in *Literacy and Power*, pp. 132–36.

Aldhelm, in addition, Daniel is the model whose hermeneutic methods exemplify the ideals of Aldhelm's monastic interpretation of the Scriptures.[55]

Having presented idealized portraits of these Old Testament virgins, Aldhelm moves on to representatives in the New Testament (John the Baptist, John the Evangelist, Thomas, Paul and Luke); he then proceeds to males and females of the Christian Church. Significant for an understanding of Aldhelm's interpretation is the fact that of the forty-eight exemplary virgins portrayed, only two do not have an identified written source. Indeed, some of them, such as the monk Amos of Nitria, are so inscribed in booklore that they had no cult or recognition in the Anglo-Saxon liturgy, calendars, or monastic office.[56] In chapter 49, Aldhelm insists that the virtues of Eustochium and Demetrias should not be excluded, he says, 'by the sheets of our writing and by parchment-leaves of our letters' ('a nostris litterarum scedulis et apicum pittaciolis'). Eustochium was particularly renowned 'throughout the western Empire for the brilliant quality of her book-learning', and for the fact that Jerome dedicated to her 'in a lengthy series of words' the eighteen-volume commentary on the prophecies of Isaiah. Here Aldhelm mentions by preterition Jerome's 'remaining commentaries' and refers to him as 'divinae legis interpres'. Although he devotes no chapter to Jerome in this prose treatise, he gives him a major section as the last but not least male in the poetic *De virginitate* (verses 1619–52). There Jerome is 'interpres et custos virgo pudoris' ('virgin guardian and interpreter [or perhaps, 'spokesman'] of chastity'), whose role as scribal interpreter encompassed both turning 'the Hebrew prophecies into Roman words' by his translation of the Bible and also unravelling 'the secret words of the prophets in a certain commentary, revealing the mysteries of things'.

Despite the fact that Aldhelm admires such interpreters as Jerome and the Fathers as commentators of Scripture, he (unlike Bede) wrote no such commentaries but worked as an interpreter in his epistles, treatises, and verses. The question is, however: if Aldhelm thought of himself as a learned interpreter of God's mysteries, why did he write a Latin 'extremely difficult and sometimes impenetrable', with 'tediously long and complicated sentences', couched in words that are 'often bizarre and arcane, sometimes inscrutable'?[57] I suppose the same question could and should be put to contemporary interpreters about their own use of interpretative language. But for Aldhelm, a first generation Christian and

[55] Lerer, *Literacy and Power*, pp. 133–34.

[56] Lapidge and Herren, *Aldhelm: Prose Works*, p. 58; Appendix III: Check-List of Sources of Aldhelm's Exemplary Virgins, pp. 176–78.

[57] Quotations from Lapidge, *Aldhelm: Prose Works*, General Introduction, p. 4.

Latinist, who had been trained in the hermeneutic style and who flaunted his command of it, this was the proper mode of interpretation, 'in tam densa totius Latinitatis silva'[58] which provided a wealth of signs, significations, meanings and interpretations, especially figurative and allegorical, to 'explicare et explanare' the biblical text. The 'opaca secreta' of the Scriptures, as Augustine calls them,[59] are interpreted by some, such as Aldhelm, with a further opacity providing still further depth and wonder. Aldhelm's purpose in creating his dense prose is to lure the students into the forest to discover the beauties and the truth concealed therein. The producer of the *Enigmata*, who invites the pupils to probe the riddling truths of the cosmos with bookish wisdom, generates as Christian pedagogue an enigmatically riddling language and style that is opaque and allusive even to the members of the restricted community of learned discourse.

This is not the mode of Venerable Bede (c. 673–735), nor of his Latin, though he too was famous, 'eximius', for his literary and biblical learning. It is a relief, after wrestling with Aldhelm's aureate Latin, to read the sober, communicative Latin of Bede. That 'clear and limpid' Latin has often been praised. The great Insular Latinist, Charles Plummer, with whom later scholars such as C. L. Wrenn and Winthrop Wetherbee are in complete agreement, remarks about the purity and ease of Bede's Latin: 'It is very seldom that we have to pause to think of the meaning of a sentence. There is no affectation of a false classicality, and no touch of the puerile pomposity of his contemporary Aldhelm, for whom, however, he cannot help feeling a kind of admiration'.[60] Bede is an educator, not a pedant. He lays out his career in the brief biographical sketch at the end of the *Historia ecclesiastica*:

> From the age of seven I have spent all my life in this monastery [of Wearmouth-Jarrow], applying myself to the study of the Scriptures; and, amid the observance of the discipline of the Rule and the daily task of singing in the church, it has always been my delight to learn or to teach or to write.

He adds that his career has been that of an *interpres*:

> From the time I became a priest until the fifty-ninth year of my life I have made it my business, for my own benefit and that of my brothers, to make brief extracts from the works of the venerable fathers on the holy

[58] Aldhelm, *De metris et enigmatibus ac pedum regulis* ('Letter to Acircius'), 8, MGH auct. antiqu., p. 77, line 5.

[59] Augustine, *Confessiones*, ed. Lucas Verheijen, CCSL 27 (Turnhout, 1981), XI.2.27.

[60] Charles Plummer, *Venerabilis Baedae opera historica*, I (Oxford, 1896), liii–liv, cited along with quotations from Wrenn and Wetherbee in notes 1 and 2 to chapter 4 of my *Bede the Venerable*, pp. 121–122.

> Scriptures, or to add notes of my own to clarify their sense and interpretation (ad formam sensus et interpretationis eorum).[61]

He then subjoins his bibliography, the fulfillment of his biography, thereby furnishing a list of his writings available for copying and interpretation. The corpus, most of it still extant, reveals that he produced works in every discipline of the monastic school system, structured to the needs and abilities of his students. Fully aware of the religious and political power of literacy and the Anglo-Saxons' need for it, striving to provide it, Bede met with resistance.

> I have intended to take into account the inertia of our nation, namely the English, which not long since, in the time of Pope Gregory, received the seed of faith and has cherished it only lukewarmly so far as reading is concerned; so I have set about not only to elucidate the meaning but also to compress the substance. For plain brevity is usually better fixed in the memory than prolix discussion.[62]

Bede was acutely aware of the need for Latin literacy for his community and, more largely, for the recently converted Anglo-Saxon nations. In embracing the pedagogical onus of making reading easier for his students in order to ensure some understanding, Bede followed the teaching of Augustine and Jerome concerning the intrinsic relationship, evident in the Latin words, between reading and understanding (*legere et intellegere*), which are the functions of the *interpres*.[63]

Bede's educational treatises, basic school texts and reference works, gave access to classical authorities and provided supplements to late antique manuals. He considered these propaedeutics to the study and interpretation of Scripture. His admirably scientific writings on computus and chronology (authoritative until the Renaissance) established a new standard. His commentaries on the Bible offered students a carefully edited and annotated synthesis of patristic sources, particularly the four Fathers of the western Church. So successful was he as editor and interpreter that by the ninth century he himself was ranked as a Father of the Church and even now he enjoys the rank of *doctor ecclesiae*.[64] The books of the Bible he chose to interpret are of two types: those that were

[61] *HE*, V.24, pp. 566–67.

[62] Prefatory letter to Eusebius (Hwætbehrt), *In Apocalypsim*, *PL* 93.134AB.

[63] Sancti Aurelii Augustini in Ioannis Euangelium Tractatus CXXIV, CCSL 36, tractate 24.2, pp. 144–45. Discussing this passage in connection with King Alfred's education, Lerer remarks, *Literacy and Power*, p. 66, '*Legere* and *intellegere*, reading and understanding, become the paired actions of the discerning interpreter'. He introduces the passage from Jerome, *In Danielem* 2.5.25/28 on p. 156, to which he adds: 'Reading, understanding, and interpreting come together in a way of making public the hidden meanings of religious texts'.

[64] See my *Bede the Venerable*, pp. 98–99.

already favourites of the Fathers, such as the commentaries on Genesis and on Luke, and those that were largely ignored by earlier exegetes, such as the commentaries on Ezra and Nehemiah and on the New Testament Catholic Epistles. Both filled pedagogical needs: the former display Bede's talents as an adapter and synthesizer, and the latter testify to Bede's originality within the exegetical tradition. In both the anthological and original kinds of commentary, Bede's interpretative mind is always at work, deciding which authority to follow, which opinion to incorporate and which to exclude, what comments to add, and what sort of synthesis to form. In doing this he asserts he is but using and developing the God-given talent referred to in the gospel parable (Matthew 25: 14–30).[65]

Bede found the treasures of God's revelation to be infinitely rich and inexhaustible. In order to delve for them, Bede, like Augustine, used whatever exegetical tools and methods deemed appropriate to the task. Therefore his hermeneutic practice is eclectic and literary, but (like Pope Gregory) usually favouring a moral interpretation over a speculative one. Though his general procedure is allegorical and sometimes, as in the *De templo*, exuberant, it is not exclusively so, since in such works as his commentary on the Acts of the Apostles he demonstrates an essentially historical, Hieronymic approach. He enuntiates the principle: 'Whoever expends effort on the allegorical sense should not leave the plain truth of history in allegorizing'.[66]

For Bede, preaching was a major form of teaching the meaning of the Scriptures, correct theological understanding, and moral rectitude; it had a special, even sacramental significance. However, according to his view, preachers are the successors of the prophets and apostles.[67] Even though in his famous letter to his erstwhile student, Bishop Egbert of York,[68] he urged missionizing and preaching among the people of Northumbria, this 'scribe trained for the kingdom of heaven' (Matthew 14: 52) himself contributed to the apostolate by composing a series of homilies, largely based on his gospel commentaries but adapted for the pulpit (or, probably more correctly, for the monastic chapterhouse). His method is to take the assigned gospel for the day's feast and probingly extract from its verses meanings for the edification of the attentive Christian. It is a meditative process of rumination, savouring the spiritual

65 *PL* 93.134A.

66 *In Genesim* I.1, CCSL 118A, p. 3, lines 30–31; cf. *In Lucam* III. 10. 29, CCSL 120, p. 222, lines 2206–9.

67 See Alan Thacker, 'Bede's Ideal of Reform', in *Ideal and Reality in Frankish and Anglo-Saxon Society*, ed. Patrick Wormald (Oxford, 1983), pp. 130–31.

68 Epistola ad Ecgbertum Episcopum, ed. C. Plummer, in *Baedae opera historica*, I, 405–23; translated by Dorothy Whitelock, in *EHD* I, no. 70.

content.[69] Within sober limits, they show a considerable range of interpretative art. Sermons for the great high feasts of joy display more overall shape, structural symmetry, figures of speech, cadenced endings, and a higher style. Homilies for vigils, Advent, and Lent show a suitably simpler mode and a more verse-by-verse approach.[70] In the introduction to the newly published Homilies of Bede, Lawrence Martin indicates some of Bede's creativity and originality in his use of patristic sources.[71]

For the genre of hagiography, Bede tells us he composed:

> a book on the life and passion of St Felix the Confessor, which I put into prose from the metrical version of Paulinus; a book on the life and passion of St Anastasius which was badly translated from the Greek by some ignorant person, which I have corrected as best I could, to clarify the meaning. I have also described the life of the holy father Cuthbert, monk and bishop, first in heroic verse and then in prose.[72]

In addition, Bede put together 'a book of hymns in various meters and rhythms', as well as 'a book of epigrams in heroic and elegiac meter', only a few of which are extant.

Bede's historical writings, for which he is most remembered now, formed a model for later medieval historiographers and are still the principal sources for information about Anglo-Saxon England through the first quarter of the eighth century. Although his history of the abbots of Wearmouth and Jarrow is a fine piece, containing precious information about the great men, Benedict Biscop, Ceolfrith, and Hwætberht, and the monastery where they were the first leaders and Bede's own superiors, it is too limited in historical scope to compete with the culminating work of his career, the *Ecclesiastical History of the English People*. After two decades of scholarly commenting on the Bible, Bede had just finished the *De templo Salomonis*. Henry Mayr-Harting has pointed out that 'the two works are complementary to each other, the *De templo* treating its subject as an allegory of the building of the universal church, partly still in pilgrimage on earth, partly reigning in

[69] On Bede's elaborate use of the biblical, patristic, and monastic meanings of *ruminatio* as an interpretative mode, see Gernot Wieland, 'Caedmon, the Clean Animal', ABR 35 (1984) 194–203, and the bibliography cited; in addition, see Lerer, *Literacy and Power*, pp. 44–48.

[70] See my *Bede the Venerable*, The Homilies, pp. 62–65.

[71] Bede the Venerable, *Homilies on the Gospels*, trans. Lawrence Martin and David Hurst (Kalamazoo, 1991), pp. xvii–xxii.

[72] *HE* V.24, pp. 568–71; see my *Bede the Venerable*, Hagiography, pp. 65–73; to which should be added, for Bede's lives of Cuthbert, Michael Lapidge, 'Bede's Metrical Vita S. Cuthberti' and Walter Berschin, 'Opus deliberatum et perfectum: Why Did the Venerable Bede Write a Second Prose Life of St Cuthbert?' in *St Cuthbert, his Cult and his Community to AD 1200*, ed. Gerald Bonner (Woodbridge, 1988), pp. 72–93, 95–102.

heaven, while the *Ecclesiastical History* describes the building up of the church amongst the English'.[73] All his mature hermeneutic skills are brought to bear on the *History*, which is based on biblical rather than classical concepts of time and event, presupposing a theocentric universe in which primary concern is focused on the sacred, and the secular is understood in terms of the sacred. It is history that traces the development of the church as it advances in time and geography to 'the ends of the earth' (Acts 1: 8), but it is also the history of one nation, the English people, now one of God's chosen tribes.

In the preface to King Ceolwulf of Northumbria, Bede lays out his sources and some of his methodology. He credits a number of personal authorities and oral tradition, but the stress is laid upon his most important sources of information, written records and accounts. Documents empower and are authoritative, but it is Bede who arranges and interprets them on every page. As Bede notes at the end of the *History*, the material was assembled 'either from ancient documents or from tradition or from my own knowledge'.[74] But the hermeneutic result is totally his art, an inscribed art.

As in all his works, *interpres* both as a word and as a concept figures largely. Bede is the authorial interpreter who, unlike Gregory of Tours in the *History of the Franks*, gently but firmly controls his narrative. He brings order out of a chaotic welter of lacunose sources, masterfully engineering a structure that coheres. Each of the five books and their parts manifests an artistic organizational symmetry. Besides ordering his material chronologically and geographically, Bede also arranges it in clusters by association with a certain person, place, or event. As Donald Fry has observed, 'Bede's *Ecclesiastical History* contains fifty-one miracles, most of them grouped in clusters, usually around a person, such as Cuthbert, a subgenre, such as visions of hell, or a place, such as the double monastery at Barking'. He unifies the clusters with particular images and symbols. For example, he unifies the Barking series (IV.7–11), with 'complicated patterns of diction and imagery invoking light and fearful confinement'.[75]

Bede's manipulative artistry is often subtle. Seth Lerer analyzes the story told in chapter 22 of Book IV, in which Imma, a thane of King

[73] Henry Mayr-Harting, *The Coming of Christianity to Anglo-Saxon England*, 3rd ed. (University Park, Penn State, 1991), p. 9. On the *HE* as a culmination of all Bede's training, see my *Bede the Venerable*, pp. 81–2, 85.

[74] *HE*, pp. 566–67.

[75] Donald K. Fry, 'Bede Fortunate in His Translator: The Barking Nuns', in *Studies in Earlier Old English Prose*, ed. Paul C. Szarmach, pp. 345–6. See also his 'The Art of Bede II: the Reliable Narrator as Persona', in *The Early Middle Ages*, Acta no. 6 (Binghamton, SUNY, 1982), pp. 63–82.

Ecfrith, is captured in a battle with King Æthelred, but afterwards can not be kept bound through the night. His captor asks him whether he has about him any 'litteras solutorias' (releasing letters, i.e., runic charms) by which he is freeing himself, but Bede explains that his daily escape is a result of the sacramental prayers of Imma's brother, a priest, who each morning at six says a Mass for what he believes is Imma's departed soul. In his analysis of this narrative, Lerer remarks:

> . . . Bede's account of the releasing letters is fragmentary and allusive. He seems to care neither for the wording of the spell not for its historical context, and I would argue that Bede remains deliberately vague on the specifics of this magic not because he wishes to deny the details of forbidden craft, but rather because he needs only to evoke in the reader's mind the impressions of superstitious belief.
>
> Bede's goal, in brief, is transformation rather than preservation. His concern lies with the representation of the Germanic past in a Christian present, and with the need to suppress or mediate the details of that past with symbolic structures of Christian narrative. The *fabulae* behind the releasing letters offer a case of pagan, oral lore juxtaposed against a Christian written *historia*.[76]

To conclude this brief discussion of Bede as interpretative historian, I want to indicate two examples of *interpres* in which Bede combines the two meanings of interpreter as translator and interpreter as negotiating agent. The first takes place in the discussion of the key event of the Council of Whitby, where the disputatious Celtic and Roman factions argue their cases for their differing ecclesiastical practices. After presenting the opposing camps under their leaders, the Irish Colman and the Anglo-Saxon Roman Wilfrid, and before having King Oswiu pronounce in favour of the Roman side, Bede interposes 'the venerable Bishop Cedd, who. . .had been consecrated long before by the Irish and who acted as a most careful interpreter for both parties at the council' ('interpres in eo concilio vigilantissimus utriusque partis').[77] Here we see that Cedd, who is a member of the Irish faction along with the great and powerful Abbess Hild, in whose monastery the council takes place, scrupulously translates and serves as the diplomatic channel by which the hostile parties can come to terms. He represents the uniting of tongues, the *adunatio linguarum,* after the disunity caused by Babel. As Mayr-Harting observes, he 'might be seen as representing at Whitby the heavenly unity of tongues and the unity of the risen church. Bede, furthermore, often shows his

[76] For a fuller appreciation of Bede's technique and purpose in the Imma story, read Lerer's whole chapter, 'The Releasing Letters: Literate Authority in Bede's Story of Imma', in *Literacy and Power*, pp. 30–60.

[77] *HE* III.25, pp. 298–99.

awareness of the need for good linguistic capacities in effective missionary work'.[78]

A similarly polyvalent use of *interpres* occurs in Book IV, in an incident that takes place again at Whitby during the rule of Abbess Hild. It is the famous story of the creation of the first known Anglo-Saxon poet, Caedmon. Chapter 24 begins:

> In the monastery of this abbess, there was a certain brother ('frater quidam') who was specially marked out by the grace of God, so that he used to compose godly and religious songs; thus, whatever he learned from the holy Scriptures by means of interpreters ('quicquid ex divinis litteris per interpretes disceret'), he quickly turned into extremely delightful and moving poetry, in English, which was his own tongue.[79]

Here the *interpretes* are the Anglo-Saxon *boceras*, the exegetes of the Latin Bible and the Christian church, who serve as the intermediaries for the unlettered but divinely graced cowherd. We learn the name of this *frater quidam*, Caedmon, at the moment he withdraws himself from the feasting to receive the gift from God. 'What we find', says Lerer, 'is a poet who is not part of the earlier traditions, a poet who receives his gift not from drink but from God . . . . If Bede strips the origins of English poetry from its ancient mythology of drink, he replaces it with a different kind of ingestion. After he enters the monastery, all Caedmon's subsequent poetic works are products not of spontaneous effusion, but of *ruminatio*'.[80] After witnessing the initial poetic performance,

> they read him a passage of sacred history or doctrine, bidding him make a song out of it, if he could, in metrical form. He undertook the task and went away; on returning next morning he repeated the passage he had been given, which he had put into excellent verse. The abbess, who recognized the grace of God which the man had received, instructed him to renounce his secular habit and to take monastic vows. She and all her people received him into the community of the brothers and ordered that he should be instructed in the whole course of sacred history. He learned all he could by listening to them and then, memorizing it and ruminating over it, like some clean animal chewing the cud ('quasi mundum animal ruminando'), he turned it into the most melodious verse: and it sounded so sweet as he recited it that his teachers became in turn his audience.[81]

The ruminating poet produces a sweet food that is given back to the *interpretes*, so that Caedmon has become the *interpres* of the Word for them. The native Anglo-Saxon unlettered poet has been absorbed into the

78 Mayr-Harting, *Coming of Christianity*, p. 9.
79 *HE* IV, 24, pp. 414–15.
80 Lerer, *Literacy and Power*, p. 44; see also pp. 45–47.
81 *HE* IV, 24, pp. 417–19.

literate culture of the Church but has also become an exemplary *interpres* between the Church and his Anglo-Saxon culture.

Aldhelm and Bede, even though very different monastic personalities, both thought of themselves as *interpretes*, go-betweens and agents, in the larger sense of theological, historical, and literary interpretation. They were negotiants between the Mediterranean Christian Latin written tradition of the Church with its Bible and interpretive texts and the recently converted, traditionally oral Anglo-Saxon peoples. What they accomplished was incalculably great not only for the faith but for literacy and literature. Aldhelm became the first northern native to compose extensively classical verses, hundreds of hexameters and other types, and became a primary exemplar of the hermeneutic prose style. Bede, with a first-rate mind and the great gift of discretion, became the glory of the English nation by his admirably sober Latin prose and more elaborate, if less brilliant, verse. His writings in every genre of the monastic curriculum served as texts for generations; his commentaries and particularly his histories are still models of their kind. Aldhelm and Bede thought of themselves as interpreters. It would help us to assess them and their work if we too considered each of them as, in a widely comprehensive sense, an *interpres*.

THE LITERATE FALLACY: INTERPRETING MEDIEVAL POPULAR NARRATIVE POETRY

KARL REICHL

In a little Irish poem from the early ninth century, written on the margins of a St Gall manuscript of Priscian's *De institutione grammatica*, the poet voices his delight in being outdoors:

> Dom-farcai fidbaidæ fál,
> fom-chain loíd luin – lúad nad cél;
> húas mo lebrán, ind línech,
> fom-chain trírech inna n-én.
>
> Fomm-chain coí menn – medair mass –
> hi mbrot glass de dindgnaib doss.
> Débrad! nom-choimmdiu coíma,
> caín-scríbaimm fo foída ross.
>
> A wall of forest looms above
> and sweetly the blackbird sings;
> all the birds make melody
> over me and my book and things.
>
> There sings to me the cuckoo
> from bush-citadels in grey hood.
> God's doom! May the Lord protect me
> writing well, under the great wood.[1]

It is an unusual setting for a very common medieval occupation. The pose of writing is depicted in innumerable illuminations, and when we think of a medieval *homme de lettres* it is probably the picture of a monk sitting behind a desk and copying a manuscript which comes first to mind. In England one of the earliest illuminations of this kind is found in the famous Codex Amiatinus, which was written around 700 in the twin monasteries of Monkwearmouth and Jarrow in Northumbria. In one of the illustrations of the Old Testament, Ezra the Scribe is seen seated in

[1] Text and translation from J. Carney, ed. and trans., *Medieval Irish Lyrics* (Dublin, 1967), pp. 22–3; for a slighly different text and a more literal translation see G. Murphy, ed. and trans., *Early Irish Lyrics. Eighth to Twelfth Century*, corr. ed. (Oxford, 1962), pp. 4–5. I would like to record my gratitude to Professors John Stevens (Cambridge) and Joseph Harris (Harvard) for their helpful comments on an earlier version of this paper.

front of an open bookcase, with a book on his knees, into which he is writing the Mosaic law. The Evangelists are also commonly represented in the process of writing, with a book or a scroll into which they are busy recording the Divine Word: St Matthew in the Lindisfarne Gospels, for instance, is closely modelled on Ezra in the Codex Amiatinus; in the Rome Gospels (of probably Mercian provenance, c. 800) the same Evangelist rests his left hand, in which he holds a pen-knife, on the book, while he dips his quill into an inkpot with his right hand.[2] Philosophers, scholars and poets are also often portrayed as writing their works in their study, in the midst of manuscripts, bookshelves, writing-desk, inkpots and quills, or in less harmonious surroundings such as Boethius in Theoderic's dungeon or Charles d'Orléans in the Tower of London. In a particularly elaborate representation of a late medieval study Jean Miélot is seen translating a book of miracles for Philippe le Bon of Burgundy (1456).[3] As readers of medieval literature we feel attuned to the stillness of the scholar's study (and perhaps nostalgic as well). For us moderns, too, the most congenial place for reading medieval literature is a well-stocked library, with Migne's *Patrologia* or the *Corpus Christianorum* on one side and the various national text-series of medieval vernacular literature on the other. Now we are ready to read a text *à la médiévale*, comparing and collating it with other texts, glossing and commenting on it, and finally trying to catch its meaning, like a fly in a spider-web, in the fine-spun tissue of intertextual relationships.

I am not arguing that our picture of the medieval intellectual as *homo scriba* is wrong, and I am not suggesting that the view of our medieval literary heritage as that of a bookish, if not monkish civilization is untenable. But these images are one-sided. We know that all through the Middle Ages there was a flourishing oral culture and that many of the works still extant have come about in an oral milieu. Often, however, their survival has been precarious. The existence of Middle English women's songs and *chansons de malmariée*, for instance, can be inferred from slight and fortuitous evidence only: a little poem scribbled on the fly-leaf of a legal manuscript in Lincoln's Inn and the refrain of an English poem prefixed to a religious Latin *contrafactum* in the Red Book of Ossory are virtually all we have.[4] A similar case of 'marginal survival'

[2] See plates 7 (A), 7 (B) and 11 (B) in M. Rickert, *Painting in Britain. The Middle Ages*, The Pelican History of Art, p. 25 (London, 1954).

[3] On Jean Miélot see P. Perdrizet, 'Jean Miélot, l'un des traducteurs de Philippe le Bon', *Revue d'Histoire littéraire de la France* 14 (1907) 472–82. Reproductions of this miniature are also found in popular books; see e.g. *Larousse Enyclopledia of Ancient and Medieval History*, ed. M. Dunan, J. Bowle (London, 1963), p. 374.

[4] For a discussion and edition of the Middle English *chanson de malmariée* see my 'Popular Poetry and Courtly Lyric: The Middle English Pastourelle', *REAL. The*

is that of the popular Italian lyrics preserved in the notary documents from Bologna (*memoriali bolognesi*).[5] But the fact that whatever literary remains from medieval times there are have of necessity been transmitted in writing, has all too often led scholars to adopt the pose of the monk in his scriptorium or the clerk in his study also when interpreting medieval literature of a popular kind. *Beowulf* has been read as a Christian allegory, the *Chanson de Roland* has been viewed as a secularized saint's legend, the Middle English dance-song 'Maiden in the Moor Lay' has been subjected to allegorical exegesis and compared to the apocryphal Book of Esdras, and there has been continued resistance to seeing the Middle English popular romances as anything but the works of literate authors.[6]

Before one argues against the interpretation of popular poetry as written literature, it has to be established that the texts in question have indeed arisen and flourished in an oral context. The terms 'oral' and 'popular' are ambiguous, and when attempting to define them rigorously one is immediately drawn into controversy. A 'truly oral poem' would ideally be a poem orally composed (either in or before performance), orally performed and orally transmitted. Poetry, lyric or narrative, which is cultivated in oral societies obviously conforms to this definition, although even here the 'purity' of an oral tradition turns out to be more often idealization than reality.[7] It is well to recognize that 'oral' is a term which stands in need of qualification; one has to make a distinction between oral composition, performance and transmission, although in the case of medieval literature such a distinction is not always easy to make. Of equal ambiguity is the word 'popular'. Benedetto Croce, in his

Yearbook of Research in English and American Literature 5 (1987) 33–61, pp. 35ff. On lost Middle English lyrical poetry see R. M. Wilson, *The Lost Literature of Medieval England*, 2nd ed. (London, 1970), pp. 159–86.

[5] Edited in S. Orlando, ed., *Rime dei memoriali bolognesi, 1279–1300*, Collezione di poesia, 170 (Torino, 1981).

[6] The strongest case for a reading of *Beowulf* as a Christian allegory has been made in M. E. Goldsmith, *The Mode and Meaning of Beowulf* (London, 1970). For an allegorical interpretation of 'Maiden in the Moor Lay' (edited in T. Silverstein, ed., *Medieval English Lyrics* [London, 1971], pp. 49–50) see D. W. Robertson, Jr., 'Historical Criticism', in *English Institute Essays 1950*, ed. A. S. Downer (New York, 1951), pp. 3–31, pp. 26ff.; for an evaluation of various interpretations of the poem see J. A. Burrow, 'Poems without Contexts', *Essays in Criticism* 29 (1979) 6–32. For a typological interpretation of the *Chanson de Roland* see R. Rütten, *Symbol und Mythus im altfranzösischen Rolandslied*, Archiv für das Studium der neueren Sprachen u. Literature, Beiheft 4 (Braunschweig, 1970). On the Middle English popular romance see below.

[7] Compare R. Finnegan, 'How Oral is Oral Literature?', *Bulletin of the School of Oriental and African Studies* 37 (1974) 52–64; R. Finnegan, *Oral Poetry. Its Nature, Significance and Social Context* (Cambridge, 1977), pp. 16ff.

Poesia popolare e poesia d'arte, points out that the borderline between 'popular poetry' and 'art poetry' is blurred if we look only at formal differences.[8] 'Anonymity', 'fluidity', 'orality' and other characteristics of popular poetry are not unique to this form of poetry, nor are they always present in a work of popular poetry. For Croce these are external characteristics, while a proper definition and appreciation of popular poetry must bring out its internal character, resulting from a particular psychological state:

> Ora, la poesia popolare è, nella sfera estetica, l'analogo di quel che il buon senso è nella sfera intellettuale e la candidezza o innocenza nella sfera morale. Essa esprime moti dell'anima che non hanno dietro di sé, come precedenti immediati, grandi travagli del pensiero e della passione; ritrae sentimenti semplici in corrispondenti semplici forme.[9]

Although this view of popular poetry comprises both poetry 'popular by origin' and 'popular by destination', it is really the former which 'naturally' exhibits the characteristics detailed by Croce.[10] One of these characteristics is the union of word and music, of song and the playing of instruments, a phenomenon which underlines the oral and performance-oriented nature of popular poetry.[11] Even if 'popular' cannot be equated with 'oral', it is the 'orality' of popular poetry which is at stake here: its existence as spoken and sung poetry, as heard rather than read poetry, as poetry performed to an audience by a professional entertainer, as poetry flourishing and (generally) originating in an oral setting.[12]

Most of the debate on orality has been concerned with the problem of demonstrating that a particular work is not only stylistically like an oral poem but genuinely belongs to the realm of oral poetry. Although there is general agreement that for a number of genres like that of the heroic lay

[8] B. Croce, *Poesia popolare e poesia d'arte. Studi sulla poesia italiana dal Tre al Cinquecento*, 2nd ed. (Bari, 1946), pp. 1ff.

[9] 'Popular poetry, then, is in the aesthetic sphere analogous to common sense in the intellectual sphere and to purity and innocence in the moral sphere. It expresses emotions behind which, as their immediate source, there are no great labours of thought or passion; it represents simple feelings in correspondingly simple forms'. *Ibid.*, p. 5.

[10] On the distinction between 'poetry popular by origin' and 'poetry popular by destination' see R. L. Greene, ed. *The Early English Carols*, 2nd rev. and enlarged ed. (Oxford, 1977), p. cxviii.

[11] 'Anche il suo [i.e. della poesia popolare] legame costante o quasi costante (come non accade nella poesia d'arte) col canto e col suono di strumenti musicali si spiega con la considerazione della sua elementarità': Croce, *Poesia popolare*, p. 11.

[12] It is in this (admittedly vague) sense of 'flourishing in an oral milieu' that I use the term 'popular' here. Other terms one would have to take into account in a more thorough discussion of 'popular' than I have space for here are 'traditional' and 'oral-derived', terms often employed in characterizing the written versions of what must originally have been oral poems such as the *chansons de geste* or the Homeric epics.

in Anglo-Saxon times or the *chanson de geste* and the popular romance in the later Middle Ages an oral background can be assumed, the extent to which the actual poems transmitted reflect this background is a matter of dispute. The methodology of the oral-formulaic theory has been unconvincing to those who do not want to be convinced, and arguments based on textual variation in the transmission of a poem have only succeeded in wrenching the admission from sceptics that perhaps texts – written texts, of course – were sometimes committed to memory.[13] The image of the scribe and the book has been too pervasive to allow a serious consideration of any other mode of literary culture. Rather than try to prove the unprovable, I will therefore concentrate on the problem of interpretation by asking what we miss if we do not read 'popular' poetry (in the sense of poetry primarily linked to an oral milieu) as popular poetry. There will hence be no attempt on my side to prove that a particular text is a piece of oral poetry. My reasoning is entirely hypothetical; I will simply explore the consequences for our understanding if we assume that a particular poem belongs to the realm of oral rather than written poetry. In doing so I will focus on Old and Middle English narrative poetry, in particular on *Beowulf* (or rather the *Lay of Finnsburh*) and on the tail-rhyme romance of *Emaré*.

Medieval literature has preserved a number of descriptions of the performance of oral poetry. One of the most elaborate is found in the Old Provençal romance *Flamenca*. At the sumptuous wedding feast of Archimbaut and Flamenca at Nemours a veritable host of jongleurs performs for the assembled company:

> Apres si levon li juglar;
> Cascus se volc faire auzir;
> Adonc auziras retentir
> Cordas de manta tempradura.
> Qui saup novella violadura,
> Ni canzo ni descort ni lais,
> Al plus que poc avan si trais.
> L'uns viola-[l] lais del Cabrefoil,
> E l'autre cel de Tintagoil;
> L'us cantet cel dels Fins amanz,
> E l'autre cel que fes Ivans.
> L'us menet arpa, l'autre viula;
> L'us flaütella, l'autre siula;

[13] For a concise introduction to the oral-formulaic theory see J. M. Foley, *The Theory of Oral Composition. History and Methodology* (Bloomington, IN, 1988); for an account of the application of the oral-formulaic theory to Middle English texts see W. Parks, 'The Oral-Formulaic Theory in Middle English Studies', *Oral Tradition* 1 (1986) 636–94.

L'us mena giga, l'autre rota,
L'us diz los motz e l'autre-ls nota. . . (592–606)[14]

Then the jongleurs got up;
Everyone of them wanted to make himself heard;
At that time you could have heard the sound
Of variously tuned strings.
Whoever knew a new melody for the vielle,
A canso, a descort, or a lai,
Came forward as well as he could.
One plays on his vielle the lai of Chèvrefeuil,
Another that of Tintagel;
One sings that of the Perfect Lovers,
Another that which was composed by Ivain.
One plays the harp, another the vielle;
One plays the flute, another the pipe;
One plays the gigue, another the rota,
One speaks the words and the other plays the music. . .

The passage continues for another hundred lines, in which a lengthy repertory of medieval narrative is enumerated. Whenever the performance of narrative poetry is explicitly described in medieval literature it is within a context of feasting. We might compare with this scene in *Flamenca* the wedding feast in Chrétien's *Erec et Enide*, where the minstrels of the country gather to tell tales, sing songs and play various instruments,[15] or the coronation feast in *Havelok*, where there was 'harping and piping ful god won' ('a full good measure') and where one could hear minstrels 'the gestes singe, / The glevmen on the tabour dinge'.[16] One of the best known passages in English literature describing the performance of oral narrative poetry is the recital of the *Lay of Finnsburh* in *Beowulf*. Here, too, the occasion is one of feasting and celebrating. After Grendel has been overcome by Beowulf, a banquet is given in the hero's honour, in the course of which there was also 'song and music':

Þær wæs sang ond swēg samod ætgædere
fore Healfdenes hildewīsan,

[14] R. Lavaud, R. Nelli, eds. and trans., *Les Troubadours. Jaufre, Flamenca, Barlaam et Josaphat* (Bruges, 1960), p. 674. The medieval vielle is a type of hurdy-gurdy, the gigue is a fiddle, the rota is a type of lyre.

[15] 'Li uns conte, li autre chante, / Li uns sifle, li autre note, / Cil sert de harpe, cil de rote, / Cil de gigue, cil de viële,/ Cil flaüte, cil chalemele. (2042–6); W. Foerster, ed., *Kristian von Troyes. Erec und Enide*, Romanische Bibliothek, 13, 3rd ed. (Halle a. S., 1934), p. 57.

[16] G. V. Smithers, ed., *Havelok* (Oxford, 1987), p. 64. The tabour is a small drum. On the performance of minstrels at feasts see also R. Crosby, 'Oral Delivery in the Middle Ages', *Speculum* 11 (1936) 88–110, pp. 92ff.

gomenwudu grēted, gid oft wrecen,
ðonne healgamen Hrōþgāres scop
æfter medobence mǣnan scolde. . . (1063–67)[17]

There was both song and music
in front of Healfdenes battle-leader,
the harp plucked, many a *gidd* recited,
when Hrothgar's scop would provide entertainment in the hall
by reciting on the meadbench. . .

What the scop then recites is a version of the *Lay of Finnsburh*, which closes with the words:

Lēoð wæs āsungen,
glēomannes gyd. Gamen eft āstāh,
beorhtode bencswēg, byrelas sealdon
wīn of wunderfatum. (1159–62)

The song was sung,
the *gidd* of the singer. Mirth arose again,
a festive noise resounded from the benches; the cup-bearers served
wine from wonderful vessels.

There are several things noteworthy about this passage. We are witnessing the performance of a professional singer, the Anglo-Saxon scop, later also called a *glēomann*.[18] The lay he is performing is referred to as a song (*lēoð*) and as a *gidd*. While the singer is reciting his lay, his audience is obviously giving him their full attention, listening in silence and possibly even refraining from drinking. It emerges from this passage not only that oral poetry solely exists in performance – which is a truism – but also that this performance needs a particular framework. Listening to an oral narrative is not like reading a book, which can be taken up or laid down at will, in whatever context we feel an inclination for reading; it is more like watching a play, which demands our continued concentration and which is tied to a particular locale (as well as a

[17] *Beowulf* quotations are from Klaeber's edition; Fr. Klaeber, ed., *Beowulf and the Fight at Finnsburg*, 3rd ed. (Lexington, MA, 1950). As with many other passages in *Beowulf*, there are some textual difficulties in this passage; see J. Hoops, *Kommentar zum Beowulf* (Heidelberg, 1932), pp. 133–4; J. R. R. Tolkien, *Finn and Hengest: The Fragment and the Episode*, ed. by A. Bliss (London, 1982), pp. 92–3.

[18] For an older and now partially outdated monograph on the Anglo-Saxon scop see L. F. Anderson, *The Anglo-Saxon Scop*, Univ. of Toronto Studies, Philological Ser., 1 (Toronto, 1903); for a linguistic study of the term *skop* see W. Wissmann, *Skop*, Sitzungsberichte der deutschen Akad. d. Wiss. zu Berlin, Kl. für Sprachen, Lit. u. Kunst, Jg 1954, Nr. 2 (Berlin, 1953), where an influence of the *mimus* on the West Germanic skop is posited; for a somewhat speculative account of the West Germanic skop see also E. Werlich, *Der westgermanische Skop. Der Aufbau seiner Dichtung und sein Vortrag* (Ph.D. Thesis Münster, 1964).

particular time of day and, in the case of seasonal drama like open-air opera or the Oberammergau Passion play, to a particular time of year).

A ceremonial framework for the performance of oral poetry can be observed in many cultures in which there is still a living oral tradition. I will give only one non-European illustration, coming from the area with which I am most familiar, Turkic oral epic poetry from Central Asia. In their study of Uzbek epic, Hadi Zarif and Viktor Žirmunskij give the following description of the performance of an Uzbek *dastan* (popular epic):

> When the singer (*baxši*) came to a village he stayed with his friends or with a person who had invited him specially and in whose house the performance was arranged. By the evening all neighbours had gathered in the house. The singer was put on the seat of honour. Around him, along the walls, but also in the middle of the room if there were many guests, the men would sit. In the old days women and children did not take part in these gatherings and would listen through the windows and the doors. The evening began with small refreshments. Then the singer sang the so-called *terma* (literally 'selection') as a prelude to the performance of the main part of his repertory: short lyric pieces of his own composition, excerpts from *dastans*, sometimes songs from Classical literature – all of these songs works of small dimensions (approximately up to 150 lines), forming a unity by their function as a prelude, attuning the singer himself and his audience to the more serious epic theme . . . .
>
> Then the performance of the *dastan* itself begins, which lasts from sunset to sunrise, with an interval at midnight. Gradually the singer enters into a state of inspiration; he 'boils' (*qaynadi*); the word 'boil' (*qaynamāq*) is used in this context in the sense of 'get excited, sing with enthusiasm'. The *baxši* himself uses at this point the expression: '*Bedawni minib haydadim*' ('Mounting the steed I rode it hard'); his *dombira* [a plucked instrument] is the *bedaw*, the good steed galloping along. Physical signs of the singer's inspired state are the sharp, rhythmic jerks of his head, with which he accompanies the 'throwing out' of each verse-line. He is covered in perspiration and takes off one after the other of the *xalats* (robes) he is wearing. Nonetheless, a good singer, a master of his art, preserves the ability to listen attentively and sensitively during the performance of a *dastan* to the reactions of the audience to his playing. Depending on the degree of interest and participation shown by the listeners, he enlarges or shortens the text of the poem. Even the choice of the plot and the more detailed elaboration of single episodes take their cue from the composition of the audience and its taste, as it is known to the singer: among old people or elderly listeners he will sing differently than among young people, etc.
>
> At midnight there is an interval. The singer interrupts the performance at a particularly interesting moment; on leaving the room he leaves his top *xalat* and his belt-scarf, in which he puts his *dombira* face down (*dombira tonkarmāq*), behind in his seat. During his absence someone in the audience spreads his belt-scarf in the middle of the room and everyone of those present puts whatever he has got ready as payment into it, payment

in kind or in money. This remuneration had been prepared by the guests earlier, but depending on the quality of the performance the size of the gifts gets larger or smaller. In addition to these presents, which they brought along, in the old days the rich gave the singer they had invited also more valuable gifts at his departure: a new *xalat*, a horse, or livestock; among these gifts a horse was held a particularly honorable present.

These performances of a singer continued for several nights, from three or four nights to a whole week and longer, sometimes in different houses in turn, by mutual agreement with the host at whose house the singer was staying.[19]

In the case of European medieval oral literature, all these aspects of a live performance are of course lost to us. They are nevertheless important elements both for the definition and the interpretation of oral and popular literature. The question of genre will serve as an illustration. It has often been argued that in Old Germanic oral poetry only the heroic lay was cultivated but not the epic. Hence *Beowulf*, which in length and narrative structure is certainly not a lay, cannot belong to the sphere of oral poetry and must be seen as a written epic.[20] The similarities between *Beowulf* and Virgil's *Aeneid* have been underlined by a number of scholars, who thus confirm the view of *Beowulf* as a bookish creation.[21] On the other hand, doubts have been voiced as to the classification of *Beowulf* as a heroic epic. The mood is very often elegiac rather than heroic and *Beowulf* has hence been characterized by some scholars as an elegiac narrative. Levin Schücking stressed the exemplary nature of the

[19] V. M. Žirmunskij, X. T. Zarifov, *Uzbekskij narodnyj geroičeskij èpos* [The Uzbek heroic folk epic] (Moscow, 1947), pp. 29–31. For a discussion of this passage and related questions see my *Turkic Oral Epic Poetry: Traditions, Forms, Poetic Structure*, The Albert Bates Lord Studies in Oral Tradition, 7 (New York, 1992), pp. 93–100.

[20] See e.g. A. Heusler, *Die altgermanische Dichtung*, Handbuch der Literaturwissenschaft, 2nd ed. (Potsdam, 1943), p. 192ff. – In order to avoid being misunderstood I should perhaps stress that I do not consider *Beowulf* as we have the poem a direct transcription of an oral performance; the text extant has certainly gone through the hands of several scribes with considerable transformations. I do, however, consider *Beowulf* as basically reflecting an oral narrative tradition and hence maintain that a reading of the poem against the oral background of Old English narrative poetry is more profitable than a reading against the equally existing background of Patristic writings. For readings of *Beowulf* in the sense intended see e.g. J. D. Niles, *Beowulf. The Poem and Its Tradition* (Cambridge, MA, 1983); compare also E. B. Irving, Jr. *Rereading 'Beowulf'* (Philadelphia, PA, 1989).

[21] 'The bookish poet of *Beowulf* may have owed the very idea of turning heroic poetry into an epic poem to his acquaintance with the *Aeneid*': J. B. Hainsworth, *The Ideal of Epic*, Eidos, 3 (Berkeley, CA, 1991), p. 137. Compare also Fr. Klaeber, 'Aeneis und Beowulf', *Archiv* 126 (1911) 40–8, 339–59; T. B. Haber, *A Comparative Study of the 'Beowulf' and the 'Aeneid'* (Princeton, NJ, 1931); T. M. Andersson, *Early Epic Scenery: Homer, Virgil and the Mediaeval Legacy* (Ithaca, NY, 1976), pp. 145–59.

hero and suggested that we see *Beowulf* as a mirror of princes. Other scholars have been puzzled by other features not fitting their respective definition of epic, and Joseph Harris has pleaded for a view of *Beowulf* as a poem *sui generis*, a kind of *summa litterarum*.[22] When determining the genre of *Beowulf* we bring to the poem the genre expectations founded on our Western literary tradition. The question asked is essentially: is *Beowulf* like those works which we consider the best representatives of the genre or not?

In an oral culture, however, this question does not arise. A genre is not defined on the basis of texts but of speech-events. Linguistics, in particular anthropological linguistics and the ethnography of communication, has in recent years elaborated the notion of a speech-event and stressed the close connection between genre or type of event with other parameters such as the reference focus of the event, its purpose or function, its setting, the participants, the act sequence, the rules for interaction, and the norms of interpretation.[23] For an oral community an 'epic' is not primarily a particular type of text, characterized by its form, content and structure, but an event: a singer performing to an audience in a context conforming to the social norms of the community and serving a specific purpose, in the case of heroic poetry generally that of reinforcing a 'heroic' ethos and system of values, sanctioned by tradition and grounded in 'tribal' or 'national' history. Reflexes of this function in medieval literature are Wace's report of Taillefer singing the *Chanson de Roland* at the battle of Hastings, the reciting of *Bjarkamál* to the troups of St Olaf, or Robert Bruce's reading the romance of *Firumbras* to his men to give them 'game and solace' during his campaign.[24]

There is certainly an awareness of genre in oral cultures, but native taxonomy, being based on the speech-event rather than the text, does not always make sense to the Western observer. It is possible that the polysemy of Old English *gidd* is due to this a-textual stance. In the *Beowulf* passage quoted, *gidd* refers to the *Lay of Finnsburh*, at least in

[22] Compare L. L. Schücking, 'Das Königsideal im Beowulf', *Englische Studien* 67 (1932) 1–14; J. Harris, 'Beowulf in Literary History', *Pacific Coast Philology* 17 (1982) 16–23 [reprinted in *Interpretations of Beowulf. A Critical Anthology*, ed. R. D. Fulk (Bloomington, IN, 1991), pp. 235–41]; J. Harris, 'Die altenglische Heldendichtung', in *Europäisches Frühmittelalter*, ed. K. von See, Neues Handbuch der Literaturwissenschaft, 6 (Wiesbaden, 1982), pp. 237–76.

[23] See M. Saville-Troike, *The Ethnography of Communication. An Introduction*, 2nd ed. (Oxford, 1989), pp. 138ff.

[24] See Robert Wace, *Le Roman de Rou*, ed. A. J. Holden, Société des Anciens Textes Français, 3 vols. (Paris, 1970–3), II, p. 183; Harris, 'Heldendichtung', p. 254; W. W. Skeat, ed., *The Bruce or The book of the most excellent and noble prince Robert de Broyss, King of Scots. Compiled by Master John Barbour, Archdeacon of Aberdeen, A.D. 1375*, EETS ES 11, 21, 29, 55, 4 vols. (1870–89), I, pp. 64–5.

line ll60 ('Lēoð wæs āsungen, / glēomannes gyd'). In other contexts, the meaning of *gidd* seems to be 'lament', as when in the Finnsburh episode Hildeburh's mourning at the funeral pile is narrated:

> Ides gnornode,
> geōmrode giddum. (1117–18)
>
> The woman mourned,
> lamented in *gidds*.

In some passages *gidd* can be glossed as 'song' or 'poem', in others 'elegiac poem'. When Beowulf describes the feast in Heorot to Hygelac he speaks of *gidd and gleo*, 'song and entertainment', later qualifying *gidd*, however, as true and sad, a qualification also found in the elegies (*soðgied* in *The Seafarer*, 1):

> Þǣr wæs gidd ond glēo; gomela Scilding,
> felafricgende feorran rehte;
> hwīlum hildedēor hearpan wynne,
> gomenwudu grētte, hwīlum gyd āwræc
> sōð ond sārlīc, hwīlum syllīc spell
> rehte æfter rihte rūmheort cyning. . . (2105–10)
>
> There was *gidd* and entertainment; the old Scilding,
> the wise man, narrated of ancient times;
> sometimes the man brave in battle played the joyful harp,
> the pleasing instrument, sometimes he recited a *gidd*,
> true and sad, sometimes the noble-spirited king
> told a wondrous tale in the right way.[25]

Later Beowulf commands the presents to be brought forward and transmits Hrothgar's message to Hygelac:

> Hēt ðā in beran eafor hēafodsegn,
> heaðostēapne helm, hāre byrnan,
> gūðsweord geatolīc, gyd æfter wræc. . . (2152–4)
>
> He then asked that the boar-standard be brought in,
> the helmet towering in battle, the grey coat of mail,
> the splendid battle-sword, and then spoke a *gidd*. . .

Here *gidd* probably means 'wise words', a meaning well attested for *gidd* in other contexts. Andreas Heusler was correct when he maintained that

[25] Commentators and translators are divided on the reference of *gomela Scilding* and *hildedēor*; some think that *gomela Scilding* and *hildedēor* refer to a singer, some that *gomela Scilding* refers to Hrothgar, but *hildedēor* to a singer, others, including myself, assume that *gomela Scilding* and *hilded*ēor refer to Hrothgar. See Klaeber, *Beowulf*, p. 205; Hoops, *Kommentar*, p. 233.

Old English *gidd* is the most general term for poetry with little specificity.[26] But we might add that this does not mean that types and genres of poetry were not differentiated; they were distinguished, but on the level of the speech-event rather than on the terminological level. For the audience in Hrothgar's hall it was clear what type of poetry the *Lay of Finnsburh* was and they reacted to it accordingly, whether they called it *leoð* or *gidd*. The context of performance disambiguated the term.

The same might be said about romance, a term as difficult to define as epic. Once again, native taxonomy is confusing: alongside 'romance' we find terms like 'geste', 'jape', 'rime', or 'yedding', all with overlapping senses.[27] While we want to define romance according to genre-expectations modelled on such disparate literature as the Hellenistic novel and Hawthorne's romances, for a medieval audience a popular romance was probably defined most clearly by the event rather than the text (although narratives were classified by their content as well, as the notorious distinction into *matières* shows).[28] The questions to be asked here are: Who performed? In what way? To whom and for what purpose? I will not pursue the question of defining the genre of romance any further here, but will turn to the key notion contained in these questions, the notion of performance.

The *Lay of Finnsburh* is available to us in two forms, a fragment of 48 lines and the episode in *Beowulf*, comprising 92 lines (1068–159). Neither of these texts gives a reliable impression of the poem; the fragment is too severely truncated and the episode presents the action only selectively and indirectly, assuming a knowledge of the poem in the audience of *Beowulf*. It is nevertheless possible to reconstruct the contents of the lay and to gain an idea of its style and narrative

[26] 'Es [sc. *giedd*] ist der allgemeinste Ausdruck für Gedicht. . .. Man bemerkt keinen Anlauf zu technischer Verengung'. A. Heusler, 'Dichtung', in *Reallexikon der germanischen Altertumskunde*, ed. J. Hoops, 4 vols. (Straßburg, 1911–19), I, pp. 439–62, p. 444. For a semasiological study of Old English *gidd* see my 'Old English *giedd*, Middle English *yedding* as Genre Terms', in *Words, Texts and Manuscripts. Studies in Anglo-Saxon Culture Presented to Helmut Gneuss on the Occasion of this Sixty-Fifth Birthday*, eds. M. Korhammer, K. Reichl, H. Sauer (Woodbridge, 1992), pp. 349–70.

[27] Compare R. Hoops, *Der Begriff 'Romance' in the mittelenglischen und frühneuenglischen Literatur* (Heidelberg, 1929); P. Strohm, 'The Origin and Meaning of Middle English *Romaunce*', *Genre* 10 (1977) 1–28.

[28] This is not the place to review the literature on romance as a genre. I will simply draw attention to Ker's distinction between epic and romance, which is still worth reading; W. P. Ker, *Epic and Romance. Essays on Medieval Literature*, 2nd ed. (London, 1908); for a stimulating account of medieval romance see J. Stevens, *Medieval Romance. Themes and Approaches* (London, 1973); for a comprehensive discussion of romance as a general narrative genre see also N. Frye, *The Secular Scripture. A Study of the Structure of Romance* (Cambridge, MA, 1976).

technique.[29] What we have then are two texts and the clues they provide for a reconstructed third text. As texts these entities are linguistic units with determinate meanings. This is not to say that these meanings are easily accessible to us nor that the assignment of meaning is unmediated by the mind of the reader. A number of literary critics have rightly stressed the role of the interpreter in interpretation, but even the most radical deconstructivist admits the ontological independence of the text.[30] However disparate the interpretations and however opaque the meaning of the text, there is always the text we can (and have to) fall back on in our dispute over its meaning. The situation is more complex in the case of oral poetry. The texts of the *Lay of Finnsburh* are fixed entities which do neither justice to the multiplicity and variability of oral poetry nor to the dynamics of performance. Rather than discuss the ontological question, however, I will focus on just one of the many aspects of performance which is not present in the fixed text, namely music.

In line 1159 the *Beowulf*-poet says: 'Lēoð wæs āsungen', the chant was sung. There can be no doubt that Old English epic poetry was indeed sung. The singing of epics is well attested from Classical Antiquity to the oral cultures still extant in this century. When Odysseus is entertained at the Phaeacian court, the blind bard Demodocus is summoned to perform for the king's guests:

> When they had satisfied their appetite and thirst, the bard was inspired by the Muse to sing of famous men. He chose a passage from a lay well known by then throughout the world, the Quarrel of Odysseus and Achilles, telling how these two had fallen out at a rich ceremonial banquet and dismayed the rest by the violence of their language, though King Agamemnon was secretly delighted to see the Achaean chieftains at loggerheads. He was reminded of the prophecy that Phoebus Apollo had made to him in sacred Pytho when he crossed the marble threshold to consult the oracle, in those days when almighty Zeus was conjuring up the great wave of disasters that was to overwhelm Trojans and Danaans alike. (*Odyssey*, VIII.72–82)[31]

The passage ends: 'this then the famous singer sang' (ταῦτ' ἄρ' ἀοιδὸς ἄειδε περικλυτός; VIII.83). Scholars have speculated on the musical side of Greek epic poetry, but all attempts at melodic and rhythmic reconstruction are, in the absence of transmitted melodies, doomed to failure.[32] The same holds true of other ancient and most medieval

[29] For such a reconstruction see Tolkien, *Finn and Hengest*.

[30] See e.g. S. Fish, *Is There a Text in this Class? The Authority of Interpretive Communities* (Cambridge, MA, 1980), pp. 303ff.

[31] Homer, *The Odyssey*, trans. by E. V. Rieu (Harmondsworth, 1946), p. 124.

[32] See Th. Georgiades, *Musik und Rhythmus bei den Griechen. Zum Ursprung der abendländischen Musik* (Hamburg, 1958), pp. 55ff.

traditions. Not a single line of melody has come down to us for Old or Middle English narrative. We are somewhat more fortunate in the case of Old French and Middle High German epic poetry. The transmitted melodies are fragmentary and often subject to controversial interpretations, but they confirm the numerous allusions in medieval texts to the singing of narrative poetry.[33] Even the *Nibelungenlied*, whose 'singability' an older generation of Germanists had emphatically denied, is today generally thought to have been sung. A record with extracts from the *Nibelungenlied* sung to the *Hildebrandston* issued in 1983 convincingly underlines what we are missing by entirely concentrating on the words and neglecting the music.[34]

There are two practical functions which the music fulfils: it helps the singer get his metrics right and it helps carry his words better. It has often been observed by field-workers that singers have difficulty in dictating their texts without singing them. The melody helps the singer perform the epic in the right rhythm and metrical arrangement. If the singer accompanies himself on an instrument, playing the instrument gives him a chance to pause in his recitation and think ahead before continuing the poem. Naturally, a singer needs a good voice; the voice of the Uzbek singer Ergaš Džumanbulbul is said to have been heard at a distance of a *tāš*, about 8 km (!) (*Bir tāš yolga bārar edi dāwuši*).[35] In *Beowulf* we hear that the voice of the scop was *swutol*, apparently meaning 'clear', 'clearly audible' (*swutol sang scopes*, l. 90). But apart from these practical aspects, there is also an aesthetic dimension to the singing of narrative poetry. Given the many possibilities of the interplay between words and music in the performance of oral epic poetry, this aesthetic dimension cannot be subsumed under a single term. I will only briefly mention some of the possibilities encountered among the Turkic peoples.

We have on the one hand traditions where epic poetry is performed in a chanting style similar to some genres of Gregorian chant. As in psalm-tones, for instance, the melodies are generally stichic, i.e. the same melody is repeated for every line of poetry. This melody may have various realizations and an epic poem might be recited to more than one melody, but the impression of 'monotony' is enhanced by the singing of consecutive verse-lines to basically the same melody (before in another

33 On the musical performance of medieval narrative poetry (with further references) see J. Stevens, *Words and Music in the Middle Ages. Song, Narrative, Dance and Drama, 1050–1350*, Cambridge Studies in Music (Cambridge, 1986), pp. 199–267.

34 See *Das Nibelungenlied. Der Kürenberger. Walther von der Vogelweide*. Im 'Hildebrandston' gesungen von Eberhard Kummer. Vienna: PAN 150005/6, 1983.

35 H. Zarif, ed., *Ergaš Džumanbulbul Oġli. Tardžimai hāl, Rawšan, Qunduz bilan Yulduz* [Ergaš Džumanbulbul-oġli. 'Autobiography', 'Rawšan', 'Qunduz and Yulduz'] (Tashkent, 1971), p. 9.

section perhaps another melody is used). This is also the way the Serbo-Croatian heroic songs are performed, and the stichic type of melody is also typical of the *chanson de geste* as far as we can tell from reconstructed melodies. In a number of Turkic traditions, on the other hand, the melodies are more complex, ranging from polymotif melodies to strophic compositions. These melodies can be song- like, and they are found in particular in those traditions in which oral narrative poetry is metrically often stanzaic (rather than laisse-like) and where the poetry is of the romance type rather than heroic poetry. In most Turkic traditions (and this is also true of other traditions of oral epic poetry, in the Balkans as well as in Africa), the singer accompanies himself on a musical instrument, generally a plucked instrument, sometimes also a type of fiddle. Only rarely, as in the Kirghiz tradition, does the singer use no instrument. The singing of poetry enhances the ceremonial and quasi-ritualistic character of the performance. As listeners we are in the presence of heightened speech, of words disconnected from everyday life, words inspired by the gods or the Muses. In more archaic traditions of northern Asia the performance of the singer and the shaman are very similar, and it can be shown that at an earlier stage in history the function of epic singer and of shaman were united in one person. In traditions where the musical side is more in the foreground of performance, the aesthetic dimension of music is further stressed. Poetry is not just pleasing as spoken sound but also as song. The form of these epics (called *dastans*) is generally prosimetric. Dramatic scenes with monologues and dialogues of the protagonists are in verse and sung, while the connecting narration is in prose. The structure of these *dastans* is not unlike that of classical opera with its change between recitative and arias, and the effect, one might add, is similar. Our appreciation of an opera will not be dependent on the text but rather on the music (many librettos make very dry reading indeed). Although in these *dastans* the text is not in the same way subordinated to the music as in a Western opera, the weight has shifted from the textual to the musical side. An interpretation of these romances purely as texts would in my opinion not do justice to their aesthetic structure. Maybe some of the Middle English popular romances would gain in our estimation if we could experience them as performed, sung narratives?

This brings me to my last point, the understanding of oral and popular poetry as traditional poetry. I will illustrate this point with the romance of *Emaré*. This romance is extant in only one manuscript (BL Cotton Caligula A.ii, 15th c.); it is in the tail-rhyme metre and comprises 1035 lines.[36] Its contents can be summarized as follows:

[36] Edited in E. Rickert, ed., *The Romance of Emaré*, EETS ES 99 (1906); T. C. Rumble, ed., *The Breton Lays in Middle English* (Detroit, 1965), pp. 97–133; M. Mills, ed.,

> The emperor Artyus has a beautiful daughter, Emaré, whom he wishes to marry after his wife has died. Although the Pope consents to this marriage, Emaré refuses and is hence banished by her father. She is put to sea in a boat without provisions or oars, but Emaré survives and reaches Galys, where the king of the country falls in love with her and marries her. During the king's absence on a military campaign in France, she gives birth to a son, Segramor. Emaré is calumniated by her mother-in-law, who had advised her son earlier against marrying the girl. She is once again put to sea in a boat, this time together with the newborn child. Emaré reaches Rome and is kindly taken in by a rich merchant. When the king of Galys hears of his mother's evil deed, he expels her from his realm and sets out on a pilgrimage to Rome. As he stays in the same house in which his wife and son have found refuge, their reunion, brought about by Segramor, is inevitable. When the emperor, too, comes to Rome to seek forgiveness, he is also happily reunited with his daughter and grandson.

This simple tale has been variously interpreted. Urs Dürmüller, in his study of the tail-rhyme romances, repeatedly stresses the poet's ineptitude, with judgements like the following: 'the author's inept handling of the tail-rhyme stanza . . . The author of *Emaré* not only lacks the gift for variation, but he is also incapable of dividing his tale according to the section structure . . . . The peculiarities of the tail-rime stanza only underline the author's lack of artistry and his incapability to control his material'.[37] Mortimer J. Donovan, in his survey of Breton lays in the 'New Wells', finds that Emaré's 'character at best is ill-defined and points to her chief purpose as exemplar of Christian virtue'.[38] Dieter Mehl has also stressed the exemplary nature of this romance: 'In contrast to romances on similar subjects, however, the colourful and pathetic adventures of the heroine are not related for the sake of entertainment, but are clearly subordinated to the central theme of the poem, the demonstration of patient suffering and the survival of true virtue through all affliction'.[39] Hanspeter Schelp, on the other hand, notes in his study of Middle English exemplary romances that *Emaré* is one of the least exemplary of this subgenre of romances.[40] He underlines,

Six Middle English Romances (London, 1973), pp. 46–74 (I am quoting from Mills' edition); see also J. Burke Severs, *A Manual of the Writings in Middle English, 1050–1500. I. Romances* (New Haven, CT, 1967), pp. 136–8, 295.

[37] U. Dürmüller, *Narrative Possibilities of the Tail-Rime Romance*, Schweizer Anglistische Arbeiten, 83 (Bern, 1975), pp. 179, 181, 182.

[38] In Severs, *Romances*, p. 138. Compare also the interpretation in M. J. Donovan, *The Breton Lay: A Guide to Varieties* (Notre Dame, IN, 1969), pp. 216–25.

[39] D. Mehl, *The Middle English Romances of the Thirteenth and Fourteenth Centuries* (London, 1968), p. 135.

[40] 'Der moderne Leser wird bei der Lektüre der Romanze *Emare* nicht ohne weiteres den Eindruck einer Geschichte deutlich christlich-exemplarischen Charakters gewinnen. . . . Von einer exemplarisch zu illustrierenden Lehre spricht er [i.e. the poet] nicht. . . . Aufs Ganze gesehen weist jedoch die Gestaltung der Handlung nicht

however, the symbolic function of the cloth which the king of Sicily sends to the emperor at the beginning of the narrative and which figures in the sequel as Emaré's cloak. This costly fabric is embroidered in its four corners with love-scenes (Amadas and Ydoine, Trystram and Isowde, Florys and Blawncheflour, the son of the sultan of Babylon and the amerayle's daughter, who embroidered the cloth) and richly studded with jewels and precious stones. For Schelp the meaning of the story is reflected in the scenes, which represent the dangers and adversities of love, and in particular in the symbolism of the stones as explained by medieval lapidaries: 'The same virtues which the jewels of Emaré's cloak possess or symbolize distinguish the exemplary type of Constance-Emaré'.[41] The romance has also been interpreted in comparison with Chaucer's and Gower's version of the Constance legend. Neil Isaacs finds, for instance, that the

> writer of *Emare* is particularly concerned with clothes and dry goods. Gower concentrates on the quality of things and people, questions of good and evil making up the bulk of his descriptions as well as of his incidents. He also betrays an interest in philology in the matter of Constance's assumed name. Chaucer's art approaches the dramatic monologue technique. The Man of Law quite naturally discusses the legal problem of *Disparitas Cultus* in connection with the Sowdan's council. In addition he betrays an upper middle-class priggishness in his frequent moral apostrophes. But the Man of Law fancies himself an authority on the arts and sciences as well, and tries to impress the company with astronomical references.[42]

What all these critical comments have in common is that they treat the romance as basically a work of written literature. It is hence natural to compare *Emaré* with Chaucer's *Man of Law's Tale* or Gower's *Tale of Constance* (in his *Confessio Amantis*). But is *Emaré* a work of written literature and is a comparison with Chaucer's or Gower's tale legitimate? Oral and written traditions mutually influenced one another all through the Middle Ages, and it would be foolish therefore to insist on a clear-cut separation of these two forms of composition, reception, and transmission. Besides, it is a well-known fact that in the Middle Ages, both in monastic and secular contexts, written literature was often read out aloud

annähernd die exemplarische Dichte z. B. eines *Sir Ysumbras* oder eines *Roberd of Cisyle* auf'. H. Schelp, *Exemplarische Romanzen im Mittelenglischen*, Palaestra, 246 (Göttingen, 1967), pp. 99, 101.

41 'Die gleichen Tugenden, die die Edelsteine des Emare-Gewandes besitzen oder symbolisieren, zeichnen den exemplarischen Typus der Constanze-Emare aus'. Schelp, *Exemplarische Romanzen*, p. 112.

42 N. D. Isaacs, 'Constance in Fourteenth-Century England', *NM* 59 (1958) 260–77, pp. 274ff.

and hence heard by an audience rather than read by a reader.[43] Medieval scribes, when copying manuscripts, were also wont to read out sotto voce what they were writing.[44] Nevertheless, the differences between a poem belonging to an oral milieu and a poem coming from the pen of a writer like Chaucer or Gower is not just a quantitative one.

Many stylistic and structural characteristics of *Emaré* point to an oral background. The romance has an unusually high proportion of repetition: lines and whole passages are repeated verbatim, an uncommon feature even of highly formulaic texts. Two examples must suffice. When the costly cloth which the king of Sicily presents to Emaré's father is described, the precious stones are twice enumerated in the same words:

> Full of stones ther hyt was pyght,
>   As thykke as hyt myght be;
> Off topaze and rubyes
> And other stones of myche prys,
>   That semely wer to se;
> Of crapowtes [toadstones] and nakette [agates],
> As thykke ar they sette,
>   Forsothe, as Y say the. (89–96)

> As full of stones ar they dyght,
>   As thykke as they may be;
> Of topase and of rubyes
> And othur stones of myche pryse,
>   That semely wer to se;
> Wyth crapawtes and nakette,
> Thykke of stones ar they sette,
>   Forsothe as Y say the. (137–44)

When Emaré lands in Galys, she is found by Syr Kadore, the king's steward:

> Every day wolde he [= Syr Kadore] go,
> And take wyth hym a sqwyer or two,
>   And play hym by the see.
> On a tyme he toke the eyr
> Wyth two knyghtus gode and fayr;
>   The wedur was lythe of le [calm and the place sheltered]. (343–8)

When she later lands in Italy, Jurdan, the merchant who finds her, is seen to have the same custom of going for a walk by the sea-side:

[43] For an early study see R. Crosby, 'Oral Delivery'; for a recent discussion, stressing the transitions between writing and speaking, listening and reading, see D. H. Green, 'Orality and Reading: The State of Research in Medieval Studies', *Speculum* 65 (1990) 267–80.

[44] Compare H. J. Chaytor, *From Script to Print. An Introduction to Medieval Vernacular Literature* (Cambridge, 1945), pp. 5–21.

Every day wolde he [= Jurdan]
Go to playe hym by the see,
The eyer forto tane. (688–90)

Apart from these and other repetitions,[45] the style conforms in its formulaic nature to that of other tail-rhyme romances, and tags like *old and yyng* (ll. 41, 65, 301, 380, 610, 725) or phrases like *wyth carefull herte and sykyng sore* (ll. 328, 676) occur repeatedly. A further indication of a popular background are the frequent allusions to minstrels and minstrelsy. On one of the corners of the precious cloth there are minstrels playing music (*And menstrellys wyth her glewe*, l. 132) and at Emaré's wedding-feast '*Ther was myche menstralse*' (l. 388). In addition to the usual reference to a book or a romance as his source (as in the tag *in romans as we rede*, l. 216), the narrator adduces also the authority of minstrels: *As Y have herd menstrelles syng in sawe* (l. 319). After the initial prayer there is a curious passage about minstrels which to my mind makes best sense if the narrator is himself a minstrel, but one who prides himself on knowing the proper way to proceed:

Menstrelles that walken fer and wyde,
Her and ther in every a syde,
In mony a dyverse londe,
Sholde at her bygynnyng
Speke of that ryghtwes kyng
That made both see and sonde.
Whoso wyll a stounde dwelle,
Of mykyll myrght Y may you telle
(And mornyng theramonge):
Of a lady fayr and fre,
Her name was called Emaré
As I here synge in songe. (13–24)

But even if the romance was not composed by a minstrel, it was clearly meant to be like a minstrel-romance, and hence to be appreciated as an orally performed, popular narrative.[46]

[45] See Rickert, *Emaré*, pp. xxvi–xxvii.

[46] As I have said above, I am not trying to prove the orality, in particular the oral composition, of a particular text. It is, however, my conviction that a number of Middle English popular romances, in particular those in the tail-rhyme metre, belong to an oral milieu and were hence part of the repertoire of minstrels and popular entertainers. The hypothesis that minstrels, who devoted their lives to performing poetry, were incapable of composing romances seems to me less likely than the hypothesis that they were not only performers but also composers of narrative poetry. By saying this, I do not wish to deny the role of writing in the transmission (and possibly composition) of these romances. Minstrels might have memorized poems composed by others and they might have used manuscripts as props. Turkic singers of the Khorezmian tradition (in Usbekistan), for instance, use manuscripts as props for

As such *Emaré* is a traditional story. It belongs like Chaucer's and Gower's tales to a group of traditional narratives, often subsumed under the heading 'Tales of the Calumniated Wife', of which the most important one is the folktale of *Crescentia* (AT 712).[47] In distinction to Chaucer's and Gower's version of the folktale, *Emaré* is neither embedded in a narrative framework nor in a larger intertextual context. To look, with E. A. Block, for 'originality' and a 'controlling purpose' in Chaucer's *Man of Law's Tale* by comparing his text with Trivet's is a meaningful critical enterprise, and although we might not share E. Clasby's view that Chaucer's tale embodies an anti-Manichean tendency under Boethian influence, the questions she asks and the methods she employs can be considered sound.[48] In *Emaré*, however, there is no dissociation of *sens* from *matière*: the meaning of the story is the story, in all its traditionality and narrative simplicity. If it is an exemplary romance then it is so because the story as such is exemplary. The narrator underlines the traditional character of his tale, not only by his reference to minstrels and to having heard it 'sung in song', but also by explicitly (and as far as we can tell, erroneously) linking it to the tradition of the narrative lai:

> Thys ys on of Brytayne layes
> That was used by olde dayes,
> Men callys 'Playn[t] Egarye'. (1030–2)

their performance; this does not call in question the basic orality of their tradition. To deny (as A. Taylor does) that any extant Middle English manuscript is a minstrel manuscript neither proves that the texts which the so-called minstrel manuscripts transmit hence never figured in a minstrel's repertoire nor that minstrels in general never used manuscripts; see A. Taylor, 'The Myth of the Minstrel Manuscript', *Speculum* 66 (1991) 43–73. On the use of manuscripts in the Khorezmian tradition of Turkic oral epic poetry and the interplay of oral and written transmission of the Middle English popular romance see my 'The Middle English Popular Romance: Minstrel versus Hack Writer', in *The Ballad and Oral Literature*, ed. J. Harris, Harvard English Studies, 17 (Cambridge, MA, 1991), pp. 243–68. On the role of memorization in the transmission of the Middle English romances compare also M. McGillivray, *Memorization in the Transmission of the Middle English Romances*, The Albert Bates Lord Studies in Oral Tradition, 5 (New York, 1990).

47 See A. Aarne, S. Thompson, *The Types of the Folktale*, FF Communications, 184, 2nd rev. ed. (Helsinki, 1961); abbreviated as AT. Others are *Griselda* (AT 887), *Oft-proved Fidelity* (AT 881), *The Maiden Without Hands* (AT 706), and *The Stone of Pity* (AT 894). See M. Schlauch, *Chaucer's Constance and Accused Queens* (New York, 1927); see also my 'Griselda and the Patient Wife: The Popular Tradition in Middle English Narrative', in *La storia di Griselda in Europa. Griselda 2*, ed. R. Morabito (L'Aquila, 1990), pp. 119–36.

48 See E. A. Block, 'Originality, Controlling Purpose, and Craftsmanship in Chaucer's Man of Law's Tale', *PMLA* 68 (1953) 572–616; E. Clasby, 'Chaucer's Constance: Womanly Virtue and the Heroic Life', *Chaucer Review* 13 (1978) 221–33.

A framework is constructed, but it is that of story-telling and not of literary reflection.

But how does the cloth with its embroideries and symbolic value fit into the picture of a popular tale? The whole episode of the cloth is odd: the cloth is handed to the emperor by the king of Sicily, who inexplicably brings this present and equally inexplicably disappears again from the story. The description of the cloth is furthermore longer and more detailed than any other description in the romance (84 lines, plus another 24 lines of framing narrative), seriously upsetting the balance of the tale. When comparing *Emaré* to other versions of the Constance legend, one begins to suspect that the plot is somewhat garbled at this point: the costly present would make more sense if the king of Sicily had come as (an unwelcome Saracen) suitor. As it is, the king of Sicily is not represented as a Saracen (although the cloth comes ultimately from the sultan) and the motif of the unwelcome suitor (as in Chaucer's *Man of Law's Tale*) has been replaced by that of the incestuous father. But even if a singer has a garbled version, he has to make sense of it for his audience. The motif of the cloth has been successfully incorporated into the romance: it is made into a robe for Emaré, which she wears at dramatic moments (such as when her father declares his intentions or when the king of Galys falls in love with her) and thus becomes associated with her beauty and innocence. The disproportionate length of the cloth's description would also fit well into an oral context. Traditional singers have been known to elaborate individual scenes, in particular when they think that the audience would appreciate this. Matthias Murko reports that one of the listeners to the performance of a Serbo-Croatian singer shouted: 'Decorate the man and the horse properly, you don't have to pay for it!'[49] This process of elaborate description has been termed 'ornamentation' by A. B. Lord and studied in particular with reference to Avdo Međedović's *Wedding of Smailagić Meho*.[50] Similar phenomena can be observed among Turkic singers.[51] I will briefly mention one case. When in *Rawšan*, an Uzbek *dastan*, the hero reaches the town in which his beloved lives, he searches for the hat-bazar because she is reported to be selling embroidered caps there. The singer Ergaš Džumanbulbul-oġli has a verse-passage comprising 303 lines in the manuscript, in which Rawšan asks various people where he can find the hat-bazar. The editors of this *dastan*, using the standards of written literature, found this passage so tedious and repetitive that they cut it down to 168 lines in an edition

49 See M. Braun, *Das serbokroatische Heldenlied*, Opera Slavica, 1 (Göttingen, 1961), p. 62.

50 See A. B. Lord, *The Singer of Tales* (Cambridge, MA, 1960), p. 88.

51 On 'ornamentation' in the epics of Kirghiz singers see my *Turkic Oral Epic Poetry*, pp. 332ff.

which was published in 1956–7. I have myself recorded a variant of this particular passage from an Uzbek singer (Čāri-šāir).[52] When listening to the performance, one realizes two things: (1) that the artistic reality of this passage does not consist only in the words but also in the music, and can therefore not be judged by purely textual criteria; and (2) that what counts in a performance is the momentary unfolding of music and poetry and not the proportionality of a closed text. If we think of *Emaré* as a romance told (or better, chanted), any sense of a lack of balance and consequently the urge to see a particular meaning in the cloth-motif will, I think, disappear.

In conclusion it must be emphasized, however, that the *Lay of Finnsburh* and the romance of *Emaré* belong to fairly different realms of popular poetry. The *Lay of Finnsburh* might be called popular in several senses: the poem is rooted in an oral culture; it is anonymous and traditional, i.e. there is no projection of a poetic individuality in it; and it does not belong to the world of bookish learning. But the *Lay of Finnsburh* is not popular in the sense of being destined for a popular (as opposed to, say, an aristocratic) audience. The art of the scop is an aristocratic art, and the very distinction between popular poetry and art poetry becomes meaningless in a preliterate society like the one in which the Germanic lay was originally cultivated. Of course, by the time the *Lay of Finnsburh* was written down the pristine state of illiteracy had long been left behind, and the way the Finnsburh episode is incorporated into *Beowulf* almost reads like a nostalgic reflection on orality by the '*Beowulf*-poet' (or redactor). As an independent poem, however, the *Lay of Finnsburh* can (and should) be viewed as a document of orality, a poem orally performed, orally transmitted, and orally composed.

With the romance of *Emaré* we enter a world in which orality has become marginal, at least as far as social power and prestige are concerned. Despite the danger of drawing an over-simplistic picture of later medieval society, it is probably true to say that the audience of popular romances like *Emaré* must be sought among those layers of society for which more sophisticated forms of literature, in English, French or Latin, were inaccessible.[53] Listening to the performance of the

[52] Later editions give a fuller version. For a translation of this passage see my German translation of the *dastan*: *Rawšan. Ein usbekisches mündliches Epos*, Asiatische Forschungen, 93 (Wiesbaden, 1985), pp. 91–9; for an edition, musical transcription and discussion of the extract recorded from Čāri-šāir in 1981 see my 'Oral Tradition and Performance of the Uzbek and Karakalpak Epic Singers', in W. Heissig, ed., *Fragen der mongolischen Heldendichtung. III*, Asiatische Forschungen, 91 (Wiesbaden, 1985), pp. 613–43, pp. 616ff.

[53] On the audience of the Middle English popular romance see D. Pearsall, 'Middle English Romance and its Audiences', *Historical and Editorial Studies in Medieval and*

popular entertainer was in the course of time replaced by reading the texts of the poetry which minstrels or *gestours* would generally recite.[54] With this shift in reception a new way of appreciation can be assumed, which eventually led to the development of popular fiction divorced from oral performance and the speech-event. It is not always easy to decide where a particular romance belongs, and there is hence no absolute certainty about the oral setting of a tail-rhyme romance like *Emaré*.

To consider the performance side of popular narrative poetry should make us aware of qualities which the texts alone cannot exhibit. Many of these qualities – the ceremonial framework of performance, the musical and gestural aspects of recitation, the singer-audience interaction – cannot be reconstructed. The realization that these various aspects existed must rather be taken as an appeal to our imagination: we cannot recreate the performance of medieval oral poetry, but we can try to take the dynamics of performance into account when interpreting these texts. If we think of these works as representatives of popular rather than written or learned poetry, we become aware that the context in which we should imagine these narratives is that of traditional story-telling rather than that of literary, intertextual discourse. In traditional narrative the story is generally known to the audience. It is neither a new story which the listeners have come to hear nor a new and ingenious retelling of an old story – such as Gottfried's version of the Tristan story or Thomas Mann's recreation of the Gregorius legend. Hearing a traditional narrative is exposing oneself to the familiar, re-experiencing a fictional world whose conventionality is both recognized and accepted. This traditionality concerns not only plot and character, but also narrative technique and diction. Alain Renoir has recently argued for a deepened understanding of Germanic traditional narrative poetry by trying to share the awareness of traditionality in style and diction with the original audience, stressing the importance of 'formulaic rhetoric' for our interpretation of this type of poetry.[55] There are many other traits characterizing traditional narrative, although formulaic diction, repetitions and set motifs, scenes, and story-patterns are probably the most obvious and striking features.[56] Literary critics who have taken an

Early Modern English for Johan Gerritsen, eds. M.-J. Arn, H. Wirtjes, H. Jansen (Groningen, 1985), pp. 37–47.

54 For evidence on the ownership (and hence readership) of romance manuscripts see H. Hudson, 'Middle English Popular Romances: The Manuscript Evidence', *Manuscripts* 28 (1984) 67–78; compare also J. Coleman, *English Literature in History, 1350–1400. Medieval Readers and Writers* (London, 1981), pp. 18ff.

55 See A. Renoir, *A Key to Old Poems. The Oral-Formulaic Approach to the Interpretation of West-Germanic Verse* (University Park, PA, 1988).

56 See Finnegan, *Oral Poetry*, pp. 126ff.; P. Zumthor *Introduction à la poésie orale* (Paris, 1983), pp. 125ff., pp. 136ff.

interest in popular and oral poetry have from the time of Herder and Percy commented on these characteristics to enhance our appreciation of this type of poetry. Herder in particular drew attention to the 'sensuous rhythm' of the language of popular poetry, and his critical observations on ballads and folk songs are mirrored in expressions such as 'la colorazione del sentimento, il ritmo, lo stesso impasto del linguaggio' which Croce uses later to describe an Italian popular song.[57] After giving a translation of the ballad of *Edward*, taken from Percy's *Reliques*, Herder asks the questions: 'Könnte der Brudermord Kains in einem Populärliede mit grausendern Zügen geschildert werden? und welche Würkung muß im lebendigen Rhythmus das Lied tun?'[58] It is this effect of popular poetry in its 'living rhythm' which we should not forget, not only when we are dealing with ballads and folk songs, but also when we interpret medieval narrative poetry for which an oral background, however opaquely perceived, can be assumed.

[57] 'The colouring of the feeling, the rhythm, the very mixture of the language': Croce, *Poesia popolare*, p. 6; see J. G. Herder, 'Über Ossian und die Lieder alter Völker', in *Von der Urpoesie der Völker*, ed. K. Nußbacher (Stuttgart, 1965), pp. 44ff. [orig. published in 1773].

[58] 'Is it possible to describe Cain's fratricide in a popular song in a more awesome style? And what must be the effect of this poem in its living rhythm?' Herder, 'Über Ossian', p. 48.

TRADUTTORE CICERONE: THE TRANSLATOR AS CROSS-CULTURAL GO-BETWEEN

JULIETTE DOR

> 'Interpretation' as that which gives language life beyond the moment and place of immediate utterance or transcription, is what I am concerned with. The French word *interprète* concentrates all the relevant values. An actor is *interprète* of Racine; a pianist gives *une interprétation* of a Beethoven sonata. Through engagement of his own identity, a critic becomes *un interprète* – a life-giving performer – of Montaigne or Mallarmé. As it does not include the world of the actor, and includes that of the musician only by analogy, the English term *interpreter* is less strong. But it is congruent with French when reaching out in another crucial direction. *Interprète / Interpreter* are commonly used to mean *translator*.[1]

George Steiner devotes the opening pages of *After Babel* to a close reading of extracts from selected English texts including Shakespeare's *Cymbeline* and Jane Austen's *Sense and Sensibility*. His point is to demonstrate *in medias res* that the reading of a not contemporary intralingual text is always a manifold act of interpretation. He subsequently argues that each synchronic *état de langue* is made up of a wide range of regional or dialectal differences, as well as of differences that are related to such components as social status, ideology, profession, age and sex, not to mention idiolects. Each of these divergences has to be fully interpreted in order to understand the exact meaning of the utterances in which they appear. Let me illustrate this with, for example, the use of dialectal forms in *The Reeve's Tale*. When John the northern clerk says that he *hopes* that his manciple is going to die,[2] what he means by 'hope' is simply 'expect'. If we are not aware of the sociolinguistic aura of the introduction of dialectal forms[3] we will miss not only Chaucer's point, but also the comic effect that is created by the discrepancy between the standard and dialectal uses of the verb.

[1] George Steiner, *After Babel. Aspects of Language and Translation* (Oxford, 1975), pp. 27–28.

[2] Larry D. Benson, general ed., *The Riverside Chaucer* (Oxford, 1988), l. 429.

[3] See Juliette Dor, 'Chaucer and Dialectology', in *Studia Anglica Posnaniensia*, t. XX (1987), pp. 59–68.

Translating from one language to another – Roman Jakobson's 'interlingual translation'[4] – poses identical problems of interpretation of the source language, as well as other specific issues that will be considered later.

The formal model of translation as a communication process is known according to a formula,[5] in which the source (S) encodes a message (M) in a specific language (A) and transmits it to a receiver (R{A}). This receiver, as translator, performs a translingual transfer (={TR}>) to encode a new message in a second language (B). The translator functions as a new source S{B} to transmit this new message to a new receiver (R{B}). Before translation can be considered the initial message has to be deciphered. If we transpose this into Jakobsonian terms, a preliminary translation is necessary: an intralingual translation in which the original linguistic signs are reworded in alternative signs of the same language. Only then can we have an interlingual translation, that is to say 'an interpretation of verbal signs by means of signs in some other language'.[6] It is as if the original text and its translation were two sides of the same coin. With the exception of a few translators or scholars who enjoy bilingual editions of texts, or who enjoy discovering how other translators have overcome difficult points, most translations are made for readers who do not read the original. As a rule, readers of a text do not turn to its translations, and vice versa. The relationship between original and translation is like that between the two sides of a coin: each ignores the other one, but both are necessary to make a coin.

The invitation to Italy in order to discuss the issues of translation reminded me of the aphorism *traduttore, traditore*. This maxim might be one of the rare points on which literary translators agree. The two words are repeated everywhere, not only because they condense much wisdom, but also because they are highly ambivalent. Let me say, in the first place, that the reader's viewpoint is different from the translator's. What is an expression of contempt for the former can be a form of irony for the latter, a mask often used to hide the experience of suffering.[7]

First of all, the translator's suffering results from the untranslatability of an indivisible whole made out of a form and a sense, sealed in a

[4] 'On Linguistic Aspects of Translation', in Reuben A. Brower, ed., *On Translation* (Cambridge, MA, 1959), pp. 232–9.

[5] S{A} - M{A} — R{A} = {TR} > S{B} - M{B} — R{B}. See, among others, James S. Holmes, *Translated! Papers on Literary Translation and Translation Studies* (Amsterdam, 1988), p. 35.

[6] Quoted by Steiner, *After Babel*, p. 260.

[7] See Antoine Berman, in A. Berman, G. Granel, A. Jaulin, G. Mailhos and H. Meschonnic, eds., *Les tours de Babel. Essais sur la traduction* (Mauvezin, 1985), p. 59.

general effect. There is no escape: they have to violate the text and to sacrifice it on the altar of betrayal. I won't dwell here on the borders of untranslatability. Let me simply recall that while it obviously applies to the poetic language,[8] it should also be extended to literary prose. I agree with Gérard Genette,[9] who prefers to distinguish between the texts that are severely damaged by the unavoidable pitfalls of translating, and those that are not. In fact, Genette, like Eugene A. Nida, draws the borderline at the point where practical language gives way to literary use. At the same time, as the French critic recalls, each language has its own specific dividing line between concepts. Once the translators have admitted that if they limit themselves to an exact rendering, a word for word translation, the result will be poor, the only solution in order to achieve a satisfactory result is to take another approach. This case is argued in greater detail by the author of *Palimpsestes*.[10] Being aware of the unavoidably distorting effect in the process of translation, translators cannot be satisfied with the result they have achieved if they have not added a further dimension to compensate for the inevitably impoverishing process of translation. And yet, in avoiding Charybdis of literalism, they should beware of running against the Scylla of endeavouring to better the original.

The polysemy of the Italian proverb *traduttore traditore* accounts for its frequency, and in a compact form it covers almost all the theoretical issues of translation. At the same time, the idea of betrayal implies an ethical obligation of fidelity. Fidelity to what? Or to whom? For treason can also be understood as the expression of the need to betray either the source text, or the target audience. As we are going to see, there are two possible orientations in translation. The emphasis can be placed either on the original, or on the target. Berman denounces what he calls 'ethnocentric' and 'hypertextual' translations,[11] the two traditional and dominant forms of literary translation. Almost by definition, these two types are, since they inevitably betray the hypotext and the original culture, unfaithful. As soon as the translator decides to focus on the audience, the communication loses its balance, because, according to Berman:

> it is *a priori* ruled by the receiver, or by the image that is made of him or her.[. . .] Translators who translate *for* a definite audience will be brought to betray the original, to prefer their audience to it, and at the same time

[8] See Stéphane Mallarmé's 'langage poétique' and Paul Valéry's indissolubility of sound and sense in poetry. Quoted by Gérard Genette, in *Palimpsestes. La littérature au second degré* (Paris, 1982), p. 239.

[9] Ibid., p. 240.

[10] Ibid., p. 241.

[11] Berman, *Les tours de Babel*, pp. 48 ff.

> their audience will be equally betrayed, because it will be presented with an 'altered' work.[12]

So, here, there is a double betrayal. In terms of communication, this was expressed by Pierre Guiraud in the following terms: 'We are torn between saying everything to nobody, and saying nothing to anybody, and the two situations are inversely proportionate'.[13] As Berman clearly concludes:

> Because it aims at fidelity, translating *originally* belongs to the ethical dimension. In its very essence it is animated by the *desire to open the Other to the translator's own linguistic space*, which does not mean that it has often been so in history. On the contrary, the West's appropriating and annexationist designs have almost always stifled the ethical vocation of translation.[14]

In other words, the general uneasiness when confronted with translation can be accounted for by the violation of the ethical concept of fidelity to the source, too often neglected in favour of the target audience's need for an easily understood text.

In his Preface to Baudelaire's *Tableaux parisiens*,[15] Walter Benjamin juxtaposed the French word *pain* to its German 'equivalent' *Brot*. He convincingly argued that while the absolute target represented by the two words – the concept of bread – is identical, the linguistic intermediaries used to express it are not interchangeable: 'The words *Brot* and *pain* "intend" the same object, but the modes of this intention are not the same'.[16] Suffice it to imagine their concrete representations and to remember that *Brot* will not evoke a *baguette* in Germany. Let me add to this that such inadequacies do not stop there, and can extend to

[12] 'Elle est régie *a priori* par le récepteur, ou l'image que l'on s'en fait.[. . .] Le traducteur qui traduit *pour* le public est amené à trahir l'original, à lui préférer son public, qu'il ne trahit d'ailleurs pas moins, puisqu'il lui présente une oeuvre "arrangée" '. (Berman, *Les tours de Babel*, p. 85)

[13] Quoted by Berman, *Les tours de Babel*, pp. 85–6: 'On est donc pris entre tout dire à personne, ne rien dire à tout le monde, et les deux situations sont inversement proportionnelles' (*Le Langage*, Pléiade, p. 461), my translation.

[14] Berman, *Les tours de Babel*, p. 89. 'La traduction, de par sa visée de fidélité, appartient *originairement* à la dimension éthique. Elle est, dans son essence même, animée du *désir d'ouvrir l'Etranger à son propre espace de langue*. Cela ne veut pas dire qu'historiquement, il en ait été souvent ainsi. Au contraire, la visée appropriatrice et annexioniste qui caractérise l'Occident a presque toujours étouffé la vocation éthique de la traduction' (my translation).

[15] 'Die Aufgabe des Übersetzers' (Heidelberg, 1923). Edited by Hans Joachim Störig, *Das Problem des Übersetzens* (Stuttgart, 1963), pp. 182–95. English translation by Harry Zohn, 'The Task of the Translator', in Walter Benjamin, *Illuminations* (London, 1973), pp. 69–82.

[16] 'The Task of the Translator', p. 74.

intralingual inconsistencies: the concrete object suggested by *pain* in the French Community of Belgium is not a *baguette* either. The German writer took this example as a part of a larger demonstration of the translators' ideal task.[17] In his view, each original text is only a writing in a given language of a hidden absolute. The translators that stick to concrete utterances in the source text miss the 'pure language' behind it. Their initial priority should be to discover the absolute signified expressed in the signifier of the source text, in order to re-convey it into the target language. As Benjamin also put it, far from hiding the original text, the genuine translation is in a position to enhance it, since, after drawing some more light from the pure language, it can shed it onto the original text. A good translation should go back to the origin of the original text,[18] ultimately to the unwritten 'hypotext'.

When Hölderlin, in his translation of *Antigon*, endeavoured to discover the etymology of the words to be translated, it was only a variant of the same quest for the hidden element behind the text.[19] Each text possesses its own stock of half hidden keywords, keynotes, key ideas. As a first step recurrent concepts and words heavily loaded with their connotations ought to be discovered; after that, translators ought to find a stock of other words conveying the same keynotes in the target language. The same words in another text would not necessarily reflect the same motif, and, consequently, equivalents would not have to be found in the translation. The word *fatalement* in French can be almost meaningless, being used merely to emphasize a statement. Yet, if one of the leading themes of a novel is 'the burden of fate', then the concept is central and must remain central. Take the semantic field of light and brightness, versus darkness in *SGGK*. At a symbolic level of reading, the Middle English poem reflects the struggle between the forces of light and of darkness. Dozens of different words are used for these concepts, and a translation that does not recreate the same richness and the same variety would miss a part of the hidden, pure language. Berman goes even further than this when he refers to 'underlying networks of signifiers':[20] below the surface of a text, there are networks of words that do not, at first sight, appear to be linked, but that are intrinsically part of its texture. To fail to carry this quality into the target text is a breach of the tissues of which it is made. In this case the distortion becomes physical; it is the very nature of the original that is torn.

More than a book would be needed to discuss the issue of absolute language. I want to focus instead on a minor point that was tackled by

[17] 'the intralinear version of the sacred text'.
[18] Berman, *Les tours de Babel*, p. 97.
[19] Berman, 'Traduction littérale et étymologisante', in *Les tours de Babel*, pp. 102–4.
[20] 'Des réseaux signifiants sous-jacents' (my translation), p. 76.

Benjamin at the end of his essay. He compared the relationship of a translation to its original with a tangent that touches a circle, and then disappears into infinity. The real meaning of the freedom implied by this comparison, Benjamin argues, was admirably expressed by Rudolf Pannwitz in his *Krisis der europäischen Kultur*.[21] Even the best of our translations into German, Pannwitz wrote, try to turn Hindi, Greek and English into German, instead of turning German into Hindi, Greek and English. They show much more respect for the ways of being of their own language than for the spirit of the foreign works.

As Friedrich Schleiermacher made clear as early as 1813,[22] translators serve two masters: the author and the reader. The point is to bring the latter – in his or her mother tongue – to an understanding of the former that is as complete as possible. Schleiermacher considered two possible methods. In the first case, it is a translation that focuses on the author. The translator brings the reader to the author and the translator's function is to replace (*ersetzen*) the reader's lack of knowledge of the original language, or, in the case of an ancient text, of another world. In other words, his text is the *translation* that could have been written in the target language by the original author. In the second case, we have the reverse situation, and everything is centred around the reader. It is the *original text* that the author himself, or herself, would have written, had he, or she, had the target language as mother-tongue. We'll return to this, let me simply say here that Schleiermacher stressed the importance of the first method, particularly because, as he said, it is through the knowledge of different languages that we become citizens of the world. Wilhelm Von Humbold defined the dilemma, according to which translators are bound to stick too much either to the original or to their own language's conventions, at about the same time as Schleiermacher wrote his article. A century later, Benjamin was not afraid to ask whether translations were actually made for the readers who did not understand the original. He overtly took sides with the first method as well:

> In the appreciation of a work of art or an art form, consideration of the receiver never proves fruitful. Not only is any reference to a certain public or its representatives misleading, but even the concept of the 'ideal' receiver is detrimental in the theoretical consideration of art[. . .]. This, actually, is the cause of another characteristic of inferior translation, which consequently we may define as the inaccurate transmission of an inessential content. This will be true whenever a translation undertakes to serve the reader. However, if it were intended for the reader, the same

[21] Nüremberg, 1947.

[22] 'Ueber die verschiedenen Methoden des Uebersetzens' (Berlin). Edited by Hans Joachim Störig, *Das Problem des Übersetzens*, pp. 38–70, under the title of 'Methoden des Übersetzens'.

> would have to apply to the original. If the original does not exist for the reader's sake, how could the translation be understood on the basis of this premise?[23]

Not only philosophers are concerned with this debate. As an example among many others, the arguments were reiterated a few years ago by the translator of the Bible, Eugene A. Nida. He too drew attention to the two basic orientations: one of formal equivalence, allowing the reader to 'identify himself as fully as possible with a person in the source-language context, and to understand as much as he can of the customs, manner of thought, and means of expression'[24] of that context. And the other, a dynamic orientation, in which an attempt was made to recreate a relationship between the receiver and the message that is 'substantially the same as that which existed between the original receptors and the message'.[25]

While Pannwitz's complaint was well-founded in the context of Germany, it could be extended to most other European countries – if not the whole world, and also to other ages. Let me concentrate on the egocentric method first. There is nothing new under the sun, we may observe when looking back at the history of translation in medieval England. David Burnley rightly remarks that:

> the transition from French to English involved a cultural descent, or at the very least a considerable broadening of appeal. Anglicisation often meant popularisation, adaptation to a new audience of less sophisticated tastes. The hallowed landmarks of aristocratic cultural reference will be omitted: the references to classical legend, the appreciative detail of physical beauty and moral perfection, connoisseurs' descriptions of objects of value or of recent fashion. Psychological subtlety and the formal analysis of character are likely to be replaced by familiar formulae and introspection by narrative action. Of more profound importance than the mere change in language used, the text undergoes a process of social adaptation.[26]

Each age, each country, and each society has its specific problems. What mattered in the special case of medieval England's so-called bilingualism was the socio-cultural gap between those with French as their mother-tongue, and those with English. But the point is that the translators focused on the target language and society, not on the source language. They were hardly concerned with the 'other'. As a result of a new

23 'The Task of the Translator', pp. 69–70.

24 Nida, *Toward a Science of Translating, With Special Reference to Principles and Procedures Involved in Bible Translating* (Leiden, 1964), p. 159.

25 Ibid.

26 'Late Medieval English Translation: Types and Reflections', in Roger Ellis, ed., *The Medieval Translator. The Theory and Practice of Translation in the Middle Ages* (Cambridge, 1989), pp. 37–53; here: p. 42.

consciousness of their own identity, what mattered to them was to provide their country with a literature in their native language. The first meaning of translation was 'to transfer from one place to another',[27] and so *to introduce* something new into another place. But in this particular case, the whole point was *to drive the French out* of the country: French literature being one of the strongholds of the invaders' power, it had to be ousted. As a result, priority was given to the culture of the adopting language which had to replace that of the sources. The culture of the 'other' could be accepted only provided it was clothed in English garments.

Allow me to use a trivial comparison. Chinese restaurants all over the world vary according to each country, with additional ingredients according to the tastes of these countries, such as green peas in Britain and cabbage in Germany. In the same way, many translators follow a recipe governed by a golden rule. It says: never forget to add several spoonfuls of local ingredients, in order not to run counter to your customers' taste. In the same way, on the other side of the English Channel, France's first genuine interest in Middle English literature was in what they understood as France transplanted to England. What they endeavoured to identify in Chaucer, for instance, was what French culture, literature, and even race had produced on a foreign soil.[28]

This issue takes us back to the famous Italian saying. As Nida rightly observed 'the human translator is not a machine, and he inevitably leaves the stamp of his own personality on any translation he makes'.[29] At some point, the level of faithfulness is left to translators. While it is obvious to everybody that the art of translation is the art of finding correspondences between two systems, the level of interpretation of such correspondences is a matter of decision, whether of individual translators or of schools, countries or ages. They are free to adopt a close rendering, with a word for word translation. They can also shift to another level, with a transposition of poetic diction from one language to another – as in the English renderings of French romances. The next stage is characterized by the substitution of motifs, such as songs, nursery rhymes, and traditional descriptions. One of the main dangers of this personal involvement of translators is a covert or overt tendency to distort the original. Some of these intrusions are simply the unconscious mirroring

[27] Chaucer still uses the word in its etymological meaning: see *Clerk's Tale*, *The Riverside Chaucer*, l. 385.

[28] Juliette Dor, 'Le Chevalier de Chatelain et la traduction des *Contes de Cantorbéry*', in *Moyen Age et XIXème siècle: le mirage des origines*, *Littérales*, 6 (1990), pp. 107–16, and 'The Wheat and the Chaff: Early Chaucer Scholarship in France', in *Etudes de linguistique et de littérature en l'honneur d'André Crépin, réunies par Danielle Buschingerb et Wolfgang Spiewok*, Greifswald *Wodan* 20, 1993, pp. 123–33.

[29] Nida, *Toward a Science of Translating*, pp. 155–6.

of personality traits. At times it is halfway between this and a conscious attempt to transform things, what Nida described as the translator's paternalistic attitude.[30] But translators are sometimes on the verge of deceit and can even be deliberately unfaithful, as is well illustrated by Chaucer in Chantecleer's famous translation of '*In principio, / Mulier est hominis confusio*' as 'Madame, the sentence of this Latyn is, / "Womman is mannes joye and al his blis" '.[31] What, apart from the function of characterizing the speaker,[32] is the point of Chantecleer's mistranslation? What the cock wants to do here is to please his audience, in this case his wife. His psychological insight prompts him to say what she wants to hear. The Latin sentence, a comic misogynist manifesto in a nutshell, is replaced by its opposite. We move from a male statement to its female counterpart, and I'd like to argue that this replacement can be seen as a metaphor for the substitution of one culture by another.

Translators' agonies of creation, or of delivery, are perhaps in vain, as we can see in the charges referred to by Brian Stone in his article 'False Friends and Strange Meters'.[33] In the case of the translation of medieval English poetry into modern English, Stone explained, the accusation of *traduttore traditore* takes two specialized forms. From a linguistic viewpoint, first, true translation can never be achieved, and, furthermore, it is unnecessary. Secondly, with regard to prosody, it is 'bad taste to bring back poetic forms when the language that sustained them has changed'. Of course, Stone agreed, it is better to read an original than a translation, but if there is a gap between the original and the present-day responses, he maintains that the translator must re-create a text that allows for a similar reinterpretation. Translators suffer, but the text

[30] 'Misled by his own paternalistic attitude into thinking that the potential receptors of his translation are so limited in understanding or experience that they must have his "built-in" explanations. Or he may believe that their language is so deficient that only by certain "improvements" (often arbitrary and artificial) can he communicate the message', Nida, *Toward a Science of Translating*, p. 155. Nida's approach here was bound to be different since his study is based on a process different from the traditional one. Most of the time, translations operate from a source language into the mother language. In the case of contemporary Bible translation, we have to do mostly with missionaries who learn the foreign language of remote language groups in order to convey the message of the Bible to them. This particular situation doubly accounts for the 'paternalistic' attitude of such translators. On the one hand, they feel personally superior to the people to whom they want to bring the Scriptures, and, on the other hand, they feel that their own mother tongue is superior in the field of biblical studies.

[31] *NPT*, *The Riverside Chaucer*, ll. 3163–6.

[32] See André Crépin, 'Chaucer and the French', in Piero Boitani and Anna Torti, eds., *Medieval and Pseudo-Medieval Literature* (Tübingen and Cambridge, 1984), pp. 55–77, p. 59.

[33] William Radice and Barbara Reynolds, eds., *The Translator's Art. Essays in Honour of Betty Radice* (Harmondsworth, 1987), pp. 175–86.

suffers as well, argues Antoine Berman, who claims that 'the private sense of the letter of the text'[34] suffers. Berman also quotes Jacques Derrida in order to demonstrate how the integrity of the text is attacked in the process:

> A verbal body does not let itself be translated or transported into another language. It is what translation ignores. Ignoring the body is the essential energy of translation . . . .[35]

Even though we try to group translations into categories, there are almost as many types of them as there are translators. What Nida calls the 'audience's decoding ability and needs'[36] can also vary. If translators are go-betweens, their task will differ according to the level of cultural integration of readers.

Time does not allow me to dwell here on my three translations of parts of the *Canterbury Tales*.[37] Let me simply say that a text written in the past requires successive adjustments in its translation as time goes by. By definition, the original is immutable; if the translation remains static, there will be a widening gap between source and translation. In other words, in order to recreate the same effects as that achieved in a first translation, there must be new translations adapted to every period. This is true because of the evolution of language and because of social and cultural changes. Reactions will be different according to the developments in the target culture; so the effects have to be created anew with due consideration for such changes. Walter Benjamin was well aware of this when he wrote:

> This, to be sure, is to admit that all translation is only a somewhat provisional way of coming to terms with the foreignness of languages. An instant and final rather than a temporary and provisional solution of this foreignness remains out of the reach of mankind; at any rate, it eludes any direct attempt.[38]

This was further demonstrated by Brian Stone's discussion of the true interpretation of 'false friends' within the same language. The reading of a poem being an act of interpretation, if a late twentieth-century English

[34] Berman, *Les tours de Babel*, p. 59: 'le sens privé de sa lettre' (my translation).
[35] Ibid.: 'Un corps verbal ne se laisse pas traduire ou transporter dans une autre langue. Il est cela même que la traduction laisse tomber. Laisser tomber le corps, telle est même l'énergie essentielle de la traduction. . .' (my translation), *L'écriture et la différence* (Paris, 1967), p. 312.
[36] Nida, *Toward a Science of Translating*, p. 156.
[37] I read a paper on the topic in the Colloquium *The Medieval Translator: The Theory and Practice of Translation in the Middle Ages*, Cardiff, 1989 ('*Les Contes de Cantorbéry, The Canterbury Tales*, Translating without Betraying?').
[38] In 'The Task of the Translator', p. 75.

audience misunderstands words that still exist in their variety of English, but had another meaning or several different meanings in a work such as *SGGK*, their interpretation and response will be affected. Here, the Italian aphorism could be rewritten: it is the absence of translation that is a betrayal. Not only are not translators betrayers, they ought to be guides through the snares and traps of linguistic and cultural differences.

'The translator enriches his tongue by allowing the source language to penetrate and modify it', argues George Steiner,[39] and Brian Stone considers introducing a word such as 'fewter' – one of the numerous terms describing weaponry – into his translation of the alliterative *Morte Arthure*.[40] I could multiply the examples, but will limit myself here to a single example of false friends between my French, and Chaucer's use of French-loanwords. It goes a stage further than what Mallarmé called 'nos mots gênés par le devoir étrange de parler une autre langue que la leur',[41] since I want to reintroduce them into the language from which they originated, but with variations of sense. The word *bachelier* in Chaucer's *WBT* means an aspirant knight. In present-day French, it refers to somebody who has successfully passed the baccalauréat. Useless to say that this is confusing. In such cases, I often resort to what Brian Stone has described as an incorporation of the annotation or interpretation in the translation.[42]

As Genette argues,[43] further aporia appear in the case of the translation from an ancient foreign language. The horizontal, synchronic difficulties are doubled by new ones, of a vertical, diachronic type this time. The only way to avoid this diachronic dimension would be to produce a translation into a language that is contemporary with the original. We may wonder what this could be, whether in English or in French, in the case of the translation of Homer's *Odyssey*, and so let me choose an easier case. I have repeatedly been asked whether I translated *The Canterbury Tales* into medieval French. Not speaking medieval French

[39] *After Babel*, p. 65.

[40] He argues for an annotated importation of the word, for which present-day English has no exact equivalent, the word 'socket' not being satisfactory, since a 'fewter' is 'the socket fixed to the saddle of a knight which is not simply a "rest", but supports the spear-butt in the charge and takes the brunt of impact', whereas 'the modern word "socket" indicates the hollow space into which a butt or shaft fits without [. . .] allowing for the violent buffer function of the medieval item of knightly equipment', Brian Stone, 'False Friends and Strange Meters', pp. 178–9.

[41] Quoted by Berman, 'Traduction littérale', p. 125.

[42] He explains that 'It was on this principle that I described the Green Knight's *ax*, which is amplified to a *spetos sparthe* in the next line, as a "hideous helmet-smasher". Modern English has just the one word "battle-axe" to describe such a weapon . . .', Stone, 'False Friends and Strange Meters', p. 179.

[43] Genette, *Palimpsestes*, p. 241.

myself, I was deeply puzzled. Being a medievalist, I have a passive knowledge of it, but would not dream of learning how to express myself that way. The main interest of the experience would be akin to a private joke between me and a very restricted audience. When I came to think about it, I realized that the point of such questions was not that they wanted me to write cryptograms, but simply that the translation into a foreign, but contemporary language was the only logical way to avoid a double transfer. As we have already seen translations are doomed to be temporary because, since the target language is developing all the time, the only way to preserve a constant relationship between translation and original text is to rewrite translations. For similar reasons, I am translating *SGGK* for the same editor as one of my Chaucer translations in a far more archaic French. Both the Gawain poet and Chaucer were the contemporaries of their contemporaries, but Chaucer wanted to write a very modern variety of fourteenth-century English, while the author of *SGGK* took part in the alliterative revival.

James S. Holmes[44] has provided a good formal model of the levels of transfer at stake in literary translation: three systems are to be shifted from the source-language to the receiver-language: the socio-cultural, the linguistic and the literary, with inter-system incompatibilities. In the case of diachronic, or 'cross-temporal' divergences, the presence of a new parameter further distorts these three levels. As Holmes goes on to argue, cross-temporal translators have to make a choice between a 'historicizing translation', that preserves an exact replica of the original, or a 'modernizing translation', in which they re-create a modern equivalent, or an intermediary stage that he calls, following Geoffrey Leech, 'standard archaic usage'.[45] What applies to cross-temporal translation also applies – in a less intricate form – to any translation, and raises the basic issue of how to translate the otherness of a source text. 'Verfremdung oder Entfremdung', wonders Hans Joachim Störig.[46] In an act that pertains both to the rewording of the original sentence and to its transfer into another language, I interpret his question as 'to convey or to destroy the original text's otherness'. Holmes takes the example of one of Charles d'Orléans's rondels, in which young men are riding on horses in order to impress girls. The historical approach would preserve the author's context and the horses, while the second choice is to transform the young men into 'motorcycle-riding "rockers" '. I have been particularly struck by this detail because it is very much the same situation as the one I came across when I determined my priorities before

44 Holmes, *Translated*, p. 36.
45 *A Linguistic Guide to English Poetry* (London, 1969), p. 13.
46 Störig, *Das Problem des Übersetzens*, p. xxvi.

translating the *Canterbury Tales*. I must confess that it never occurred to me I should make Chaucer's pilgrims drive and wear jeans. Of course, Chaucer was his contemporaries' contemporary, and if we preserve a historical background we distort a part of the original effect, but, on the other hand, jeans and motor-bikes are anachronisms, since one of the basic features of the work is that it belongs to the late fourtheenth century.

The situation is in some ways comparable to that we find in the stage production of plays. The same issues are raised by costumes, although there is a major difference due to the visual aspect of a performance. Any production is an interpretation for a specific audience, at a specific time, and is created by a group of people aware that their art is ephemeral.

We shift here to Jakobson's third level of relationship between signs and meaning. After rewording and translation proper, there is transmutation: an intersemiotic process in which verbal signs are interpreted by means of non-verbal sign systems which may be pictorial, gestural, mathematical, or musical. In the case of Charles d'Orléans, a consideration of various translations allowed Holmes to conclude that none of them modernized at all three levels. Most of the translations combined historicizing approaches with modernizing ones, in the prosody, in the 'temporal dialect', or the cultural background. The link with the past cannot be totally dismissed, and, obviously, the socio-cultural sphere seems to be the most resistant bastion.

The idea that it is important to convey the sense of the other culture was central in early 19th-century Germany's great translations, as is well illustrated by Wilhelm von Humboldt's introduction to *Agammemnon*.[47] In his introduction to *Das Problem des Übersetzens*, Hans Joachim Störig quotes Friedrich Schleiermacher, who considered that the world to be translated was far away (in distance, and/or in time), and so 'fremd', other. As a result,

> The translator is a pontifex, a builder of bridges, and what he must bridge here is a considerable crevasse. Here his work should rely on both pillars:

[47] 'The fact that translating has in itself a certain colour of foreignness is necessarily connected with this viewpoint. The translation has reached its highest aim provided it is not the foreignness but the otherness that is felt. But if the foreignness appears for itself and is even likely to hide the otherness, the translator shows that he was not worthy of the original' ('Mit dieser Ansicht ist freilich nothwendig verbunden, dass die Uebersetzung eine gewisse Farbe der Fremdheit an sich trägt[. . .]. Solange nicht der Fremdheit, sondern das Fremde gefühlt wird, hat die Uebersetzung ihre höchsten Zwecke erreicht; wo aber die Fremdheit an sich erscheint, und vielleicht gar das Fremde verdunkelt, da verräth der Uebersetzer, dass er seinem Original nicht gewachsen ist'), 'Einleitung zu *Agamemnon*', in Hans Joachim Störig, ed., *Das Problem des Übersetzens*, p. 83 (my translation).

> on the one hand, he is responsible before his creator, on the other hand, he translates *always* for an audience, for a country, for an age.[48]

Störig further shows that the quality of otherness in the original can be due to its particular *realia*. If an Oriental poet compares a woman with a flower that is unknown to us, what should we do? It is all the more difficult to provide an answer because we cannot be sure of the exact meaning of the comparison. Should the translator leave the name of the unknown flower, or should he replace it by a rose, for instance? One of the other issues here is also the audience's traditional representation, as in the case the Last Supper. Should we redress things and describe Jesus and his disciples as lying down even reclining though the Middle Ages had transformed the Last Supper into an event in which the participants were sitting? Should the translator preserve the foreign, exotic character of the translated text for the reader? Schleiermacher uses a striking verb to convey this idea: *fortpflanzen*, to transplant the otherness in the target text. Berman provides the same answer to these questions when he denounces the ethnocentric trend of our translations. He shows that translating idiomatic phrases is not the same as trying to find equivalences, as illustrated by an example drawn from Conrad's Typhoon:

> He did not care *a tinker curse Damme*, if this ship isn't worse than Bedlam'(underlying of the phrases mine), translated by 'Il s'en fichait comme du juron d'un étameur, que le diable m'emporte si l'on ne se croirait pas à Bedlam![49]

A comparatist, Berman reports, reproached Gide with not translating by 's'en fichait comme d'une guigne' and not replacing Bedlam by Charenton, an equivalent French asylum. The point is that such idiomatic phrases convey the sense of Englishness. Had Gide referred to Charenton, we would have felt at home, of course, but would have missed a sense of otherness. We would have missed part of Berman's 'parlance du texte':

> To improve a work by suppressing its foreign character in order to *facilitate* its reading will lead to no more than to disfigure it, and, hence, to

[48] 'Der Übersetzer ist ja ein pontifex, ein Brückenbauer, und hier muss er eine beträchtliche Kluft überbrücken. Dabei soll sein Werk aber auf beiden Pfeilern sicher ruhen: er ist einerseits dem Original und seinem Schöpfer verpflichtet, auf der anderen Seite übersetzt er *stets* für ein Publikum, für ein Land, für ein Zeitalter.', in Störig, *Das Problem des Übersetzens*, p. xxvi (my translation).

[49] Berman, *Les tours de Babel*, pp. 79–80.

betray the reader that it pretends to serve. What we would need instead, would be, as in science, a *training to otherness*.[50]

My discussion of the contribution of translators to such a new dimension often agrees with the concept of an absolute language that is being developed by 'traductologists'[51] and by current trends of philosophy. One only has to think of Walter Benjamin's ideas on translation, and of Martin Heidegger, who conceives translation and interpretation as two closely interwoven operations with a feed back process. Heidegger writes:

> Any translation is in itself an interpretation. It bears in itself, without giving them a voice, all the bases, the openings and the levels of interpretation that were present at its origin. And interpretation, in its turn, is only the accomplishment of the still silent translation, the translation that has not been expressed in a completed word. Essentially, interpretation and translation are one and same thing.[52]

It is also of crucial importance to discover that translators can compensate for the inevitable loss in the course of the journey from one language into another by providing clues to the discovery of other cultures. I see this opening to 'otherness' as a wonderful bonus that can make up for the losses incurred in the act of translation. Good translations should try to grasp the absolute, the pure language hidden in the languages, the unity which existed before Babel, 'the predestined, hitherto inaccessible realm of reconciliation and fulfillment of languages'.[53] At the same time, they should reflect diversity, and the differences between cultures. Translators are in a position to prevent a standardization of European diversity, the marked reduction in the vigour of individual cultures. This has been called the 'Trans-Europ-Repress':

> Cut across by businessmen trains – with windows tightly sealed, attaché cases, and suits and ties, Europe, once loved by a god, is now, as

[50] 'Amender une oeuvre de ses étrangetés pour *faciliter* sa lecture n'aboutit qu'à la défigurer et, donc, à tromper le lecteur que l'on prétend servir. Il faut donc plutôt, comme dans le cas de la science, une *éducation à l'étrangeté*', in Berman, *Les tours de Babel*, p. 86 (my translation).

[51] Following Antoine Berman's definition of 'Traductology: translation's reflection on itself, on the basis of its nature of experience' ('La traductologie: la réflexion de la traduction sur elle-même à partir de sa propre expérience'), *Les tours de Babel*, Introduction, p. 39.

[52] 'Denn jede Übersetzung ist in sich schon eine Auslegung. Unausgesprochen trägt sie bei sich alle Ansätze, Hinsichten, Ebenen der Auslegung, der sie entstammt. Die Auslegung selbst wiederum ist nur der Vollzug der noch schweigenden, noch nicht in das vollendende Wort eingegangenen Übersetzung. Auslegung und Übersetzung sind in ihrem Wesenskern dasselbe' (my translation), *Heraklit*, *Gesamtausgabe* (Frankfurt am Main, 1979, Band 55), p. 63.

[53] Benjamin, *Illuminations*, p. 75.

> everybody knows, no more than a 'Space' made out of several other spaces that have been piled up or intertwined: the economic space, the technological space, the judicial space (that is to say the police's), and the moral-ideological space: in all, the space of the repression of the very possibility to exist.[54]

Yes, translators are betrayers. But they can sublimate the suffering of the unsatisfactory creation. As long as they see themselves as second-rate creators, as the craftsmen of a work that is bound to be inferior to the original, they will remain iconoclastic, second-rate writers. Their mission is to bridge cultural gaps, to train their fellow-readers to the otherness of different literatures, of different ways of being. And what a splendid achievement whenever, through their halting efforts, distrust and suspicion give way to the exhilaration of discovery.

[54] 'T.E.R. Editions Trans-Europ-Repress. Sillonnée par les trains d'affaires – fenêtres bloquées, attaché-cases et complet-cravate – l'Europe, jadis aimée d'un dieu, n'est plus désormais, comme chacun sait, qu'un 'Espace' fait de plusieurs autres empilés ou entre-croisés: l'espace économique, l'espace technologique, l'espace judiciaire (c'est-à-dire policier), l'espace idéologico-moral. Au total, l'espace de la répression de la possibilité même d'exister'. (Berman, *Les tours de Babel*; my translation).

INTERPRETATION OF GENRES AND BY GENRES IN THE MIDDLE AGES

H. ANSGAR KELLY

I wish to deal here with some ways in which interpretation followed upon generic ideas of structure or content in the Middle Ages. But first let me make some general observations about literature and genre theory.

According to Tzvetan Todorov in his *Introduction to Poetics*, the study of literature has been divided between poetics (the scientific analysis of form and structure) and interpretation (the search for meaning); he believes that there has been a massive imbalance in favour of interpretation, which he would like to redress.[1] But Lubomír Doležel, who has a similar notion of poetics, distinguishes it not from interpretation but from criticism, that is, the placing of value-judgments on works of literature.[2] I think that most observers will agree that both interpretation and criticism have always played a prominent role not only in reader-response to literature but also in author-production of literature; they correspond in many ways to the twin goals of poetry in Horace's classic formulation, the *utile* and the *dulce*, instruction and pleasure.

Todorov implies that the New Critics were particularly prominent in emphasizing interpretation over structure; but I would say rather that they subordinated both structure and interpretation to criticism. They devalued interpretation especially by ignoring or despising the didactic aspect of literature and by promoting ambiguity as a positive aesthetic value. Post-structuralism by definition downplays structure, and the deconstructivist branch takes the new-critical emphasis on ambiguity to the point of radical skepticism, so that all meanings and values in a given work are open to question. But there has been more conscious attention paid to deconstructionism's rejection of definite meanings in literature

[1] Tzvetan Todorov, *Introduction to Poetics*, tr. Richard Howard (Minneapolis, 1981), esp. pp. 7, 12. See also Robert M. Jordan, 'Todorov, Vinsauf, and Chaucerian Textuality', *Studies in the Age of Chaucer Proceedings* 2 (1986) 51–7. Todorov's work was originally published as *Qu'est-ce que le structuralisme: Poétique* in 1968 and revised in 1973; he supplied a new preface, dated May 1980, to the English edition (pp. xx–xxxii).

[2] Lubomír Doležel, *Occidental Poetics: Tradition and Progress* (Lincoln, Nebr., 1990), Chap. 1: 'Aristotle: Poetics and Criticism', pp. 11–32.

than to its corollary consequences for aesthetic criticism. However, the aesthetic approach to literature was already under attack from other quarters. Northrop Frye's call for a scientific poetics, in which value judgements based on taste had no place, was particularly influential,[3] and Todorov endorses this stand in his major work on genre theory, *The Fantastic*.[4]

I wish to go beyond Frye and Todorov and set aside, at least for the time being, not only evaluative criticism but also interpretation and scientific or structural poetics as well. I freely acknowledge that modern theorists have made valuable interpretative and structural conclusions that can profitably be applied to medieval literature. For instance, what Frye has to say about genres in his *Anatomy of Criticism* is extraordinarily provocative, not only in his theory of genres but even more so in his theories of modes and myths.[5] More recently, I have found Doležel's concept of 'narrative worlds', which he derives from modal logic, to be very helpful.[6] But I am more interested at present in finding out what we can about the views of writers in the Middle Ages. Hans Robert Jauss has done much to move us in this direction by outlining how to go about analyzing actual medieval generic concepts: we must abandon the procedures of the literary handbooks, 'according to which one promiscuously uses original characterizations, classical genre concepts, and later classifications', and limit ourselves instead to medieval 'horizons of expectations'.[7] Jonathan Culler puts it another

[3] Northrop Frye, *Anatomy of Criticism: Four Essays* (Princeton, 1957), 'Polemical Introduction', esp. pp. 8, 18–28.

[4] Tzvetan Todorov, *The Fantastic: A Structural Approach to a Literary Genre*, tr. Richard Howard (Ithaca, 1973), from *Introduction à la littérature fantastique* (1970). I would also like to point to the 'Marxist' approach of the art historian Otto Karl Werckmeister in 'Marx on Ideology and Art', *New Literary History* 4 (1972–73) 501–19. Werckmeister considers himself a Marxist because he agrees with Karl Marx that no valid philosophy of aesthetics is possible, and that therefore it is not the business of art historians to make value judgments on what is beautiful and not beautiful. Rather, their efforts should be directed towards trying to determine the aesthetic preoccupations of the artists and their patrons.

[5] Frye says in his prefatory statement, 'What is here offered is pure critical theory, and the omission of all specific criticism, even, in three of the four essays, of quotation, is deliberate' (p. vii). For an account of this and other general systems of genres, see Alastair Fowler, *Kinds of Literature: An Introduction to the Theory of Genres and Modes* (Oxford, 1982), pp. 235–55. See also Fredric Jameson, *The Political Unconscious: Narrative as a Socially Symbolic Act* (Ithaca, 1981), esp. Chap. 2: 'Magical Narratives: On the Dialectical Use of Genre Criticism', pp. 103–50. I should note that Fowler's treatment of 'Genre Labels in the Middle Ages', pp. 142–7, is very superficial and misleading, and demonstrates the need for more spadework.

[6] Lubomír Doležel, 'Narrative Worlds', in *Sound, Sign, and Meaning: Quinquagenary of the Prague Linguistic Circle*, ed. Ladislav Matejka (Ann Arbor, 1976), pp. 542–52.

[7] Hans Robert Jauss, 'Theorie der Gattungen und Literatur des Mittelalters', *Grundriss der romanischen Literaturen des Mittelalters*, part 1: *Généralités*, ed. Maurice

way: 'An account of genres should be an attempt to define the classes which have been functional in the processes of reading and writing, the sets of expectations which have enabled readers to naturalize texts and give them a relation to the world or, if one prefers to look at it in another way, the possible functions of language which were available to writers at any given period'.[8]

Most historical accounts of genres suffer from methodological confusion and a lack of attention to primary evidence. The most serious offenses have resulted from an unacknowledged mixture of poetics and criticism: often what is meant to be pure poetics is criticism in disguise; it becomes, in Doležel's phrase, a 'hidden axiology'.[9] Let me give a specific, and what should be notorious, example. A judgmental conclusion in chapter 13 of Aristotle's *Poetics*, that the best tragedy involves the fall of a basically good man through some *hamartia*, has been mistakenly taken to be part of his general understanding of tragedy, with the implication that he allowed only dramas of this sort within the category of tragedy. This misreading, which seems to be almost universally accepted as accurate, would have the effect, if consistently applied to the surviving Greek tragedies, of eliminating almost all of them from the tragic genre. The plays that end with Medea and Electra successful in their vengeance, or with Orestes absolved, or with Iphigenia saved from committing fratricide by a last-minute recognition of her brother Orestes, or the story of Odysseus finally being united with Penelope, would be generic rejects or outcasts. Aristotle himself, of course, includes all such dramas and stories within the 'scientific' genre of tragedy, even when he ranks them critically from the point of view of effectiveness or lack of effectiveness: some are good tragedies, some are defective, others are downright bad; but all are tragedies.

Aristotle's most general understanding of tragedy is that it encompasses all stories that deal with 'spudean' (that is, noble, or at least

Delbouille (Heidelberg, 1972), pp. 107–38, esp. 107, 110. It is reprinted, with original pagination, in Jauss's collected essays, *Alterität und Modernität der mittelalterlichen Literatur* (Munich, 1977), essay no. 10. The French version that appeared in *Poétique* 1 (1970) 79-98, seems to have been translated from a preliminary and incomplete draft. The German version appears in a good English translation by Timothy Bahti with other of Jauss's essays, in *Toward an Aesthetic of Reception* (Minneapolis, 1982), as 'Theory of Genres and Medieval Literature', pp. 76-109, 205–11 (for the quotations above, see pp. 77 and 79), but the original is mistakenly said to have appeared in 'volume 6' of the *Grundriss*. The confusion is no doubt due to the fact that Jauss edited part 6 of the *Grundriss*, which appeared in two volumes, in 1968 and 1970. For a good application of Jauss's ideas (as they appear in the *Poétique* version), see Paul Strohm, 'Middle English Narrative Genres', *Genre* 13 (1980) 379–88, esp. 385–8.

[8] Jonathan Culler, *Structuralist Poetics: Structuralism, Linguistics, and the Study of Literature* (Ithaca, 1975), p. 136.

[9] Doležel, *Occidental Poetics*, p. 29.

better than average) characters or situations. This allows him to incorporate epics like the *Iliad* and the *Odyssey* into the category of tragedy. But there is another fundamental principle of categorization that Aristotle as a good scientist was acting upon: any work that is called a tragedy by its author, or that is considered by the author to be a tragedy, is a tragedy. This principle, of course, would exclude epics. But both principles necessitated the inclusion of plots with happy endings within the category of tragedy. Euripides's *Iphigenia Among the Taurians*, for instance, which ends with Iphigenia joyfully welcoming Orestes, is a tragedy not only because it has spudean characters and action but also because Euripides himself designed it as a tragedy. It also, I might add, vies with Sophocles's *Oedipus rex* for Aristotle's choice of best tragedy.

We can call the first of these two Aristotelian principles or procedures 'definitional', since it is based on a fixed idea of a genre, and the other 'nominalist', based on a common term with possibly different meanings in various instantiations. Todorov, like Frye, follows the definitional approach. For instance, when Todorov discusses the question of how much fieldwork is necessary for the study of a genre, it is clear that he has a theoretical generic notion in mind from the beginning. He asks, 'Are we entitled to discuss a genre without having studied (or at least read) all the works which constitute it?' and answers in the affirmative: the scientific method proceeds by deducing hypotheses from a limited number of instances. He concludes, 'Let us leave exhaustiveness, then, to those who have no other recourse'.[10] The nominalist approach, however, does not reduce itself to a choice between induction and deduction, or to a choice between limited induction and complete induction, since no hypothesis is sought. Rather, the object is simply to find out what the generic terms meant to the users. This enterprise, moreover, often precludes a Jaussian search for horizons of expectations, for frequently a genre word will come into use only as a result of a solitary act of haphazard reading or idiosyncratic deduction.

I have spent the last several years applying the nominalist approach to tragedy. That is, I have been trying to come up with as complete and as objective a characterization as possible of the various ideas and forms of tragedy that can be be found from Aristotle's time through the Middle Ages. From this perspective, the name of tragedy is a sufficient and necessary condition for being a tragedy. In other words, everything that is called or considered a tragedy is a tragedy, and only what is called a tragedy is a tragedy. Tragedies are tragedies only to those who consider them to be tragedies, and only according to their own understanding of the term. The subjective aspect is the essential factor.[11]

[10] Todorov, *The Fantastic*, pp. 3–4.

[11] See H. A. Kelly, *Ideas and Forms of Tragedy from Aristotle to the Middle Ages*

In this paper I wish to extend my approach beyond tragedy to genres in general. I am restricting myself to two kinds of situations: to cases of authorial awareness of genres in composing their own works – I call this the interpretation *of* genres; and to cases where writers apply generic categories to already existing works – this is interpretation *by* genres. Dante's conception of his *Inferno* as a comedy is an example of the first;[12] his reference to the *Aeneid* as a tragedy is an example of the second,[13] as is the whole tradition of commentary on Dante's completed *Comedy*. For a work to qualify as an interpretation of a genre in the sense that I am using it here, it is not enough for its author to call it by a generic name; he must be consciously using it in a generic sense. The example from Dante holds, because we know from the *De vulgari eloquentia* that he had definite ideas about the meaning of the term comedy. Similarly, it is not enough for a writer simply to refer to the works of others by generic names to enable us to conclude that he is interpreting them by those genres unless there is some indication that he is actually indulging in generic thinking. In the case of Peter of Blois, who refers to stories of Arthurian heroism as tragedies,[14] one might easily suppose that he was

(Cambridge, 1993). Another study, *Chaucerian Tragedy*, in preparation, deals with the tragedies of Chaucer, Lydgate, and Henryson and the non-tragedies of Boccaccio's *De casibus*.

12 Dante, *Inferno* 16.128; 20.2.

13 Ibid., 20.113.

14 Peter of Blois, *Liber de confessione sacramentali*, PL 207:1088–1089: 'Vera siquidem penitentia non in lacrymis momentaneis aut horaria compunctione consistit. Nulla etiam affectio pia meritoria est ad salutem nisi ex Christi dilectione procedat. Sepe in tragediis et aliis carminibus poetarum, in joculatorum cantilenis, describitur aliquis vir prudens, decorus, fortis, amabilis, et per omnia gratiosus. Recitantur etiam pressure vel injurie eidem crudeliter irrogate, sicut de Arturo et Gangano [*lege* Gaugano] et Tristanno fabulosa quedam referunt histriones, quorum auditu concutiuntur ad compassionem audientium corda et usque ad lacrymas compunguntur. Qui ergo de fabule recitatione ad misericordiam commoveris, si de Domino aliquid pium legi audias quod extorqueat tibi lacrymas, nunquid propter hoc de Dei dilectione potes dictare sententiam? Qui compateris Deo, compateris et Arturo. Ideoque utrasque lacrymas pariter perdis, si non diligis Deum, si de fontibus Salvatoris, spe, scilicet, fide, et caritate, devotionis et penitentie lacrymas non effundis'. True penitence, he says, does not consist in momentary tears, and meritorious affection must proceed from the love of Christ: 'Often in tragedies and other works of poets, and in the songs of jougleurs, there is described some man who is prudent, decent, strong, lovable, and graceful in all things; and then there are recited the acts of oppressions or injuries cruelly visited on him. Such are the fabulous accounts told by histrions of Arthur and Gaugan and Tristan; and when the audience hears about them, their hearts are struck and moved to compassion, and they feel such sorrow that they shed tears. Therefore, if you are moved to pity by the recitation of a fable, do you think you can say something about the love of God just because hearing something pious read about Our Lord squeezes tears out of you? You feel sympathy for God, but you feel sympathy for Arthur as well. You will therefore shed both sets of tears in vain if you do not love God, if you do not shed tears of devotion and penitence from the fonts of Our Savior, that is, hope, faith, and charity'.

using the term in a technical sense, since his brother William was the author of tragedies.[15] But in fact Peter is simply copying a similar observation made by Aelred of Rievaulx.[16]

In my study of the occurrences and meanings of the word tragedy over the centuries, I have been struck by how rare the term was and how seldom it was used as a genre in the Middle Ages. But when I broaden my view to take in genres as a whole, I conclude that generic thinking of all kinds was comparatively rare. James J. Murphy judges the theoretical treatment of poetry in the rhetorical tradition to be essentially without genre.[17] The commentary tradition, particularly as isolated by A. J. Minnis, is just as thin, it seems, except when forced by the work itself or its title to deal with generic concepts, as in the case of the commentaries on Dante.[18]

Medieval characterizations of generic terms, beginning with those of Isidore of Seville, were often made in the dark, that is, in ignorance of actual examples of the categories in question. In the eighth book of his *Etymologies*, Isidore distinguishes four kinds of poets: the lyric, the tragic, the comic (including the new comic or satiric), and the theological. The lyric writers were so called from the variety of their poems; the tragic wrote realistic and mournful accounts of public affairs and kings; the comic dealt with cheerful events and the deeds of private men, with the older sort like Plautus, Accius, and Terence stressing the laughable, while the newer satirists like 'Flaccus', Persius, and Juvenal emphasized vicious behaviour; and the theological poets wrote poems of the gods.[19] He goes on to remark that a writer like Lucan is not considered to be a poet because his subjects are not realistic but real; that is, he is seen as a writer of histories.[20] Isidore knows, of course, that Lucan wrote in dactylic hexameters, for he cites the *Pharsalia* elsewhere (8.9.2). He does not mention Virgil's similar work, the *Aeneid*, in this connection; it is obviously not purely historical, but if it is to be fitted under any of the four categories mentioned, it would have to be tragedy

15 Peter of Blois, *Epistles* 76 and 93 (PL 207:235, 291–293).

16 Aelred of Rievaulx, *Speculum caritatis* 2.17.50–51, ed. C. H. Talbot, *Aelredi Rievallensis opera omnia* 1 (Turnhout, 1971) 90.

17 James J. Murphy, 'Poetry Without Genre: The Metapoetics of the Middle Ages', *Poetica: An International Journal of Linguistic-Literary Studies* (Tokyo) no. 11 (1979) 1–8.

18 See A. J. Minnis, *Medieval Theory of Authorship: Scholastic Literary Attitudes in the Later Middle Ages* (London, 1984): he has only a few specific references to genres (see his Index under comedy, satire, and tragedy) and no discussion of genres in general. See also A. J. Minnis and A. B. Scott, *Medieval Literary Theory and Criticism, c.1100–c.1375: The Commentary-Tradition* (Oxford, 1988; rev. ed., 1991).

19 Isidore, *Etymologies* 8.7.4–9, ed. W. M. Lindsay, 2 vols. (Oxford, 1911).

20 Ibid., 8.7.10.

or theology. However, he does go on to distinguish the *Aeneid* from comedies and tragedies, in which only characters speak, and the *Georgics*, in which only the poet speaks; for in the *Aeneid* both the poet and characters speak.[21]

Five hundred years later, in the early twelfth century, Honorius Augustodunensis also speaks of four kinds of poetry, corresponding, perhaps coincidentally, to Isidore's first two categories and his subdivided third: 'The books of the poets are divided into four species, namely, tragedies, comedies, satiric pieces, and lyrics. Tragedies deal with war, as in Lucan; comedies sing of wedding celebrations, as with Terence; satires record reproofs, like those of Persius; and lyrics sound forth odes, that is, praises of the gods or of kings, with hymnic voice, and Horace is an example of this kind of poet'.[22]

We note that both Isidore and Honorius make their sometimes odd divisions not on the basis of style but on subject matter and purpose. But style is uppermost in Matthew of Vendôme's account of the species of poetry. Whereas Honorius likens the four kinds of poetry to four villas belonging to the city of grammar (which is one of the cities of the soul's exile from its homeland of true wisdom, Holy Scripture),[23] Matthew in his *Ars versificatoria*, written around the middle of the twelfth century,[24] envisages his four genres of Tragedy, Satire, Comedy, and Elegy, as four female attendants upon Lady Philosophy in the idyllic spring setting of a dream. Philosophy herself is based in part on the figure in Boethius's *Consolation of Philosophy*, but the same can hardly be said for her attendants. In Boethius, Philosophy speaks of tragedies as clamorously weeping and bewailing overturned kingdoms, but Matthew's Tragedy is a vociferous loudmouth who bellows threats and hurls forth her pot-bellied jugs and sesquipedalian words from the added height her buskins give her (Matthew interprets the *projicit* of Horace's 'Projicit ampullas et sesquipedalia uerba' to mean not 'lays aside' but 'uses as projectiles'). The shamelessly naked Satire is cross-eyed and garrulous, and Comedy dresses in common work clothes and shuns all festiveness, while Elegy flirtatiously sings of love and has a charming limp (a reference to the elegiac distichs she uses).[25] Furthermore, just as these stylistic figures

21 Isidore, *Etymologies*, 8.7.11.

22 Honorius, *De anime exsilio et patria* 2 (PL 172:1243D): 'Libri poetarum. . .in quattuor species dividuntur, scilicet in tragedias, in comedias, in satyrica, in lyrica. Tragedie sunt que bella tractant, ut Lucanus. Comedie sunt que nuptialia cantant, ut Terentius. Satyre que reprehensiva scribunt, ut Persius. Lyrica que odas, id est, laudes deorum vel regum hymnilega voce resonant, ut Horatius'.

23 Ibid. 2, 12 (PL 172:1243CD, 1245C).

24 See Franco Munari, ed., *Mathei Vindocinensis opera*, 3 vols. (Rome, 1977–88).

25 Matthew of Vendôme, *Ars versificatoria* 2.5–8 (Munari 3: pp. 135–6), 2:23–25.

show no descent from the *Consolation*, they show no influence on Matthew's own poetic works. His *Milo*, for instance, which resembles the so-called 'elegiac comedies' of his era, is in elegiac distichs, but it has no noticeable resemblance to the Comedy or to the Elegy of his dream.[26]

Early in the next century, Geoffrey of Vinsauf updated Horace in another way by omitting all consideration of tragedy and saying that the old understanding of comedy was obsolete; in place of comedy he treats jocose matter, *res jocosa*.[27] However, in an expanded version of his *Documentum de arte versificandi*, he comes up with a long list of genres, some perhaps deriving from Isidore's discussion of metres.[28] He rarely gives examples, and those he does give are fairly standard: for instance, Aesop and Avianus wrote *apologi*, that is, beast fables; and the three satiric poets (the only three, he seems to suggest) are Horace, Persius, and Juvenal. Comedy, broadly speaking, is any jocose poem, but strictly it is a rustic song dealing with humble persons, beginning in sadness and ending in joy, and containing five parts dealing with 'lasciviousness'; such comedy is no longer in use, but on the ancient form Horace can be consulted for theory and Terence for practice. Tragedy deals with contempt of Fortune, showing the misfortunes of grave persons, beginning in joy and ending in grief; it takes its name from *tragos*, which means goat, to indicate the filthiness of its subject. He cites Horace's line about the poet who competed for a goat with a tragic poem, but he names no practitioner of the genre.[29]

John of Garland adapted Vinsauf's latter-day listing of genres to his own purposes,[30] and he went one step further and composed some examples of his own. One is a poem that is simultaneously elegiac (dealing with the misery of love), amabeous (representing the characteristics of lovers), bucolic (with a pastoral setting and using humble style), and, finally, ethical (a hermeneutic category, meaning that it has an

[26] Matthew, *Milo* (Munari 2: pp. 57–72).

[27] Geoffrey of Vinsauf, *Documentum de arte versificandi* 2.3.162–163, ed. Edmond Faral, *Les arts poétiques du xiie et xiiie siècle* (Paris 1924), p. 317; cf. *Poetria nova* 1885–1909 (ibid., p. 255).

[28] Isidore, *Etymologies* 1.39.

[29] Geoffrey of Vinsauf, expanded *Documentum*, excerpts given by Traugott Lawler, *The Parisiana Poetria of John of Garland* (New Haven, 1974), pp. 330–2; see *Ars poetica* 220: 'Carmine qui tragico vilem certavit ob hircum'. Geoffrey, who puts *carmen* for *carmine*, is probably drawing directly or indirectly on Isidore 8.7.5, who, however, cites it correctly and does not speak of *fetor materie*, *contemptus Fortune*, *infortunia personarum gravium*, or movement *a gaudio in luctum*. I should note that when Garland uses *lacivia* in connection with the parts of comedy, following Geoffrey, Lawler translates it 'light entertainment' (*Parisiana poetria* 5.12, pp. 84–85).

[30] For other kinds of generic divisions in Garland, see Edgar de Bruyne, *Études d'ésthétique médiévale*, 3 vols. (Bruges, 1946, reprint Geneva, 1975), 2: pp. 18–23.

allegorical Christian dimension).[31] Another freshly composed example is a comedy in the new loose sense, a humorous narrative using low sentiments and humble style, but nevertheless employing a certain amount of rhetorical ornamentation.[32] Garland must have been aware of the ancient comedies of Terence, which conformed to the pattern described by Horace, if only from Vinsauf's reference, and he clearly must have assumed that there was an abundance of comedies in the broader sense. But he somehow came to the conclusion that only one tragedy had ever been written: it was by Ovid, and it was lost. Therefore, his own tragedy presented here was only the second of its kind, and the only one extant.[33]

Although at one point he copies Vinsauf's stipulation that the parts of tragedy concern grave persons,[34] he makes no such claim for his tragedy, advisedly so, since the main characters are two *lotrices*, washerwomen, who supply a garrison of 60 soldiers with the services of washing and copulating, *vices lavandi et coeundi*. Even though the garrison is under siege, this arrangement seems enough to qualify the beginning of the piece as one of joy, which gives way to tears at the end (one of the women kills the other, and betrays the whole garrison to cover up her crime), thus fulfilling one of the tragedy's properties. The other two properties named are that it is in grave style, and that it deals with shameful and wicked actions.[35] Like his comedy, it is in dactylic hexameters.[36]

Garland seems to have written his *Poetria* around 1220, and though he revised it fifteen or so years later,[37] he did not return to his generic experiments during the rest of his long life. He points out in his preface that the *Poetria* was meant to be an art of eloquence, designed to teach his readers how to write 'in any kind of composition, whether it be a legal or academic letter, or an elegiac poem, or a comedy, or a tragedy, or a satire, or a history'.[38] But as the last of his breed, he was without known

31 John of Garland, *Parisiana poetria* 1.394–456 (Lawler, pp. 24–6).

32 Ibid., 4.416–474 (pp. 78–80).

33 Ibid., 7.4–7 (p. 136).

34 Ibid., 5.13–14 (p. 84)

35 Ibid., 5.24–26 (p. 136): 'Hujus tragedie proprietates sunt tales: gravi stilo describitur; pudibunda proferuntur et celerata; incipit a gaudio et in lacrimas terminatur'. *Celerata* means *scelerata*, which was connected with the subject of tragedy in Isidore's treatment of the theater, *Etymologies* 18.45: 'Tragoedi sunt qui antiqua gesta atque facinora sceleratorum regum luctuosa carmine spectante populo concinebant'.

36 Garland, 7.28–153 (pp. 136–42).

37 See Louis John Paetow, *The Arts Course at Medieval Universities with Special Reference to Grammar and Rhetoric* (Urbana, 1910), p. 17.

38 Garland, Prologue (trans. Lawler, p. 3). The Latin reads (p. 2, lines 15–6): 'in quolibet genere dicendi, sive sint littere curiales sive scolastice, sive elegiacum carmen tradatur, vel comedia, vel tragedia, vel satyra, vel hystoria'. See Murphy, pp. 2–3.

followers or imitators, and his treatise seems to have received little attention. The lack of influence in Italy, to which we now turn, is particularly noticeable, for none of the surviving six manuscripts of the *Parisiana poetria* have Italian connections.[39]

Two practitioners of genre theory command our attention at the turn of the fourteenth century: Albertino Mussato of Padua and Dante Alighieri. Mussato was inspired by the newly discovered tragedies of Seneca to write a tragedy of his own, the *Ecerinis* or story of the fall of Ezzelino da Romano, 'tyrant' of Padua, who died in 1259. That is, he interpreted Ezzelino's life generically by imitating the form of Seneca's dramas, but he did so in the context of more general theorizing about the genre of tragedy. He could have taken advantage of Aristotle's observations, for Mussato is the only known medieval user of William of Moerbeke's accurate translation of the *Poetics*, but he drew on it only for minor points not connected with tragedy.[40] Guizzardo of Bologna, who wrote a commentary on the *Ecerinis*, drew on Averroes's commentary on the *Poetics* in a similarly superficial way: he did not penetrate far enough into it to realize that Aristotle (and Averroes) was dealing with tragedy.[41] The same is true of Benvenuto of Imola in his commentaries on Dante's *Comedy*.[42] Mussato drew on other sources to define tragedy as *alte materie stilus*, 'a style of high matter', which takes two basic forms: when the events being dealt with concern the falls of great kings and princes, iambic metre is employed, as in Sophocles's *Maidens of Trachis* and Seneca's ten tragedies; but when military triumphs are being described, then the heroic metre is used, as in Ennius, Lucan, Virgil, and Statius, and, of course, Homer (citing Horace).[43]

As for Dante, I accept the arguments of Giorgio Brugnoli that he never came to know about the tragedies of Seneca,[44] and I believe it to be true also of the comedies of Terence and Plautus. His peculiar understanding of tragedy set forth in the *De vulgari eloquentia* is based on traditions as

39 See Lawler, pp. xix–xxi.

40 H. A. Kelly, 'Aristotle-Averroes-Alemannus on Tragedy: The Influence of the *Poetics* on the Latin Middle Ages', *Viator* 10 (1979) 161–209, esp. p. 188.

41 Ibid., pp. 193–5. Mussato wrote the *Ecerinis* in 1314 or 1315, and Guizzardo finished his commentary in 1317.

42 Ibid., pp. 200–4.

43 Ibid., pp. 192–3, citing Mussato's *Lucii Annei Senece Cordubensis vita et mores*, ed. Anastasios Ch. Megas, *Ho prooumanistikos kuklos tēs Padouas* (Salonika, 1967), pp. 154–61, esp. pp. 159–60; Mussato takes *Ars poetica* 73–4, 'Res gestae regumque ducumque et tristia bella / Quo scribi possent numero, monstravit Homerus', to indicate the subject matter and form of this sort of triumphalist tragedy.

44 Giorgio Brugnoli, 'Ut patet per Senecam in suis tragediis', *Rivista di cultura classica e medioevale* 5 (1963) 146–63; see also his edition of the *Epistle to Cangrande*, in *Opere minori*, vol. 2, ed. P. V. Mengaldo et al. (Florence, 1979), pp. 512–21, 598–643, esp. pp. 617–9.

yet not clearly understood. It is obvious, however, that he did not have this notion of tragedy when he wrote his love lyrics and his commentary on them in the *Vita nova*. In the *De vulgari* he reinterprets the lyrics as tragedies: they fulfil his three criteria treating of the highest subject matter, using high style, and being in the best forms. He repeatedly singles out the *Donne ch'avete intelletto d'amore* in this regard.

Dantists have not joined Dante in considering his lyrics to be tragedies or even in thinking that he thought them to be tragedies. The consensus is that he was speaking only of tragic style. The reason for this failure to come to the obvious conclusion is that modern readers of Dante have their own ideas of how they think tragedy was understood in the Middle Ages, and, of course, many of them believe that Dante himself discoursed on the subject in the *Epistle to Cangrande*. For my part, I hold with the old majority view, which seems to be gaining ground again in recent times, that *Cangrande* is not by Dante, and I have offered further evidence to that effect.[45]

Be that as it may, in terms of how Dante understood tragedy when he wrote the *De vulgari eloquentia*, we can conclude that he categorized as tragedies not only his own lyrics but also the lyrics of the poets whom he singles out for praise throughout his discussion, notably those he lists as having treated the worthiest subjects: namely, Bertran of Born on arms, Arnaut Daniel on love, Giraut of Bornelh on rectitude, and Cino of Pistoia on the love that is associated with rectitude.[46] When Dante reinterpreted these poems as tragedies, they did not change in themselves, but only in his own mind, by being placed into a new generic category. But this was a real change. As Culler says, speaking of more modern ideas of tragedy, 'To read a text as a tragedy is to give it a framework which allows order and complexity to appear'.[47] But when Dante was writing the *Inferno*, he was actually composing it as a comedy. He seems to have understood comedy to be a poem that uses a range of styles and covers a range of subjects.[48] He contrasts his own comedy with Virgil's 'high tragedy', the *Aeneid*, which consistently maintains a high style and a high subject matter.

Towards the end of *Paradiso*, Dante says, in effect, that the task of describing Beatrice adequately would be beyond the powers of any tragedic or comic poet (30.22–24). This shows that he could not at the same time have written an introduction to *Paradiso* in a letter to

[45] H. A. Kelly, *Tragedy and Comedy from Dante to Pseudo-Dante* (Berkeley, 1989).
[46] *De vulgari eloquentia* 2.8.8
[47] Culler, *Structuralist Poetics*, p. 136.
[48] See Kelly, *Tragedy and Comedy*, pp 7–10, where I argue for this as Dante's understanding of comedy, based ultimately on Papias and Horace.

Cangrande della Scala in which he set forth a notion of tragedy that absolutely contradicted his earlier definition of the genre as dealing with the noble subjects of love, virtue, and honourable self-defence, a definition that allowed him to say that both his own lyric poems and Virgil's *Aeneid* were tragedies. According to the contrasting definition of *Cangrande*, tragedy begins in an admirable state but ends in horror. A tragedic poet in this view could, it is true, introduce a noble subject, like Beatrice, but only to chronicle its degradation into some kind of filthy and abominable misery.[49]

According to my analysis, *Cangrande* derives its definition of tragedy from Guido da Pisa,[50] who shows himself to be unaware of Dante's own discussion of tragedy in the *De vulgari eloquentia*, and the same is true of Dante's son Pietro, whom I take to be the source of the *Cangrande* assumption that Dante called his work a comedy rather than a tragedy because the vernacular could not be a vehicle for tragedy.[51] Pietro either had not comprehended his father's defense of the *lingua vulgaris illustris*, or he let an inappropriate generic description override his knowledge. Similarly, when Guido illustrates his characterization of tragedy by referring to the tragedies of Seneca, not only for the filth and horror of their endings but also, by implication, for the admirable and pleasing quality of their beginnings, he, like the *Cangrande* author who follows him, is making a generic misinterpretation of the plays; for none of them has such a beginning. The characterization of the plays of Terence as beginning in asperity is hardly more accurate, especially in the absence of any reference to humour, since the asperity is defined by juxtaposing it with the punishments of hell.

Boccaccio, however, professed to find the parallels between the beginnings of the plays of Terence and Plautus to be very similar to the *Inferno* and their ends to bear a striking likeness to the *Paradiso*. Of the fourteenth-century critics of Dante's poem, apart from Petrarch, who said that he had no idea why Dante called his poem a comedy,[52] Boccaccio had the most difficulty with Dante's title. By the time that he came to give his lectures on Dante, he clearly believed that the only true comedies were those that had been composed in classical antiquity. His analysis of these comedies suggested various characteristics of the genre, namely, base matter, humble style, restriction to dialogue, lack of

[49] *Epistle to Cangrande* 10.29 (see Brugnoli's edition, noted above).

[50] Guido da Pisa, *Expositiones et glose super Comediam Dantis*, ed. Vincenzo Cioffari (Albany, NY, 1974).

[51] *Petri Allegherii super Dantis ipsius genitoris Comediam commentarium*, ed. Vincenzo Nannucci (Florence, 1845), pp. 9–10.

[52] In a lost letter reported by Francesco da Buti, *Commento sopra la Divina comedia*, ed. Crescentino Giannini, 3 vols. (Pisa, 1858–62), 1: p. 543.

examples and similes, fictional events, and division into scenes, none of which were to be found in Dante's work. That left only the characteristic of movement of events from discord to tranquillity, which he seems to have found in an *accessus* to Dante's poem that was later incorporated into the *Epistle to Cangrande*. However, he concluded that this characteristic was not enough to make the poem a comedy in reality, but only figuratively.

The only fourteenth-century commentator on Dante who explicitly acknowledged the existence of postclassical comedies other than Dante's was the jurist Alberigo da Rosciate. He considered comedies to be versified accounts of the great events of the time or of the deeds of great lords, which were recited by pairs of minstrels.[53] It does seem, however, that Boccaccio in his more youthful years had named a work of his own a comedy, whether literally or figuratively, namely, the *Comedy of the Florentine Nymphs*.

The frequent assumption of modern scholars that Boccaccio considered the individual accounts of his *De casibus virorum illustrium* to be tragedies is not borne out by an analysis of the work, for he restricts his references to tragedy to classical times and forms.[54] However, Geoffrey Chaucer, who came upon a definition of tragedy as a poem beginning in prosperity and ending in adversity, doubtless did consider Boccaccio's accounts to be tragedies, and he went on to write new tragedies of his own, later assigned to the Monk in the *Canterbury Tales*. The subtitle of the *Monk's Tale* in a primitive version of the text is *De casibus virorum illustrium*, and Chaucer draws upon Boccaccio's *De casibus* for his tragedy of Zenobia, and, arguably, for that of Hugelino. He seems also to have drawn on Boccaccio's *De claris mulieribus* for the Zenobia account, and he may have considered many of the accounts there to be tragedies.[55]

In interpreting Boccaccio's falls to be tragedies, Chaucer tranformed them to his own generic understanding of the form: The purpose of tragedies is to bewail misfortunes (he is drawing on Fortune's characterization of tragedies in the *Consolation*) and to teach lessons of caution, when appropriate, and resignation when hopeless.[56] Boccaccio, in contrast, set up his series not to lament falls but to show that they are caused by sinful overreaching. Chaucer went on to adapt a longer work

[53] Alberigo da Rosciate, Introduction to his Latin translation of Jacopo della Lana, ed. Antonio Fiammazzo, *Il commento dantesco di Graziolo de' Bambaglioli* (Savona, 1915), p. 110.

[54] H. A. Kelly, 'Chaucer and Shakespeare on Tragedy', *Leeds Studies in English* 20 (1989) 191–206, esp. p. 192.

[55] Geoffrey Chaucer, *The Monk's Tale*, in *The Riverside Chaucer*, gen. ed. Larry D. Benson (Boston, 1987); see the note on pp. 929–30.

[56] See the first stanza of the *Monk's Tale*.

of Boccaccio's into a tragedy, namely, the *Filostrato*, which he turned into the *Troilus and Criseyde*.

We must not think that Chaucer considered all stories that ended in sorrow to be tragedies, or at least, pure tragedies. Specifically, his tales in the *Legend of Good Women* are at least in part adaptations of another genre, the *vita sancti*, or, more specifically, the *passio martyris*, like the legend of St Cecilia, which Chaucer versified in the *Second Nun's Tale*. The purpose of such *passiones*, stories of the persecution and unjust execution or murder of saints, was not lamentation but praise, and the lesson to be learned was not caution but emulation. Chaucer's legends of pagan women who come to grief over love seem to combine aspects of both genres, tragedy and the martyr's passion.

Chaucer's ambition to write a comedy, stated at the end of his tragedy of Troilus, must remain something of a puzzle, because he never explains what his understanding of comedy is. But if, as is likely, it is the opposite of tragedy, then a work like the *Knight's Tale* would qualify.

Chaucer was unaware of Seneca's tragedies, so that one might consider it easier for him to identify Boccaccio's series of narratives as consisting of tragedies than for someone who did know Seneca. But there was one other man of letters in the Middle Ages who was acquainted with the dramatic tragedies and yet who came to a similar conclusion about the *De casibus*, seemingly through commentaries on Dante: I refer to the Marquis of Santillana. And he also, like Chaucer, set about composing his own tragedy, dealing with the defeat of the Aragonese navy off the coast of Gaeta in Italy in the year 1435. But while he was composing the piece, the king of Aragon and his brothers were released from captivity, and so he decided to turn it into a comedy, calling it the *Comedieta de Ponza*.[57]

Other users of Boccaccio's *De casibus* did not come to the conclusion that the work was cast in the genre of tragedy: this holds for Laurence of Premierfait in his two translations or adaptations into French, and also for George Chastelain, who in his *Temple of Boccaccio* saw himself as continuing the *De casibus*.[58] This work, finished in 1465 dedicated to Margaret of Anjou, Queen of England, received several generic characterizations by its various copyists, such as mirror for princes,

[57] Iñigo López de Mendoza, Marqués de Santillana, *Comedieta de Ponça*, ed. crit., ed. Maxim P. A. Kerkhof (Madrid, 1987). He explains his understanding of tragedy, and of Boccaccio as writing tragedies, in a letter of 1443, ed. Kerkhof, pp. 269–77; see esp., pp. 271–4. Boccaccio is introduced as a character in the *Comedieta*, functioning as he does in the *De casibus*, as the recorder of the misfortunes of great men.

[58] George Chastelain, *Le temple de Bocace*, ed. Susanna Bliggenstorfer, Romanica helvetica 104 (Bern, 1988).

complaint, and consolation, but tragedy was not one of them.[59] John Lydgate, however, in adapting Premierfait's second version of the *De casibus* into English as *The Fall of Princes*, did call the stories of disaster tragedies; but he was imitating Chaucer. Lydgate's example in turn inspired the authors of *A Mirror for Magistrates*, which brought the theory and practice of Chaucerian tragedy into Shakespeare's time, and, I argue, into Shakespeare's own practice.[60] Furthermore, Robert Henryson was imitating Chaucer in conceiving his *Testament of Cresseid* as a tragedy.

Thus Chaucer, in addition to being one of a small number of generic innovators in the Middle Ages, was an even rarer bird. He not only reinterpreted a genre and put it into practice himself, as Dante did, but he also had a following of practitioners. Dante left only admirers in his wake, and not imitators, perhaps because his feat was unimitable, but perhaps also because his implicit generic concepts were fundamentally untraditional. As for the Marquis of Santillana, neither his own example nor the studies of Dante and Seneca that he fostered produced generic imitations or inspired generic variations. Later Iberian tragedies are *sui generis*. One member of Santillana's circle, Pedro of Portugal, wrote *The Tragedy of the Celebrated Queen, Lady Isabel* (c.1455), but it is little more than an account of his own sorrow on losing a beloved sister.[61] The brief *Tragedy of Caldesa* by Johan Roiç de Corella (c.1458) is also an autobiographical account of sorrow, this one caused by discovering that his beloved was carrying on a liaison with someone else.[62] The fragmentary *Tragedy of Lancelot* by Mossèn Gras, published in Barcelona in 1496, deals with the misunderstandings and troubles between Lancelot and Guinevere stemming from jealousy; but it caused only a temporary setback, for they were reconciled and their love was sustained through the final ordeals of their life.[63] It was therefore a tragedy with a happy ending, of sorts.

59 See Bliggenstorfer, pp. *23–*24. She says, 'Ainsi le *Temple de Bocace* devient à la fois un miroir de prince, un consolation, une complainte, le récit d'un cas et de *remoustrances*, une imitation ou bien un traité de fortune, selon l'importance que veut accorder un scribe à telle ou telle partie du texte'.

60 Kelly, 'Chaucer and Shakespeare on Tragedy'.

61 Pedro de Portugal, *Tragedia de la insigne reina dona Isabel*, ed. Luís Adão da Fonseca, *Obras completas do condestável dom Pedro de Portugal* (Lisbon, 1975).

62 Johan Roiç de Corella, *Tragèdia*, ed. Josep Almiñana Vallés, *Obres de Joan Roiç de Corella*, 2 vols. (Valencia, 1984–5), 2: pp. 683–6.

63 *Tragèdia ordenade per mossèn Gras, la qual és part de la gran obra dels actes del famós cavaller Lançalot del Lac, en la qual se mostra clarament quant les solàsias* [sic, for *gelòsias*?] *in les coses de amor danyen, e com als qui vertaderament amen ninguna cosa los desobliga*, ed. Martín de Riquer, 'La *Tragèdia de Lançalot*, texto artúrico catalán del siglo xv', *Filologia romanza* 2 (1955) 113–39, text on pp. 131–9.

Another Spanish work of the time was a comedy with a very unhappy ending, namely, the so-called *Celestina* of Fernando de Rojas, a Castilian play or dialogue published just after Gras's tragedy.[64] Rojas first called it, *Comedy of Calisto and Melibea*. It is the story of an illicit love affair, which ends with Calisto falling off a ladder to his death and Melibea committing suicide. When Dante referred to his poem as a comedy, his commentators found that it called for an explanation, but only Petrarch seems to have objected to it altogether. With Rojas, critical reader response was immediate: he was told that the work should be called a tragedy rather than a comedy, since it ended in sadness. In a preface to a new edition Rojas revealed that, unlike Dante, he had not been engaging in an act of generic interpretation when he called his work a comedy. Rather he was simply finishing up a work begun by another author, and it was that author who had called it a comedy. Rojas assumes that he did so because of the pleasant beginning of the story, whereas it seems entirely likely that the the pleasantness was intended to continue through to the end, with the lovers getting married, as in the underlying story of *Pamphilus de amore*. Rojas tried to placate his critics while remaining true (he thought) to his predecessor, by renaming his work a tragicomedy; the 'tragi'- part was meant to account for the ending, and the 'comedy' for the beginning. It is unlikely that his critics were satisfied, since their definition of tragedy undoubtedly provided for a pleasant beginning as well as an unhappy ending, but we have no record of their further reaction.

We see in this last example a mixture of horizontal expectations on the part of the audience and an almost total generic obliviousness on the part of the author. As such, it can be used to typify the variety of traditional interpretations, thoughtful reinterpretations, and quirky misinterpretations of genres and generic names to be found during the course of the Middle Ages.

[64] Fernando de Rojas, *Celestina: Tragicomedia de Calisto y Melibea*, ed. Miguel Marciales, 2 vols. (Urbana, 1985).

INTERPRETATION WITHIN THE *DECAMERON*

FRANCESCO BRUNI

1. A few tales of the *Decameron* represent or presuppose, in their narrative situation or development, aspects of verbal and non-verbal communication which are easier to perceive today, due to modern linguistic achievements. Boccaccio indeed did not adhere to any modern school of linguistics, but his curriculum included grammar or *gramatica* (i.e. the Latin language), rhetoric, Latin and vulgar literature, astronomy and other medieval sciences or disciplines (*artes trivii et quadrivii*). Grammar and logic, as is well known, dealt with the natural or conventional relation between words and their meaning (*signifiant* and *signifié*, in Saussurean terms), a problem which went back to the linguistic thought or, rather, to the logical and philosophical thought of Plato and Aristotle; the main aim of rhetoric was persuasion, but it also dealt with the science of gestures, which medieval monks used to practise but which could also be put into practice by lovers.

The interlacing of verbal and non-verbal communication can be observed in the story of Simona and Pasquino (IV 7), two humble Florentine lovers working in the textile industry, which was so important for the economic growth of medieval Florence.

It happens that Simona and Pasquino, one Sunday, decide to go to a garden:

> In that part of the garden to which Simona and Pasquino had retired, there was a splendid and very large clump of sage, at the foot of which they settled down to amuse themselves at their leisure. Some time later, having made frequent mention of a picnic they were intending to take, there in the garden, after they had rested from their exertions, Pasquino turned to the huge clump of sage and detached one of its leaves, with which he began to rub his teeth and gums, claiming that sage prevented food from sticking to the teeth after a meal. After rubbing them thus for a while, he returned to the subject of the picnic about which he had been talking earlier. But before he had got very far, a radical change came over his features, and very soon afterwards he lost all power of sight and speech. A few minutes later he was dead . . . .[1]

[1] English quotations are taken from the translation by G. H. McWilliam (London, 1972); for the Italian text, see *Decameron*, a cura di V. Branca (Torino, 1992, 6th edition).

A friend of Pasquino charges Simona with Pasquino's death, and the young woman is taken to the Magistrate's palace:

> A judge was persuaded to interrogate her forthwith about the circumstances of Pasquino's death. But being unable to conceive how Simona could have practised any deceit, or how she could possibly be guilty, he insisted that she should accompany him to the site of the occurrence, *so that, by getting her to show him the manner of it* and seeing the dead body for himself, *he could form a clearer impression of the matter than he had been able to obtain from her words alone*. Without creating any disturbance, he therefore had her conveyed to the spot where Pasquino's body lay, still swollen up like a barrel, and shortly afterwards he went there himself. Gazing at the body in astonishment, he asked her to show him precisely how it had happened, whereupon Simona walked over the clump of sage, and, having told the judge what they had been doing together so as to place him fully in possession of the facts, she did as Pasquino had done, and rubbed one of the sage-leaves against her teeth.

Simona also dies shortly, and her innocence is proved. The judge discovers that the sage was poisoned by a huge toad, and the two unlucky lovers are buried in the same church, like the famous lovers Tristan and Isolde.

The point is that when Simona is in the presence of the judge, verbal language cannot represent non-linguistic experience, so that she explains the event by copying Pasquino's actions. Rubbing her teeth with a leaf of the poisoned sage causes her death, as it had caused Pasquino's. Simona does not succeed in expressing herself with words and has to appeal to gestural communication because of the situation. The accused is in front of the judge, and a social gap divides the lower-class worker from a member of the upper class. Many centuries before sociolinguistics highlighted situations and role relations, Boccaccio understood the rules underlying this kind of communication between unequals and used them as the basis for the pathetic dénouement of his story.

2. After this prologue, I would like to discuss six tales in which the topic of understanding versus misunderstanding plays a special role. The number of stories could be greater, but I have preferred to select three tales in which appear what may be termed astute or perceptive characters, and three in which the opposite side emerges, that of simple-mindedness: *'semplici' and 'intendenti'* could be an appropriate subtitle for my paper.

The tale I have chosen to start with relates how Bergamino managed to overcome a difficult situation (*Decameron* I 7). Cangrande della Scala, Lord of Verona, renowned for his munificence (Dante Alighieri, who was given hospitality by him, praised his guest's generosity in a famous passage of the *Paradiso* XVII, 76–93), plans to give a feast and calls many courtiers to Verona. But he suddenly changes his mind and, after compensating them for their trouble, sends them away. A certain Bergamino, however, a jester, whom the tale describes as 'presto parlatore e ornato' ('a conversationalist of quite extraordinary wit and brilliance'), remains, without receiving his compensation. But Cangrande

> had the fixed idea that whatever he gave to this man would be more surely wasted than if he had thrown it into the fire. He did not, however, say anything personally to Bergamino about this, nor did he have him told by others.

The unexpected avarice of Cangrande is the element which gives the tale its interest: the term *novella*, connected with *nuovo*, 'new', carried with it the concept of an unexpected or surprising event.

To pay the hotel keeper, Bergamino is compelled to give him one of three suits of clothes he has brought with him. Then, he has to give him another. Then he begins to live off the third, having decided to stay until he has seen how long it will last, before going away.

One day he meets Cangrande, who asks him why he is so melancholy; depressed we would say. Bergamino tells him a story, which constitutes the central part of the tale and demonstrates the ready speech (*presto parlatore*) attributed to him.

We might call the Bergamino and Cangrande story the first-level tale, and the story told by Bergamino the second-level tale. The hero of the second-level tale is the medieval Latin poet Primasso (who lived in Cologne in the first half of the XIII century). Primasso is presented by Bergamino as 'grande e presto versificatore', that is a 'quick and gifted versifier'. Since Boccaccio has called Bergamino 'quick in speaking', the text suggests an identification between the two characters. Having been told about the Abbot of Cluny's munificence, Primasso moves to Cluny in order to see for himself the truth about the Abbot's fame.

When Primasso arrives at Cluny, the Abbot is suddenly overtaken by an attack of avarice and refuses to go to the table:

> it was a custom of the house that neither wine nor bread nor any other food or drink was ever placed on the tables till the Abbot came and occupied his seat.

Bergamino is tired and hungry from his journey; he has brought three bread rolls with him, and while waiting for the Abbot he eats one of the rolls, and then another. Then he begins to eat the third.

The relationship between the first- and the second-level tale is very clear: both Cangrande and the Abbot become unexpectedly mean, while Bergamino's three suits of clothes correspond to Primasso's three bread rolls. Up until this point in the story, the second-level tale is shaped like the first. The first-level tale has been temporarily interrupted, while the second-level story continues. The Abbot's attendants inform him of Primasso's conduct and the Abbot repents of his meanness. He receives Primasso with honour, and

> he saw that he was richly clothed, provided him with money and a saddle-horse, and offered him the freedom of his household.

At this point, the second-level tale ends, and the first-level tale begins again. The parallel between the two continues, but this time the direction is inverted because the first-level tale becomes influenced by the second-level tale:

> Can Grande saw that the innkeeper's account was settled, then dressed Bergamino most sumptuously in one of his own robes, provided him with money and a saddle-horse, and offered him the freedom of his household for the rest of his stay.

In telling his story, Bergamino solves a difficult problem: it would be impolite or even risky for him to ask Cangrande for money and permission to leave, so he avoids confronting Cangrande with a direct request and instead resorts to the allusivity of the story of Primasso and the Abbot of Cluny. For his part, Cangrande, who was an intelligent lord ('il quale *intendente* signore era', as the text says), shows his own perceptiveness and proves his own astuteness in switching from the first-level to the second-level tale, and vice versa. Bergamino's story offers Cangrande the chance to escape from an awkward situation, allowing him to settle the problem without losing face. Direct confrontation is avoided by the example of the story of Primasso and the Abbot, but such a solution is possible only in as much as the two characters share the ability to grasp what is hidden behind the explicit message. Bergamino's tale might be considered a little chapter of Boccaccio's *Essay on Human Understanding*.

3. I would like to turn now to one of the briefest stories of the *Decameron*, the first of the sixth day. Since the *Decameron* consists of one hundred tales (ten tales for ten days), the first of the sixth day opens the second half of the book and is the central story. As with classical or medieval works, such as the *Aeneid*, the *De planctu Naturae*, the *Roman de la Rose*, the *Divina Commedia*, the central part of the *Decameron* accords with the principles of narrative strategy. The first tale of the sixth day does not explain how a short story should be told, but how it should not.

The heroine is Madonna Oretta, an anagram of *attore*, that is *auctor*:

One day, finding herself in the countryside[. . .], and proceeding from place to place, by way of recreation, with a party of knights and ladies whom she had entertained to a meal in her house earlier in the day, one of the knights turned to her, and, perhaps because they were having to travel a long way, on foot, to the place they all desired to reach, he said: 'Madonna Oretta, if you like I shall take you riding along a goodly stretch of our journey by telling you one of the finest tales in the world'.
'Sir,' replied the lady, 'I beseech you most earnestly to do so, and I shall look upon it as a great favour.'
Whereupon this worthy knight, whose swordplay was doubtless on a par with his storytelling, began to recite his tale, which in itself was indeed excellent. But by constantly repeating the same phrases, and recapitulating sections of the plot, and every so often declaring that he had 'made a mess of that bit', and regularly confusing the names of the characters, he ruined it completely. Moreover, his mode of delivery was totally out of keeping with the characters and the incidents he was describing, so that it was painful for Madonna Oretta to listen to him. She began to perspire freely, and her heart missed several beats, as though she had fallen ill and was about to give up the ghost. And in the end, when she could endure it no longer, having perceived that the knight had tied himself inextricably in knots, she said to him, in affable tones:
'Sir, you have taken me riding on a horse that trots very jerkily. Pray be good enough to set me down.'
The knight, who was apparently far more capable of taking a hint than of telling a tale [il cavaliere, il quale per avventura era molto migliore *intenditor* che novellatore . . .], saw the joke and took it in the cheerfullest of spirits. Leaving aside the story he had begun and so ineptly handled, he turned his attention to telling her tales of quite another sort.

In this tale, the horse metaphor plays the same role that the second-level tale plays in the story of Bergamino and Cangrande. The knight starts to tell Madonna Oretta a story using the riding image. Madonna Oretta puts an end to his clumsy story-telling. After accepting to mount the horse, she begs him to let her down. The knight's bad rendition of the tale is placed between the opening invitation and the final rejection, both expressed by two links of the same metaphoric chain. The knight redeems his narrative incompetence with his perception of the connection between his story-telling and the woman's ultimate rejection.

4. The third short story of the group based on wit concerns Guido Cavalcanti's walk in the heart of Florence, from Orsammichele through the Corso degli Adimari (today, Via dei Calzaiuoli) to the Piazza del Duomo (*Decameron* VI 9).[2] Now it is the old town, in Boccaccio's time it was simply the centre of Florence.

[2] Cf. the recent paper of P. F. Watson, 'On Seeing Guido Cavalcanti and the Houses of the Dead', *Studi sul Boccaccio* 18 (1989) 301–18, with the identification of the tombs

Guido Cavalcanti was well known both as a philosopher and as a lyrical poet of the second half of the XIIIth century. Boccaccio's tale portrays the typical philosopher, solitary and devoted to his meditation. Public opinion (from which the author keeps his distance) was that Cavalcanti's speculations 'were exclusively concerned with whether it could be shown that God did not exist'. But Cavalcanti 'was an exceedingly charming and sophisticated man, with a marked gift for conversation, and he outshone all his contemporaries in every activity pertaining to a gentleman that he chose to undertake'. For this reason a group of Florentines, led by Messer Betto Brunelleschi, wanted to include him in the entertainments they often organized:

> Now, one day, Guido had walked from Orsammichele along the Corso degli Adimari as far as San Giovanni, which was a favourite walk of his because it took him past those great marble tombs, now to be found in Santa Reparata, and the numerous other graves that lie all around San Giovanni. As he was threading his way among the tombs, between the porphyry columns that stand in that spot and the door of San Giovanni, which was locked, Messer Betto and his friends came riding through the piazza of Santa Reparata, and on seeing Guido among all these tombs, they said:
> 'Let's go and torment him.'
> And so, spurring their horses and making a mock charge, they were upon him before he had time to notice, and they began to taunt him, saying:
> 'Guido, you spurn our company; but supposing you find that God doesn't exist, what good will it do you?'
> Finding himself sorrounded, Guido promptly [prestamente] replied:
> 'Gentlemen, in your own house you may say whatever you like to me.'
> Then, placing a hand on one of the tombstones, which were very tall, he vaulted over the top of it, being very light and nimble, and landed on the other side, whence, having escaped from their clutches, he proceeded on his way.

At the outset, nobody understands Cavalcanti's answer. Finally, the leader of the group, Betto Brunelleschi, explains the obscure words:

> 'You're the ones who are out of your minds, if you can't see what he meant. In a few words he has neatly paid us the most back-handed compliment I ever heard, because when you come to consider it, these tombs are the houses of the dead, this being the place where the dead are laid to rest and where they take up their abode. By describing it as our house, he wanted to show us that, by comparison with himself and other men of learning, all men who are as uncouth and unlettered as ourselves

alluded to in the tale. The discussion of the Cavalcanti tale and of the following tales takes up points dealt with in F. Bruni, *Boccaccio. L'invenzione della letteratura mezzana* (Bologna, 1990).

are worse off than the dead. So that, being in a graveyard, we are in our own house.'

A structure which was characteristic of the medieval transmission of learning is easily detectable in the episode; that is, the doctrinal and scholastic system at whose highest level the search for truth is the task of the *auctor*. The *auctor*'s words and works and sentences are to be explained by the commentator or glossator or *expositor*. Finally, the *rudes* or *scholares* receive the *glossa*. The answer given by Cavalcanti, whose role corresponds to that of a modern *auctor*, would not be understood, were not Betto Brunelleschi (commentator) there to explain his words to the audience. Betto, after reflection, grasps the distinction between physical and intellectual death, so he is deemed an 'intendente e sottile cavaliere': the group 'looked upon Messer Betto as a paragon of shrewdness and intelligence'.[3]

In the three tales the protagonists, Bergamino, Oretta and Cavalcanti, test the perspicacity of their antagonists; Cangrande della Scala, the anonymous knight and Betto Brunelleschi show their subtlety in correctly interpreting a story (the second-level tale) that merely alludes to the real situation (the first-level tale), in picking up on the metaphor already established by the protagonist, in explaining an answer with a double meaning.

5. We must now take the second group of tales into consideration. In certain comic stories, communication does not work or works in a very particular and distorted way, not at all casual, to give rise to a comic effect.

In the world of the *Decameron*, jealousy is a sin, possibly a deadly sin, and deserves punishment: a jealous husband is destined to be betrayed by his wife. Among others, such is the case of Ferondo, 'an exceedingly coarse and unimaginative fellow', 'fatuous and stupid' ('uomo materiale e grosso senza modo', 'semplice e dissipato'; *Decameron* III 8). As we shall see, simple-mindedness is quite the opposite of perspicacity and subtlety. Persecuted by her husband's jealousy, Ferondo's wife, of course a very beautiful woman, rouses the interest of a family friend, an Abbot, who tries to think of the best way of having a good time with her. With the woman's consent, the Abbot makes Ferondo drink a narcotic, which causes Ferondo's catalepsy. Since everybody thinks he is dead, Ferondo is buried and carried to the cellar of the monastery.

[3] The tale which preceeds Cavalcanti's relates how Fresco da Celatico's sharp criticism of his niece Cesca misses its target because Cesca does not understand her uncle's words, and there is no *interpres* in the story to explain to Cesca Fresco's subtle observation. The contiguity of the two tales is not casual.

Let us leave the Abbot and Ferondo's wife, or rather widow, to take pleasure in each other, and follow Ferondo's strange destiny. When Ferondo wakes he finds himself in an eschatological framework, along with a monk, an accomplice of the Abbot. The task of the monk is twofold: Ferondo being dead, the monk makes him believe the place where they are is Purgatory; so he beats Ferondo in expiation of the latter's jealousy. Ferondo being alive, the monk has to feed him. Furthermore, Ferondo is a stupid but curious man, so he raises many questions, asking the monk where they are, whether the dead eat, how many people there are in Purgatory and why he cannot see them. There is also a pseudo-theological explanation concerning the sin of jealousy and the punishment it deserves.

In medieval didactic literature the organization of the composition could follow the question and answer pattern: the *auditor* (the pupil) asks the *magister* (the master), and the *magister* answers, satisfying the former's desire for knowledge. Boccaccio parodies this genre of didactic literature. Let me point out a passage of the dialogue between Ferondo and the monk:

> 'And how far are we away from home?'
> 'Oho! Far more miles than one of our turds would travel.'
> 'Crikey! that's a fair distance. I should think we must have left the earth behind entirely.'

The monk's quip can hardly be directly translated into English. The Italian text reads as follows:

> 'Ohioh!' disse il monaco 'sèvi di lungi [you are far from there, from the village] delle miglia più di ben [much more miles] la cacheremo [we shall shit it]'.

The monk's words are a string of phrases devoid of sense and this explains why Boccaccio uses a vulgar word; normally, in fact, he avoids scatological or sexual terms.

However, for our purposes the main fact is that Ferondo seems to understand the monk's reply as if it were the clearest answer; Ferondo interprets an inane sentence, giving meaning to a statement which has no meaning. In my opinion, Boccaccio is able to build such a dialogue because he knows well that questions often do not really require information. Asking how far Purgatory is from the world, Ferondo expects to be confirmed in what he already knows, or in what he thinks he knows. How could Purgatory conceivably be just down the road? Purgatory must be as far away as possible, and even further. The monk has only to utter such words as *lungi* and *miglia* (that is 'far' and 'miles') for Ferondo to understand that Purgatory is an extremely remote place.

What I am trying to say is that Boccaccio perceived those features of real conversation which modern linguistics defines as the system of expectations; he has represented the role which presupposition plays in a dialogue with an artistic aim. What we expect to hear shapes our comprehension, and such is the case with Ferondo: he interprets as meaningful a meaningless statement, whereas the more discerning, the *intendenti*, are able to understand the polysemy of a sentence or of a tale.

6. The hero of stupidity is, as every reader of the *Decameron* knows, Calandrino, who is the chief character of four tales. Heliotrope, the magic stone that makes one invisible, is the subject of one of them (*Decameron* VIII 3). The simple-minded Calandrino meets the cunning Maso del Saggio in a Florentine church. Maso tricks his interlocutor by recounting to him the marvels of a very special country, Cockaigne, or the land of Plenty. In Cockaigne, which Maso del Saggio calls Bengodi and could be translated as 'Good Time Land' or 'Have-a-good-time-land',

> vines are tied up with sausages, and you could buy a goose for a penny, with a gosling thrown in for good measure. And in those parts there was a mountain made entirely of grated Parmesan cheese, on whose slopes there were people who spent their whole time making macaroni and ravioli, which they cooked in chicken broth and then cast it to the four winds, and the faster you could pick it up, the more you got of it. And not far away, there was a stream of Vernaccia wine, the finest that was ever drunk, without a single drop of water in it.
> 'That's a marvellous place, by the sound of it,' said Calandrino, 'but tell me, what do they do with all the chickens they cook?'
> 'They are all eaten by the Basques,' Maso replied.
> Then Calandrino asked him whether he had ever been there himself, and Maso replied:
> 'Been there myself? If I've been there once, I've been there a thousand times at least.'
> Whereupon Calandrino asked:
> 'How many miles away is it?'
> 'More than a milling, that spends the night trilling,' said Maso.
> 'In that case,' said Calandrino, 'it must be further than the Abruzzi.'
> 'It is indeed,' Maso replied, 'just a trifle.'

The Italian text reads:

> 'Di' tu se io vi fu' mai? [Do you ask whether I was ever there?] Sì vi sono stato così una volta come mille [I was there as once as a thousand times]',

which is a contradictory statement. But Calandrino, like Ferondo, receives these words as being perfectly consistent. Like Ferondo, Calandrino ignores the world outside his city, and is ready to hear that

Maso del Saggio is a great traveller, and has visited Cockaigne many times. So only the word *mille* (one thousand) reaches his mind, while the other words which make up Maso's statement are disregarded.

As to Maso's reply to the question regarding the distance of Cockaigne from Florence (again, as in the Ferondo tale), it sounds as follows:

> 'haccene più di millanta, che tutta notte canta', that is, literally: 'there are more than a thousand [miles], that [or: because it] sings all the night'.

My translation, however, fails to capture the rhyme *millanta : canta*, and does not fully render *millantare*, a verb which is connected with *mille* (one thousand) but means *to boast*. Of course, Calandrino interprets Maso's answer as if it had been: 'I was there a thousand times'.

Maso's last statement is also ambiguous:

> 'Sì bene, sì è cavelle', which might be translated: 'Yes, of course, yes-and-no'.

But the literal sense is not completely clear even in the Italian text.

Anyway, Calandrino would like to go to Cockaigne, but it is too far. In the neighbourhood of Florence, however, – so Maso del Saggio makes his naïve interlocutor believe – stones of marvellous powers do exist. One of them is heliotrope. Let us listen to Maso's words:

> 'a stone that we lapidaries call the heliotrope, which has the miraculous power of *making people invisible when they are out of sight*, provided they are carrying it on their person [qualunque persona la porta sopra di sé, mentre la tiene, *non è da alcuna altra persona veduto dove non è*]'.

Since the information focuses on the marvellous power of heliotrope, it is not so strange that Calandrino should hear what Maso says, but fail to take in the meaning of the last few words. It is not necessary to think of these words as being pronounced as a theatrical aside; such a convention was unknown in Boccaccio's time, and the text may be interpreted in the way suggested above. It is pointless to say that heliotrope makes a person invisible wherever that person is not, because this is true for every kind of stone, or for everything.

As Calandrino is ready to believe in the magic power of heliotrope and its availability in the neighbourhood of Florence, Maso can deny the premise of his own discourse, and deceive Calandrino by telling him the truth about heliotrope.

7. The apex of equivocation and misunderstanding, which depends on Boccaccio's sound perception of the system of expectations involved in communication, is to be found in Friar Cipolla's tale (*Decameron* VI 10). Cipolla is a personal name, but it is also comical because *cipolla* (with a small letter) means 'onion'. The action of the story takes place in Certaldo, the Tuscan village from which Boccaccio's family originated (Boccaccio himself was born in Certaldo or in Florence) and which, according to the tale, 'produces onions that are famous throughout the whole of Tuscany'. The text then suggests a relationship between the protagonist (and his name) on the one hand, and the rural context of the action on the other.

Let us read part of the portrait of the protagonist:

> This Friar Cipolla[. . .]was quite illiterate, but he was such a lively and excellent speaker [sì ottimo parlatore e pronto era], that anyone hearing him for the first time would have concluded, not only that he was some great master of rhetoric, but that he was Cicero in person, or perhaps Quintilian.

Friar Cipolla plans to deliver a sermon to the peasants of Certaldo, in order to receive gifts from them; if he did not study rhetoric, Boccaccio did, and the author developes his knowledge of *ars dictaminis* and of para-scholastic literature which flourished on the fringes of the rhetoric classes.

Friar Cipolla announces to the people of Certaldo that he is going to give a sermon; furthermore, he says:

> since I know how deeply devoted you all are to the Lord Saint Anthony, I shall show you, by way of special favour, a most sacred and beautiful relic, which I myself brought back from a visit I once paid to the Holy Land across the sea; and this is one of the feathers of the Angel Gabriel, which was left behind in the bedchamber of the Virgin Mary when he came to annunciate her in Nazareth.

But two friends of Friar Cipolla play a trick on him, and substitute the relic with charcoal. When Friar Cipolla becomes aware of the substitution, he soon finds a remedy, and changes his story. He says that when he was a young man he made a long journey to the Holy Land, and brought back marvellous relics. This is the beginning of his oration:

> Ladies and gentlemen, I must explain to you that when I was still very young, I was sent by my superior into those parts where the sun appears . . .

'Those parts where the sun appears': but the sun appears everywhere, so it is not necessary to move toward the east. Nevertheless, Friar Cipolla's audience is ready to hear about the preacher's pilgrimage to the Holy Land, and is tricked by him into believing that the Friar embarked on such a dangerous enterprise.

And a little later he says:

> After crossing the Straits of Penury, I found myself passing through Funland and Laughland, both of which countries are thickly populated, besides containing a lot of people. Then I went on to Liarland, where I found a large number of friars belonging to various religious orders including my own, all of whom were *forsaking* a life of discomfort for the love of God, and paying little heed to the exertions of *others* so long as they led to *their own* profit [poco dell'*altrui* fatiche curandosi dove la *loro* utilità vedessero seguitare].

The clownish geography of the false pilgrim is judged authentic by Friar Cipolla's listeners, who connect those mysterious terms to lands extremely distant, unknown, dangerous.

Concerning the second part of the passage, what do people attending a sermon expect to hear? The normal, pious message should be that Friar Cipolla was a lover of poverty; on the contrary, he says he forsook it, therefore uttering the opposite of what he would be expected to say. But the people do not notice anything strange, because they unconsciously turn upside down what Friar Cipolla had consciously turned upside down, taking the message back to its etymon, to its origin. Friar Cipolla's *parole*, again in Saussurean terms, is taken back to what the *langue* of a sermon should be, to the *langue* a preacher is expected to deliver. Mental decoding does not recognize the novelty of the message. Even if Friar Cipolla's sermon is quite the opposite of a pious one, his audience reverses the message, restoring to it what he ought to have said.

As to the last words of the quotation, the normal message may be obtained by simply exchanging the position of the possessive adjectives, as spoken by Friar Cipolla:

> poco dell'*altrui* fatiche curandosi dove la *loro* utilità vedessero seguitare > *poco delle *loro* fatiche curandosi dove l'*altrui* utilità vedessero seguitare.

To lie by telling the truth: the same trick we observed with Calandrino and the heliotrope emerges when Friar Cipolla speaks about the mountains 'where all the waters flow downwards'. Friar Cipolla reverses the *adynaton* figure, but the audience is fooled into believing that in those mountains the 'waters flow upwards'.

At the moment of blessing the people with the charcoal, Friar Cipolla says:

> I must tell you that all those who are marked with the sign of the cross by these coals may rest assured that for a whole year they will never be touched by fire *without getting burnt* [chiunque da questi carboni è tocco, tutto quello anno può viver sicuro che fuoco nol cocerà *che non si senta*].

We have already observed the same device in the definition of heliotrope. If I have chosen Friar Cipolla's tale as the conclusion of my paper, thus suggesting a kind of *climax*, the reason is that puns, amphibologies and so on are much more dense in this tale and, above all, work in a more complex communicative context.

In fact, Friar Cipolla's sermon is lengthy, and it is based on a double meaning addressed to two different audiences. The orator's words convey a meaning which seems to refer to a pilgrimage to the Holy Land, yet, at the same time, denies it, communicating a somewhat less spiritual enterprise.

Simple-minded people, that is the people of Certaldo, take the first meaning for granted. Among Friar Cipolla's listeners, however, are his two friends who substituted the feather of the Angel Gabriel with charcoal, and have understood the real meaning:

> Having attended his sermon and observed the ingenious manner in which he had turned the situation to his advantage with his preposterous rigmarole, the two young men laughed until they thought their sides would split.

Therefore, Friar Cipolla's audience includes both simple-minded and astute listeners (*semplici* and *intendenti*), who decode the same sermon in two different ways. The simple-minded, who draw a moralistic meaning from the sermon, coexist with the two friends who interpret the Friar's words differently. Within the tale, the two friends play the role of the astute audience and foreshadow the behaviour and comments of the listeners outside the tale within the frame of the *Decameron* (no longer the listeners of the sermon, but of the tale which contains it):

> The whole company was vastly pleased and entertained by Dioneo's tale, and they all laughed heartily over Friar Cipolla, especially at his pilgrimage and at the relics, both the ones he had seen and those he had brought back with him.

So, the two friends and the group in the *Decameron* frame share the same interpretation of the sermon; outside the text, the readers of the *Decameron* are expected to understand the text according to the two friends and the group, and not according to the peasants of Certaldo.

In conclusion, the same text – Friar Cipolla's sermon – conveys two different meanings, addressed to two different kinds of audience.

8. In one of his last works, the *Genealogie deorum gentilium*, Boccaccio tries to show that poetry and theology are similar. One aspect of this theory is that a literary work should be read according to the method of allegorical interpretation, with the consequent distinction of literal sense from allegorical sense. I suggest that the *Decameron* is unrelated to the theories Boccaccio was to produce at the time of the *Genealogie*: the rhetorical and communicative devices of the *Decameron*

I have discussed pertain to the domain of literal sense; the *Decameron* lacks the allegorical dimension. According to Servius's commentary on Virgil, *simpliciter* means *literally*,[4] but in the exegetical tradition, literal sense includes rhetorical figures and the expressive devices put into practice in the *Decameron*. Therefore, *simpliciter* means *literally* but this does not imply that deciphering a double meaning is an operation belonging to a different level of interpretation. A passage which is relevant to the point may be quoted from Minnis's valuable *Medieval Theory of Authorship*:

> there are various kinds of literal sense: sometimes, the *auctor* may speak plainly and directly; sometimes he may employ figurative expressions. All kinds of figurative language, including metaphors, parables and similitudes, involve significative words and are, therefore, part of the literal sense.[5]

The method of biblical exegesis is at the basis of this doctrine; but it can be extended to the domain of literature. Bergamino's second-level story, the metaphor of Madonna Oretta, Friar Cipolla's sermon, all pertain to the domain of literal sense, which admits rhetorical devices and figures.

[4] See C. Lazzarini, 'Historia/fabula: forme della costruzione poetica virgiliana nel commento di Servio all'Eneide', *Materiali e discussioni per l'analisi dei testi classici*, 12 (1984) 117–44, p. 138 e n. 32.

[5] A. J. Minnis, *Medieval Theory of Authorship* (London, 1988, 2nd ed.), pp. 73–4. See also R. Copeland, 'Rhetoric and the Politics of the Literal Sense in Medieval Literary Theory: Aquinas, Wyclif, and the Lollards' in this volume.

POSTCARDS FROM THE EDGE: INTERPRETING THE INEFFABLE IN THE MIDDLE ENGLISH MYSTICS[1]

VINCENT GILLESPIE

When Lancelot arrives at the threshold of the grail chamber at Corbenic he finds the door firmly closed against him. In a manner typical of his muscular christianity, he beats against it, seeking access to the mystery he has so long pursued:

> He pushed against it, thinking to open it, but he could not; he tried again and again but nothing he did could gain him entry.[2]

In response to his clamour he hears strains of ineffable music, 'so sweet that it seemed no mortal voice could utter it', in which he fancies that he is able to discern a doxology of praise to the Father of Heaven. Kneeling down and with a swelling heart, this trace of the ineffable provokes in him a prayer of longing and petition:

> Most sweet Lord Jesus Christ, if ever I did anything that pleased Thee, then of Thy pity, gracious Lord, spurn me not now, denying me all sight of that which I have been seeking.[3]

On looking up, he finds the door of the chamber miraculously open and a great light flooding out into the rest of the palace. Lancelot's 'joy and his desire to see the source of the light grew so intense that he forgot everything beside'. He is on the point of crossing the threshold when he is forbidden entry by a hidden voice. Obedient, he gazes round the room from the threshold. His vision is resonant with the iconography and symbolism of affective eucharistic imagery:

> So he let his gaze run round the room and observed the Holy Vessel standing beneath a cloth of bright red samite upon a silver table. And all around were ministering angels, some swinging silver censers, others

[1] This paper owes much of its approach and many of its ideas to a collaborative study of Julian of Norwich in progress with Sr Martha Reeves (Maggie Ross).

[2] *The Quest of the Holy Grail*, translated with an introduction by P. M. Matarasso (Harmondsworth, 1969), p. 261. All quotations are taken from this translation. For the French text, see *La Queste del Saint Graal*, ed. A. Pauphilet, Les Classiques Français du Moyen Age (Paris, 1967), p. 254.

[3] Matarasso, p. 261; Pauphilet, p. 254.

> holding lighted candles, crosses and other altar furnishings. . .Before the Holy Vessel was an aged man in priestly vestments, engaged to all appearances in the consecration of the Mass. When he came to elevate the host, Lancelot thought he saw, above his outstretched hands, three men, two of whom were placing the youngest in the hands of the priest who raised him aloft as though he were showing him to the people.[4]

Seeing the priest stagger under the burden, Lancelot is characteristically moved to assist him, crosses the threshold and breaks the prohibition:

> With that he crossed the threshold and made towards the silver table. As he drew near he felt a puff of wind which seemed to him shot through with flame, so hot it was, and as it fanned his features with its scorching breath he thought his face was burned. He stood rooted to the ground like a man paralysed, bereft of sight and hearing, and powerless in every limb. Then he felt himself seized by many hands and carried away. And when they had grabbed him by the arms and legs they pitched him out and left him where he fell.[5]

In this passage Lancelot's approach to the threshold of the ineffable has the typical ingredients of prayer and praise, but his spiritual maturity is still inadequate to allow him access to the hidden secrets. His prayer stresses his sense of his own deserving, suggesting that his service has earned him access to the mysteries. He tries to storm the bastion of the apophatic, beating on the door that conceals it, and he interprets what he is shown in the referential terms of devotional affectivity. His quasi-pentecostal experience inside the room is parodic of the ecstasy of spiritual insight and mystical vision, but he is unprepared and incapable of bearing the cost of his violation.[6]

Lingering between life and death for 24 days he awakes with a recognition that his eyes had been blinded and sullied by looking on the midden of this world. His seeing is still bodily, his interpretation still

[4] Matarasso, p. 262; Pauphilet, p. 255.

[5] Matarasso, pp. 262–3; cf. her notes pp. 301–2; Pauphilet, p. 256. Lancelot's punishment is similar to King Mordrain's earlier in the text (Matarasso, pp. 106–7). Lancelot's denial has been foretold in a vision to Sir Hector. Lancelot stoops to drink from a spring which hides itself from his sight (Matarasso, p. 164; Pauphilet, pp. 149–50). The inevitable hermeneutical hermit explains that the spring is 'the Holy Grail, the grace of the Holy Ghost', in the presence of which Lancelot's eyes will lose their sight (Matarasso, pp. 172–3; Pauphilet, pp. 158–9).

[6] The traditional reading of this passage sees Lancelot receiving an ecstatic vision. My reading is in agreement with that of P. M. Matarasso, *The Redemption of Chivalry: A Study of the Queste del Saint Graal*, Histoire des Idées et Critique Littéraire, 180 (Geneva, 1979), pp. 137–42, who sees the quasi-pentecostal wind as the *ventus urens* of the Old Testament. For the traditional view, see especially E. Gilson, 'La Mystique de la Grace dans La Queste del Saint Graal', in *Les Idées et les Lettres* (Paris, 1932), pp. 59–91.

fleshly. In the *Cloud*-author's terms, he makes a bodily conceit of a ghostly thing. Gesturing towards the ineffable in impeccably Pauline terms, it is clear that the eyes of his soul have not been fully opened:

> I have seen. . .such glories and felicity that my tongue could never reveal their magnitude, nor could my heart conceive it. For this was no earthly but a spiritual vision. And but for my grievous sins and my most evil plight I should have seen still more, had I not lost the sight of my eyes and all power over my body, on account of the infamy that God had seen in me.[7]

Lancelot's failure lies in his impetuosity and self-reliance. On entering the castle he has been rebuked for carrying his knightly arms to protect himself instead of trusting in the mercy of God.[8] In taking the initiative in crossing the threshold, he has violated the essential mystical decorum that requires God to have the initiative in all revelation.[9]

Lancelot's bruising encounter with the ineffable contrasts powerfully with that of his son Galahad. As a figure of the unfulfilled spiritual perfection of his father, Galahad's innocence of the ways of the world, his virginity and chastity and his ability to occupy the Siege Perilous all signify that his route to perfection will be less troubled than his father's.[10] Unwillingly forced to accept earthly kingship, he recreates the ark of the covenant as a housing for the grail, shielding it from prying and inquisitive eyes. At this new Holy of Holies he performs regular liturgical observances. Returning one dawn to 'the palace which men termed spiritual', he sees 'a noble-looking man in the vestments of a bishop' celebrating mass using the Grail. Unlike his impetuous father, Galahad waits until he is invited forward to 'look on that you have so ardently desired to see'. Responding to the divine initiative, he 'drew near and looked into the Holy Vessel':

> He had but glanced within when a violent trembling seized his mortal flesh at the contemplation of the spiritual mysteries. Then lifting up his hands to heaven, he said: 'Lord, I worship Thee and give Thee thanks that thou hast

7 Matarasso, p. 264; Pauphilet, p. 258.

8 'O man of little faith and most infirm belief, why placest thou greater trust in thine own arm than in thy Maker? Thou art but a sorry wretch to hold that He whom thou didst choose to serve can stand thee in no better stead than shield and sword' (Matarasso, p. 260; Pauphilet, p. 253).

9 As Vladimir Lossky puts it, 'If he (the lord of Israel) excludes images and condemns the curiosity of those who would pry into his transcendent nature, it is because the initiative of revelation belongs to him alone in the history of the people he has chosen', 'The Theology of the Image', *Sobornost* 3 (1957–8), p. 22, cited A. Nicholls, *The Art of God Incarnate* (London, 1980), p. 23.

10 Most critics see Galahad as a complex figure of Christ; see Matarasso, *Redemption*, pp. 33–95.

granted my desire, for now I see what tongue could not relate or heart conceive.[11]

Galahad's behaviour is paradigmatic. He obeys his destiny without wilfulness or ambition, without assertion or explicit aspiration, but with a focused longing in his heart. He accepts worldly responsibility but sees it as a distraction from his desire for contemplation. Most notably, his contemplation of the mysteries within the grail has none of the anthropomorphic iconography deployed in Lancelot's encounter. By looking *into* the grail at the non-figural apophatic surface of the water and wine at the point of liturgical transubstantiation ('the solemn part of the mass') Galahad's perception is itself transfigured and transubstantiated. His ineffable experience allows him to pass over the threshold of earthly signification into the glory of the apophatic. His liminality in the experience urges him to pray for release from earthly life:

I pray Thee now that *in this state* Thou suffer me to pass from earthly life to life eternal.

Unlike his father, who is returned after balancing between life and death, Galahad is allowed to pass over the Jordan into the promised land:

for his soul had already fled its house of flesh and was borne to heaven by angels making jubilation and blessing the name of Our Lord.[12]

Both Lancelot and Galahad are unable to articulate or describe their experience of the ineffable: rather they reinforce its ineffability in the transfiguration of their languages and their lives. They bear the trace of the ineffable in their longing to achieve union with it. They yearn for it with no prospect of comprehending it and circumscribing it.

Mystical language seeks to deliver us to the threshold of ineffability. Mystical imagery seeks to deliver us to the brink of the apophatic. Together they constitute a repertoire of liminal signifiers which gesture beyond themselves into the realm of unmediated wisdom and the paradise of the Transcendental Signified from which we have been excluded by the fall.[13] Mystical writing can only ever be about thresholds: the

[11] Matarasso, pp. 282–3; Pauphilet, pp. 277–8. For discussion, see Matarasso, *Redemption*, pp. 180–204.

[12] Matarasso, p. 283; Pauphilet, p. 278.

[13] On ineffability and the apophatic tradition, see the valuable summary accounts and bibliography in B. McGinn, *The Foundations of Mysticism*, The Presence of God: A History of Western Christian Mysticism, 1 (London, 1992), s.v.; V. Lossky, *The Mystical Theology of the Eastern Church* (London, 1957, repr. Cambridge, 1991), pp. 23–43; R. A. Lees, *The Negative Language of the Dionysian School of Mystical Theology: An Approach to the Cloud of Unknowing*, Analecta Cartusiana, 107 (1983); A. Louth, *Denys the Areopagite*, Outstanding Christian Thinkers Series, (London, 1989); G. R. Evans, 'The Borrowed Meaning: Grammar, Logic and the Problem of

thresholds of language, the thresholds of perception, the thresholds of interpretation. Interpreting the ineffable strains human endeavour to the limit. God cannot be comprehended or circumscribed within the repertoires of human hermeneutics.[14] Human language and human understanding fall away when faced with the glory of the revealed Word.

This may partly explain the apparent anti-intellectualism of so much mystical writing, as *clergie* and learning can be seen to usurp the divine prerogative of ineffable self-revelation. *The Book of Privy Counselling*, one of the works of the author of *The Cloud of Unknowing*, persistently teaches the surrender of our discursive consciousness and the abandonment of the intellectual *curiositas* that seeks to entrap God in the world of referentiality and figurality:

> Trewly I telle þee þat ȝif a soule, þat is þus ocupied, had tonge & langage to sey as it feliþ, þan alle þe clerkes of Cristendome schuld wondre on þat wisdam. ȝe! & in comparison of it, al here grete clergie schuld seme apeerte foly. & þerfore no wondre þof I kan not telle þee þe worþines of þis werk wiþ my boystouse beestly tonge. & God forbede þat it scholde be so defoulid in it-self for to be streynid vnder þe steringes of a fleschly tonge! Nay, it may not be, & certes it wil not be, & God forbede þat I schuld coueyte it![15] (*BPC* 153.12–20)

The 'goostly werk' of the *Cloud*-author hinges on a letting go of the intellectual procedures and interpretative strategies of the world and a

Theological Language in the Twelfth-Century Schools', *Downside Review* 96 (1978) 165–75; M. Ross, 'The Apophatic Ordinary', *Anglican Theological Review* 74 (1992), 456–64; 'Apophatic Prayer as a Theological Model: Notes for a Quantum Theology', *Literature and Theology* (forthcoming).

14 On medieval language theory, see M. L. Colish, *The Mirror of Language: A Study in the Medieval Theory of Knowledge*, revised edition (London, 1968), chapters 1–3; J. M. Gellrich, *The Idea of the Book in the Middle Ages* (Ithaca, 1985), chapters 1–3.

15 *The Cloud of Unknowing and the Book of Privy Counselling*, ed. P. Hodgson, EETS OS, 218 (1944, revised reprint 1973). Subsequent references to *Cloud* and *BPC* by page and line number of this edition. Hodgson produced a new edition, with rather few textual changes but with an expanded and modified introduction and notes, as *The Cloud of Unknowing and Related Treatises*, Analecta Cartusiana, 3 (1982). As Hodgson points out, *BPC* is here quoting the opening of Aristotle's *Metaphysics*. My thinking on the *Cloud*-author has been decisively influenced by the work of Dr René Tixier of the University of Toulouse, whose thesis *Mystique et Pédagogie dans The Cloud of Unknowing* (unpublished Doctorat Nouveau Régime, Université de Nancy, 1988), is a sustained and detailed analysis of the verbal and pedagogic strategies of the *Cloud*. See also his '*This louely blinde werk*: Contemplation in *The Cloud of Unknowing* and related treatises', in *The Medieval Mystical Tradition in England*, ed. W. Pollard (forthcoming). On *curiositas*, see E. Gilson, *The Mystical Theology of St. Bernard* (London, 1940), Appendix 1.

stilling of the analytical instincts of the discursive mind.[16]. Recognizing that our 'wittys' find that such abnegation starves them of the meat of intellection, he writes:

> Late hem faste awhile, I preie þee, from here kyndely delite in here kunnyng; for, as it is wel seide, a man kyndely desireþ for to kunne; bot certes he may not taast of goostly felyng in God bot only by grace, haue he neuer so moche kunnyng of clergie ne of kynde. & þerfore, I preie þee, seche more after felyng þen after kunning; for kunnyng oft-tymes disceyuiþ wiþ pride, bot meek louely felyng may not begile. Sciencia inflat, karitas edificat. In knowyng is trauaile, in feling is rest.
>
> (*BPC* 171.22–172.3)

The technologizing of knowledge, he complains, has led scholars to criticize the difficulty of his teaching. In reality, he says, turning their learning against them in a typically paradoxical peripeteia, their 'coryous kunnyng of clergie' (*BPC* 137.16) makes them as incapable of understanding the book's simple teaching as a child who is learning his ABC is of understanding 'þe kunnyng of þe grettest clerk in scole' (137.21).[17] The school of love requires the surrender of intellectual

[16] Cf. E. R. Elder, 'William of St Thierry: Rational and Affective Spirituality' in *The Spirituality of Western Christendom*, ed. E. R. Elder, Cistercian Studies, 30 (Kalamazoo, 1976), pp. 85–105: 'If reason first bows itself beneath the lintel of faith, if reason stoops beneath him who claimed to be the door, then reason, humbled by faith under the yoke of authority, may enter into the knowledge of God's very truth' (p. 95), paraphrasing *Speculum Fidei*, 24. *The Clensyng of Mannes Soule* makes a similar point: 'Perfectioun of resoun in þis liif is to be rauysched aboue hym self goostly to se our lord god be an inward and intellectuale knowinge þorouȝ purite of þe soule wiþout eny ymaginacouns or bodily liknes and wiþ[out] eny argumentz of naturel resoun', Oxford, Bodleian Library MS Bodley 923, fols 150v–151r.

[17] See Hodgson, Analecta, p. 176 on this anti-intellectual outburst. Rolle is similarly scathing in *Incendium Amoris*: 'An old woman can be more expert in the love of God. . .than your theologian with his useless studying. He does it for vanity, to get a reputation, to obtain stipends and official positions. Such a fellow ought to be entitled not "Doctor" but "Fool"!', *The Fire of Love*, translated by Clifton Wolters (Harmondsworth, 1972), p. 61; cf. p. 46. On Rolle's apparent 'anti-intellectualism', see V. Gillespie, 'Mystic's Foot: Rolle and Affectivity', in *The Medieval Mystical Tradition in England*, 2, ed. M Glasscoe (Exeter, 1982), pp. 207–9. See also the virtuosic study by N. Watson, *Richard Rolle and the Invention of Authority*, Cambridge Studies in Medieval Literature, 13 (Cambridge, 1991), for a profoundly revisionist reading of Rolle's textual strategies. There is evidence for seeing such 'anti-intellectual' postures as rhetorical tropes of *diminutio*, but the opposition between the schools of love and logic is widespread: Margarete Porete describes the Holy Spirit writing on the precious parchment of the soul: 'þere is yholden þe diuine scole wiþ mouþe closed, þat no wit of men may putte in speche', *Margaret Porete: The Mirror of Simple Souls, A Middle English Translation*, ed. M. Doiron, *Archivio Italiano per la Storia della Pietà* 5 (1968) 241–382, p. 303. For a sixteenth-century example, see 'Robert Parkyn: Devotional Treatises', ed. A. G. Dickens in *Tudor Treatises*, *Yorkshire Archaeological Society: Record Series*, 125 (1959), pp. 61–3. On Parkyn

curiosity and the abandonment of exegetical fervour. God's freedom to move in a mysterious way requires the martyrdom of our self-consciousness:

> For siþ in þe first biginnyng of Holy Chirche in þe tyme of persecucion, dyuerse soules & many weren so merueylously touchid in sodeynte of grace þat sodenly, wiþoutyn menes of oþer werkes comyng before, þei kasten here instrumentes, men of craftes, of here hondes, children here tables in þe scole, & ronnen wiþ-outyn ransakyng of reson to þe martirdom wiþ seintes. (*BPC* 151.1–6)

This passage alludes to many distinctive features of the encounter with the ineffable. The suddenness of the working of grace, described as a touching; the suspicion and rejection of *menes* and works; the rejection of the procedures of the schools; the abandonment of reason in favour of desire and love.

The translator's preface to *The Seven Points of True Wisdom*, extracted from Suso's *Orologium Sapientiae*, makes a similar point in the text it takes as its epigraph:

> Feliþ of oure Lorde in goodnesse and sechiþ him in symplenesse of herte, for he ys foundene of hem þat temptene him not, and he apperiþ to hem þat hauene feith into hym.[18]

The point is reinforced by the work's introductory parable of a devout disciple of wisdom who attended 'diuerse scoles' to learn many 'sciences of mannis doctrine and wordelye wisdam'. Being touched by grace, he comes to consider such studies 'veyne trauayle' and prays to be brought to the knowledge and understanding of 'soþefast and souereyne philosophie'. Restlessly passing from school to school, he finds only 'an ymage or a lykenesse' of the wisdom he seeks, until 'þere apperid to his sighte as hit were a wondir gret and large rownde hows lyke to þe spere of þe firmamente' which is divided in the middle into two mansions, each containing doctors, teachers and disciples. The lower mansion contains students of earthly crafts and sciences 'þe wheche alle hadden as hit were a manere veyle vpon here faces'. These are comforted in their labours by

(ob.1580), see A. G. Dickens, 'The Last Medieval Englishman', in *Christian Spirituality: Essays in Honour of Gordon Rupp* (London, 1975), pp. 143–81.

[18] All quotations are taken from Aberystwyth, National Library of Wales MS Porkington 19, the base text for the forthcoming critical edition by Dr Christina von Nolcken of the University of Chicago, to whom I am indebted for a copy of her transcription. The prologue occupies pp. 7–13 of this manuscript. For a printed text, see K. Horstmann, '*Orologium Sapientiae* or The Seven Poyntes of Trewe Wisdom aus MS. Douce 114', *Archiv* 10 (1887) 323–89. On the popularity of the *Orologium* in England, see R. Lovatt, 'Henry Suso and the Medieval Mystical Tradition in England', in *The Medieval Mystical Tradition*, 2, ed. Glasscoe (1982), pp. 47–62.

a drink which fails to quench their thirst but rather serves to increase it. The disciple's stomach revolts from this drink, and he goes up to the threshold of the second house and sees an inscription over the door:

> Þis is þe scole of soþfaste diuinite, where þe maystresse is Euerlastynge Wisdam, þe doctrine is verite and treuþe, and þe ende euerlastynge felicite.

He does not hesitate to cross the threshold, hoping to find the fulfilment of his desires. Within he finds three groups of teachers and pupils. The first, seated on the ground by the door, looks back toward things that lie outside the door. The second group 'profited not feruentlye, but in manere semede as þei stodene stille'. The third group sit close to the master, and:

> drinkynge þe watere of helefulle wisdam þat came out of his mowþe, þei were made so drunkyn þat þei forȝetene hemself and alle oþer worldely þingis, hauynge here hertis and here eyȝen euer vpwarde to þe mayster and feruentlye rauysched into his loue and heuenely þingis.[19]

Although the text expounds this vision as describing three manners of studying holy writ, its imagery and vocabulary clearly also align it with progression in the work of contemplation and liberation from the parched pursuit of signification in the language and images of the world.

The Cloud of Unknowing, as so often, encapsulates the problems of mystical language and imagery:

> Alle þe reuelacions þat euer sawe any man here in bodely licnes in þis liif, þei haue goostly bemenynges. & I trowe þat & þei vnto whome þei were schewid, or we for whome þei were schewid, had been so goostly, or couþe haue conceyuid þeire bemenynges goostly, þat þan þei had neuer ben schewed bodily. & þerfore late us pike of þe rouȝ bark, & fede us of þe swete kyrnel. (c.58; 107.11–16)

In gesturing towards the most commonplace medieval image of the process of interpretation, the *Cloud* engages with the core hermeneutical problem of mystical experience.[20] How do we speak of the ineffable, how do we read the languages of the threshold? Not, it is clear, by rejecting language altogether. We should not feed off the fruit and despise the tree, or drink the wine and throw the cup against a wall (107.20–108.7).

[19] Compare the hermit's similar exegesis of Hector's dream in the *Grail*: 'The waters of this spring will never fail, however deep the draughts one draws from it: it is the Holy Grail, the grace of the Holy Ghost. This spring is the gentle rain, the Gospel's dulcet words, from which the heart of the penitent derives such sweet refreshment that the more he savours it the greater his craving: it is the grace of the Holy Grail' (Matarasso, p. 172; Pauphilet, pp. 158–9).

[20] This image is used in other works by the *Cloud*-author, and in other English mystical works, see Hodgson, EETS, p. 201.

If ghostly fruit is contained in language, imagery or other means to bring men to recognize and foster their naked yearning for God, then these *means* should be valued.[21] As Galahad teaches us, the grail of language is properly valued not for itself but for the apophatic and eucharistic truths that it contains. Means must not become ends in themselves. The challenge to the mystical writer is to get his audience to look beyond the superficial beauty of the linguistic grail and to gaze into the apophatic surfaces of its contents, and to taste the wisdom of the ineffable:

> In þis werk men schul use no menes, ne ȝit men mowe not come þerto wiþ menes. Alle good menes hangen upon it, & it on no mene; ne no mene may lede þerto. (*Cloud* c.34; 71.7–10)

Wisdom, popularly etymologized as a 'sauoury science', differs from knowledge because it is based on experience. Knowledge makes us learned but feeling makes us wise, claims St Bernard. A man knows good wine when he sees it fair in a glass, 'but by the gifte of sapience a man knoweth as he knoweth the wyne by the drynkyng'.[22] Only this drink will slake the existential thirst of the human soul.

Language, as a repertoire of conventional signs, operates by a system of differences. The reader learns the grammar and syntax of his language to enable the process of differentiation and signifying to unfold in his consciousness and to respond to the conceptual stimuli generated by his

[21] Cf. *Cloud* c.61; 114. 3–10. For discussion see V. Gillespie and M. Ross, 'The Apophatic Image: The Poetics of Effacement in Julian of Norwich', in *The Medieval Mystical Tradition in England*, 5, ed. M. Glasscoe (Cambridge, 1992), pp. 53–77, for parallel discussion of this issue; J. Burrow, 'Fantasy and Language in *The Cloud of Unknowing*', *Essays in Criticism* 27 (1977) 283–98. The issue is, of course, closely related to the debate on the status and use of images: for a brief discussion see V. Gillespie, 'Strange Images of Death: The Passion in Later Medieval English Devotional and Mystical Writing', in *Zeit, Tod und Ewigkeit in der Renaissance Literatur*, 3, Analecta Cartusiana, 117 (1987), pp. 111–59, supplemented by J. Pelikan, *Imago Dei: The Byzantine Apologia for Icons* (New Haven, 1990); M. Aston, *England's Iconoclasts*, 1: *Laws Against Images* (Oxford, 1988).

[22] *Disce Mori* in Oxford, Bodleian Library MS Laud Misc. 99, fol 179r. The image is also found in the *Somme le Roi* and its main English version *The Book of Vices and Virtues*, ed. W. N. Francis, EETS, OS, 217 (1942), p. 272. On metaphors of spiritual sense perception, see W. Riehle, *The Middle English Mystics*, translated by B. Standring (London, 1981), pp. 104–27. On the distinction between *scientia* and *sapientia* as reflected in some Middle English texts, see Gillespie, 'Mystic's Foot', pp. 199–211; M. C. Davlin, 'Kynde Knowynge as a Middle English Equivalent for 'Wisdom' in *Piers Plowman* B', *Medium Ævum* 50 (1981) 5–18; J. Simpson, 'The Role of *Scientia* in *Piers Plowman*', in *Medieval English Religious and Ethical Literature: Essays in Honour of G. H. Russell*, eds. G. Kratzmann and J. Simpson (Cambridge, 1986), pp. 49–65.

mind, memory and imagination by relating them to and assessing them against the mental archive of words, concepts, images and symbols. New sense data, new images, new concepts are assessed and assigned a place in the taxonomy of knowledge through assimilation into the syntax of the mental language. This taxonomy itself operates by a system of difference and distinction: an analytical and interpretative assessment that articulates itself in terms of quality, quantity, nature of the concept. The discursive consciousness cannot prevent itself from engaging in such processes of assessment and hierarchizing. 'Curiositee of the wittys' is a kind of intellectual covetousness; a thirst for control and certainty. Such acts of interpretation are a function of our exile from the paradise of unmediated knowledge, an exile symbolized by the primal act of intellectual covetousness towards the tree of the knowledge of good and evil. The fall of language is precipitated by the relentless desire to interpret and discriminate. The aspiration to distinguish knowledge into good and evil is the first interpretative act, an act of will and of self-assertion.

But the ineffable nature of God is beyond the hermeneutical grasp of men's minds. Neither negation nor affirmation can define him:

> Þer is of hym no settyng ne doyng awey; bot whan we affermingly set or deniingly do awey alle or any of þoo þinges þat ben not he, hym we mowe neiþer set ne do awey, ne on any vnderstondable maner afferme him, ne denie him. For þe parfite & þe singuleer cause of al most nedelynges be wiþoutyn comparison of þe moost hiȝe heiȝt abouen alle, boþe settyng & doyng awey. And his not-vnderstondable ouerpassyng is vn-vnderstondabely abouen alle affermyng and deniinge.[23]

God resists the taxonomy of analysis: he is 'wiþoutyn comparison'. God simply IS: his being, which may be deduced from his energies, tracked from his traces in the book of creation, and articulated by the incarnation of the logos remains beyond the differentiating grasp of the discursive consciousness:

> For þer is no name, ne felyng ne beholdyng more, ne so moche, acordyng vnto euer-lastyngnes, þe whiche is God, as is þat þe whiche may be had, seen & felt in þe blinde & þe louely beholding of þis worde IS. For ȝif þou sey 'Good' or 'Faire Lord', or 'Swete', 'Merciful' or 'Riȝtwise', 'Wise' or 'Alwitty', 'Miȝti' or 'Almiȝti', 'Witte' or 'Wisdome', 'Miȝte' or

[23] From *Deonise hid Diuinite*, the *Cloud*-author's version of *The Mystical Theology* of Pseudo-Denys, ed. P. Hodgson, EETS OS, 231 (1955 for 1949), p. 10, 15–23. cf. his comment in *A Pistle of Discrecioun of Stirings*: 'For to him þat wil be sped of his purpos goostly, it suffiseþ to him for a mene, and him nediþ no mo bot þe actuele minde of good God only, wiþ a reuerent stering of lastyng loue; so þat mene vnto God gete þee none bot God, ȝif þou kepe hole þi stering of loue' (Hodgson, EETS, 231, p. 75.8–12).

> 'Strengþe', 'Loue' or 'Charite', or what oþer soche þing þat þou sey of God: al it is hid & enstorid in þis litil worde IS. (*BPC* 143.19–26)

God cannot be spoken, only spoken of and, all too often, special thought about God creates a self-referential and solipsistic looping of abstraction and image-making that talks only to itself.

One of the favourite paradoxes of the medieval schoolmen was the proposition that God is 'an intelligible sphere whose centre is everywhere and whose circumference nowhere'.[24] God is the still centre who circumscribes creation but is not circumscribed by it. Language, therefore, is predicated by him, but not of him. As Derrida puts it

> It has always been thought that the center, which is by definition unique, constituted that very thing within a structure which, while governing the structure, escapes structurality. . .the center is paradoxically, *within* the structure and *outside it*.[25]

God's ineffability is an absent presence that escapes structurality. The *Deus absconditus* of Christian tradition inhabits the non-dimensional silence beyond the grasp of men's structuring consciousness. Yet God is present and absent. The play of absence and presence in his communion with men is a powerful trace of his ineffable essence.[26] Because of this, mystical language has as its characteristic tone longing for presence and yearning for liberation from absence. Mystical writers, in seeking to interpret this trace and to transcribe it for their readers aspire to a mode of interpretation that 'seeks to decipher, dreams of deciphering a truth or an origin which escapes play and the order of the sign, and which lives the necessity of interpretation as an exile'.[27]

The order of the sign, the referentiality of language, depend upon structurality and difference. The repertoires and codes that condition and

24 St Bonaventure, *The Mind's Road to God*, translated by G. Boas, The Library of Liberal Arts (New York, 1953), cap. 5.8. The *Itinerarium Mentis in Deum* is shot through with the influence of Pseudo-Denys, mediated by Thomas Gallus; see J. G. Bougerol, 'Saint Bonaventure et le pseudo-Denys l'Areopagite', in *Etudes Franciscaines: Actes du Colloque Saint Bonaventure*, *Orsay*, 18, supplement annuel (1968), pp. 33–123; A. J. Minnis, 'Affection and Imagination in *The Cloud of Unknowing* and Hilton's *Scale of Perfection*', *Traditio* 39 (1983) 323–66.

25 J. Derrida, 'Structure, Sign and Play in the Discourse of the Human Sciences', in *Writing and Difference*, translated by A. Bass (London,1978), pp. 278–92, p. 279, where he also notes that 'the movement of any archaeology, like that of any eschatology, is an accomplice of this reduction of the structurality of structure, and always attempts to conceive of structure on the basis of full presence which is beyond play'.

26 Gillespie, 'Strange Images', pp. 142–3 and notes; Gillespie and Ross, 'Apophatic Image', *passim*; R. Tixier, '*Good gamesumli pley*: Games of Love in *The Cloud of Unknowing*', *Downside Review* 108 (1990) 235–53.

27 Derrida, 'Structure', p. 292.

interpret our response to phenomena operate, for the most part, within systems of linear causality and temporal sequence. Syntax operates in thought and imagery as well as in language. Images, for example, work within iconographical systems that attribute conventional valencies and excite easily codifiable responses. Even symbols and metaphors develop a decorum of procedure, a rhetorical framework, a circumference of accepted and convenient structure which serves to limit the play of their signification. While offering the possibility of limited escape from simple referentiality, figural and analogical tropes soon fossilize into programmatic and conventional triggers for stock responses. Religious imagery in general, and Passion images in particular, soon acquire, as the *Cloud*-author notes, approved significations and authorized resonances, creating a self-fuelling chain of low level affective responses.[28]

Symbolic and verbal languages operate in time even when they seek to bring us to the brink of eternity and the threshold of the apophatic. As Julian learns from her showings, sin and syntax are both products of the fall into time and causality.[29] Mystical writing aspires to pass over from referentiality to a promised land without spatial or temporal coordinates:

> For tyme, stede, & body, þees þre schuld be forȝeten in alle goostly worching. (*Cloud* c.59; 111.4–5)

God's being informs structure without being comprehended by it. The initiative lies with him. Only in the incarnation of the Word does the ineffability of God's being manifest itself in time and structure. The linguistic implications of the incarnation are explored in a remarkable poem by St Ephrem the Syrian that anticipates in many ways the teachings of the Dionysian tradition:

> It is *our* metaphors that he put on – though he did not literally do so; He took them off – without actually doing so: when wearing them, He was at

[28] *Cloud* c.7; 26.13–29.6. See Gillespie, 'Strange Images', 111–31. Lees, *Negative Language*, pp. 24, 83, discusses Gregory of Nyssa's struggle with man's spatial perception.

[29] See her discussion in chapter 27, where the pain of sin 'is somethyng, as to my syte, for a tyme, for it purgith and makyth us to knowen ourselfe and askyn mercy'. Sin is 'behovabil', but all shall be well: 'And in these same words I saw a mervelous hey privite hid in God, which privity he shall openly make knowen to us in hevyn; in which knowyng we shal verily see the cause why he suffrid synne to come; in which syte we shall endlesly ioyen in our lord God'; *Julian of Norwich: A Revelation of Love*, ed. M. Glasscoe (Exeter, 1976), pp. 28–9. All Julian quotations are taken from this edition of London, British Library MS Sloane 2499 (S1). For a defence of S1's superiority over the Paris manuscript used as base by Colledge and Walsh, see M. Glasscoe, 'Visions and Revisions: A Further Look at the Manuscripts of Julian of Norwich', *Studies in Bibliography* 42 (1989) 103–20; Gillespie and Ross, 'Apophatic Image', elaborates our preference for S1.

> the same time stripped of them. He puts one on when it is beneficial, then strips it off in exchange for another; the fact that he strips off and puts on all sorts of metaphors tells us that the metaphor does not apply to His true Being: because that Being is hidden, He has depicted it by means of what is visible.[30]

God's metaphors are metaphorical. This double displacement prevents simple codification and interpretative stylization:

> He wished to teach us two things: that He became flesh, yet He did not come into being. In his love He made for himself a countenance so that his servants might behold Him; but lest we be harmed by imagining he was really like this, He moved from one likeness to another, to teach us that He has no likeness. And though he did not depart from the form of humanity, yet in his Transfiguration He did depart.

The motive for this play of absence and presence, then, is to lead men to seek transfiguration in imitation of the transfigured Christ: 'He clothed himself in our language so that He might clothe us in his way of life'.

In a manner characteristic of mystical writing, the playful paradoxes and provisionalites of Ephrem's language taunt our interpretative expectations of referentiality and figurality. The images flicker and tease to allow our thoughts and responses to gather, focus and penetrate into the mysteries that he seeks to address. But ultimately, as his strategies of effacement suggest, we are no nearer possessing God when we possess his metaphors, unless we are prepared to transfigure our perceptions, strip ourselves of our expectations and focus ourselves into a naked and blind yearning of love that reaches out across the threshold of language. 'If I touche bot þe hemme of his cloþing, I schal be saaf', the words of the woman afflicted with an issue of blood, are used on *The Book of Privy Counselling* to describe the wounded self-consciousness of the human soul. The remedy is simple : 'Take good gracyous God as he is, plat & pleyn as a plastre, & legge it to þi seek self as þou arte' (138.28–9), but it involves the denial of the usual workings of the world of analysis and discursiveness:

> It chargeþ not now in þee bot þat þi blynde beholdyng of þi nakid beyng be gladli born up in listines of loue, to be knittid & onid in grace & in spirit to þe precious beyng of God in him-self only as he is, with-outen more. (*BPC* 139.11–14)

30 *Hymns on Faith* no 31, edited and translated by S. Brock in *A Garland of Hymns from the Early Church*, (McLean, Virginia, 1989); see the discussion by S. Brock, *The Luminous Eye: The Spiritual World Vision of St. Ephrem*, Placid Lectures (Rome, 1985), pp. 43–8. On similar themes in Gregory of Nyssa and Pseudo-Denys, see Lees, *Negative Language*, pp. 13–155; McGinn, *Foundations*, pp. 139–42, 157–82.

Fantasy and 'corious seching' hinder the 'naked felyng of þi blynde beyng' by drawing attention away from the stillness of contemplation into the realm of analogy, metaphor and difference. By contrast the progressive loss of self-consciousness liberates the soul from the burden of analysis and interpretation. Self-consciousness becomes a barrier between the soul and God:

> Þan wol þee þenk it a wel heuy & a ful peynful birþen of þi-self. . .For þan arte þi-self a cros to þi-self. & þis is trewe worching & wey to oure Lorde, as him-self seiþ: 'Late hym bere his cros', first in the peynfulnes of hym-self, & siþ 'folow me' into blis or into þe mounte of perfeccion, taastyng þe softenes of my loue in godly felyng of my-self.
>
> (*BPC* 157.13–14;16–20)

The incarnation and the passion are acts in time, but they are also the literal foot of a complex theological metaphor. To be understood properly we must make of them, in the *Cloud*'s words, a (properly ordered) 'goostly conseyte of a bodely þing' (c.65; 117.16) before we can escape from the constricted perspective of sin and time, of syntax and provisionality.[31]

The metaphoricity of Christ leads us away from time to eternity, from trace to presence, from interpretation to bliss. Christ, the incarnate Word, is the liminal signifier of the ineffable and the apophatic. St Bonaventure likens him to the propitiatory suspended over the ark of the covenant in the Holy of Holies:

> He who with full face looks to this propitiatory by looking upon Him suspended on the cross in faith, hope and charity, in devotion, wonder, exultation, appreciation, praise and jubilation, makes a passover. . .that he may pass over the Red Sea by the staff of the cross from Egypt into the desert, where he may taste the hidden manna and with Christ may rest in the tomb as if outwardly dead, yet knowing, as far as possible in our earthly condition, what was said on the cross to the thief cleaving to Christ: 'Today thou shalt be with me in Paradise'.[32]

In this passover, Christ is the way and the door. Meditation on the suffering humanity of Christ is an inescapable prerequisite for contemplation of his divinity: one is predicated on the other; they are two halves of a single divine metaphor. As the *Stimulus Amoris* puts it:

> Who-so wenyth to come to contemplacioun of criste and cometh not by þis dore ne bi þis wey ne bi þe bitternesse of crist in his manhede, he is but a

[31] I am indebted to Denis Renevey for the suggestion that a 'goostly conseyte of a bodely þing' may be the *Cloud*-author's term for metaphor.

[32] *The Mind's Road to God*, cap. 7.2, pp. 43–4; *Itinerarium Mentis in Deum* in *S. Bonaventurae Opera Omnia* (Quaracchi, 1882–1902), V, 312.

> þeef and a mychere, for whenne he weneth to be with-inne, he is ful fer wiþ-outen.[33]

Walter Hilton, who translated the *Stimulus Amoris* into Middle English, glosses this passage in *The Scale of Perfection*:

> No body can come to the contemplation of the Deity unless he be first reformed by fullness of humility and charity to the likeness of Jesus in his manhood. (*Scale* 1.91)[34]

This reformation of the self in meekness and charity is acquired by transfiguring ourselves into the mind of Christ:

> For let this mind be in you which was also in Christ Jesus, who. . .[did not consider equality with God a thing to be grasped, but] emptied himself, taking the form of a servant, being made in the likeness of men and in habit found as a man. He humbled himself, becoming obedient unto death, even to the death of the cross. Therefore (for which cause) God hath exalted him, and hath given him a name which is above all names.
>
> (Philippians 2: 5–9)[35]

The paradox of humility and exaltation which is rooted in the refusal to grasp equality with God leads to the reward of the transfigured name which is above all names. The incarnation, death and exaltation of Christ offers a metaphorical paradigm, an immanent model for the trajectory of mystical experience.

Self-emptying – *kenosis* – is the model for the humility, meekness and obedience, the loss of self-consciousness, the yielding of the initiative to God that prepares us for transfiguration into ineffable knowing. 'For it is

33 *The Prickynge of Love*, ed. H. Kane, Salzburg Studies in English Literature, Elizabethan and Renaissance Studies, 92:10 (1983), p. 124. On Hilton's authorship of the translation, see J. P. H. Clark, 'Walter Hilton and the *Stimulus Amoris*', *Downside Review* 102 (1984) 79–118.

34 In the absence of a Middle English text, references are to *Walter Hilton: The Scale of Perfection*, translated by J. P. H. Clark and R. Dorward, The Classics of Western Spirituality (New York, 1991), which uses the same base texts as the forthcoming Early English Text Society edition. This quote, p. 160.

35 I have used the Douay-Rheims translation, corrected against RSV within the square brackets. Julian's Short Text explicitly alludes to this passage (*A Book of Showings to the Anchoress Julian of Norwich*, ed. E. Colledge and J. Walsh, Pontifical Institute of Mediæval Studies, Studies and Texts, 35 (Toronto, 1979), p. 234), and the Long Text showing of the Lord and the Servant contains a possible echo (Glasscoe, c.51., p. 59; Colledge and Walsh, p. 535). See Gillespie and Ross, 'Apophatic Image', n.22, to which references should be added J.P.H. Clark, 'Time and Eternity in Julian of Norwich', *Downside Review* 109 (1991) 259–76, p. 268, who refers to the Augustinian use of the passage in *De Trinitate*; J. M. Nuth, *Wisdom's Daughter: The Theology of Julian of Norwich* (New York, 1991), pp. 50–2; Tixier, '*Louely blinde werk*', n.8.

God who works in you both to will and to accomplish according to his good will' (Philippians 2: 13). We must learn to inhabit the paradox of Christ's dual nature, to sustain and nurture it. We must resist and yield up the natural inclination to resolve it into a linear proposition. His metaphoricity is a signifier of the complex significations that it invites us to pass into. We must engage in a kind of interpretative *kenosis*, a stilling of the workings of the discursive consciousness in favour of a meek, blind and naked yearning for the unmediated knowing of God. The mystic, refusing to grasp equality with God, longs to be comprehended by God rather than to comprehend Him.

For *The Book of Privy Counselling*, imaginative meditation may help to bring to the threshold, may indeed be the only true way of approach. But unless these *means* are shed and denied then, like Lancelot and Suso's scholars, the contemplative will find his way barred or his gaze misdirected:

> For many weneþ þat þei ben wiþ-inne þe goostly dore, & ȝit stonden þei þer-oute, & scholen do vnto þe tyme þat þey sechen meekly þe dore. (*BPC* 158.27–159.2)

Christ's humanity is the doorway into 'goostlines', but entry is under the control and at the initiative of his 'Godheed'. However, the incarnation opens up a 'comoun pleyne wey & an open entre to alle þat wolen come' (159.15). To remain rooted in the manhood means looking back from the threshold into the world 'in beholdyng of þe peyne of his manheed'. Suso's scholars at the threshold lacked 'trewe taste of dyuinite' because they were 'copiose and habundaunt [in] þe lettrere-science wiþoute þe sperite'. They were literal readers 'blowene and fillid wiþ pride'. Lancelot's spiritual failure was because of 'bobbaunce and pride of the worlde'.[36] *Privy Counselling* warns that such men must remain at the threshold:

> til þe grete rust of his boistous bodelynes be in grete party rubbid awei, his counseil & his concience to witnes; and namely, euer to he be clepid innermore bi þe priue teching of þe spirit of God, þe whiche techyng is þe rediest & þe sekerist witnes þat may be had in þis liif of þe clepyng & þe drawyng of a soule innermore to more special worching of grace.
> (*BPC* 161.2–7)

To enter into the gate of contemplation, we must die to the world and enter into what Hilton calls the darkness of self-knowing, so that we can say with St Paul 'the world is slain and crucified to me and I to the world':

36 *Malory: Works*, ed. E. Vinaver, second edition (Oxford, 1977), p. 557.

> The man who can bring himself first to nothing through grace of humility, and in this way die, he is in the gate, for he is dead to the world and lives to God. St Paul speaks of it like this:. . .You are dead: that is, you that for the love of God forsake all the love of the world are dead to the world; but your life is hidden from worldly men, as Christ lives and is hidden in his divinity from the love and the sight of carnal lovers. (*Scale* 2.27; p.245)

Hilton's argument by analogy makes it clear how the noughting of the soul at the threshold is predicated on the metaphor of Christ's transfigured life in God. Eckhart says that God called himself a Word: besides the word man is an adverb: *quasi*.[37] As Ephrem says, 'He clothed Himself in our language so that He might clothe us in His mode of life'.

Mystical writers send despatches from the threshold, artists' impressions of the apophatic, postcards from the edge. Language falters in the face of the ineffable:

> Fewe ben þi wordes, bot ful of frute & of fiir. A schorte worde of þi mouþ conteneþ a woreld ful of wisdam, ȝit semeþ it bot foly to hem þat wonen in here wittis. (*BPC* 166.24–167.1)

Contemplative prayer struggles to break free of earthly syntax and aspires to the condition of heavenly song. *The Cloud of Unknowing* recommends short words, ideally of one syllable only. The single, uninflected, syntactically uninhibited word aspires to escape from referentiality and from the chains of signification of earthly discourse. It resists interpretation:

> & ȝif he profre þee of his grete clergie to expoune þee þat worde & to telle þee þe condicions of þat worde, sey him þat þou wilt haue it al hole, & not broken ne vndon. (c.7; 29.1–4)

'Schort preier peersiþ heuen'.[38] Such prayer aspires to its own effacement:

> Prayer is not a preamble, an accessory mode of access. It constitutes an essential moment, it adjusts discursive asceticism, the passage through the

[37] Eckhart's *quasi* is discussed in an important recent essay by Derrida where he articulates the similarities and differences between his approach and that of Pseudo-Denys and the negative theologians, seeking (not totally successfully) to distance himself from their procedures and assumptions: J. Derrida, 'How to Avoid Speaking: Denials', in *Languages of the Unsayable: The Play of Negativity in Literature*, ed. S. Budick and W. Iser, Irvine Studies in the Humanities (New York, 1989), pp. 3–70, p. 46; the same volume has a perceptive commentary on Derrida's essay by Frank Kermode: 'Endings, Continued', pp. 71–94, esp. pp. 72–81.

[38] *Cloud*, c.37; 75.5. On the popular currency of this aphorism, see J. A. Alford, 'Some Unidentified Quotations in *Piers Plowman*', *Modern Philology* 72 (1974–5) 390–9, pp. 390–1.

> desert of discourse, the apparent referential vacuity which will only avoid empty deliria and prattling, by addressing itself from the start to the other.[39]

Contemplative prayer and praise, the jubilation so often described in mystical experience, reach out beyond language.[40] Like the *neume* at the end of an antiphon it seeks 'pure vocalization, form of an inarticulate song without speech, whose name means breath, which is inspired in us by God and may address only Him'.[41] As Augustine says:

> For whom is such a jubilation suitable unless to an ineffable being, and how can we celebrate this ineffable being, since we cannot be silent, or find any thing in our transports which can express them unless unarticulated sounds.

Derrida, in his discussion of Rousseau's *Essay on the Origin of Languages*, describes the aspiration of such songs as:

> A speaking and a singing breath, breath of language which is nonetheless inarticulate. . . to speak before knowing how to speak, not to be able either to be silent or to speak, this limit of origin is indeed that of pure presence, present enough to be living, to be felt in jouissance but pure enough to have remained unblemished by the work of difference, inarticulate enough for self-delight not to be corrupted by interval, discontinuity, alterity.[42]

Such a speech relates to no object and knows no articulation.

Most mystical language seeks to transcribe the approach to and return from the ineffable. Few are audacious enough to go beyond language. Richard Rolle's experience of a transcendental *canor* provoked him into attempting to capture something of its inarticulate joy.:

> In my prayer I was reaching out to heaven with heartfelt longing when I became aware, in a way I cannot explain, of a symphony of song, and in myself I sensed a corresponding harmony at once wholly delectable and heavenly, which persisted in my mind. Then and there my thinking itself turned into melodious song, and my meditation became a poem, and my

39 Derrida, 'How to Avoid Speaking', p. 41.

40 Cf. Cassian's comment: '[This prayer] is not concerned with any consideration of an image, nor characterized by any sound nor set of words. It comes forth from a fiery mental intention through an ineffable rapture of the heart (*excessus cordis*) by means of an inexplicable burst of the spirit. Freed from all sensations and visible concerns, the mind pours itself out to God with unspeakable groans and sighs (Romans 8: 26)', *Conlationes* 10.11, cited McGinn, *Foundations*, p. 224.

41 J. Derrida, 'Genesis and Structure of the *Essay on the Origin of Languages*', in *Of Grammatology*, translated by G. C. Spivak (Baltimore, 1976), p. 249, which includes the next quotation from Augustine. Cf. McGinn, *Foundations*, pp. 232–43. On musical metaphors in English mystical writing, see Riehle, pp. 119–22.

42 P. 249.

> very prayers and psalms took up the same sound. The effect of this inner sweetness was that I began to sing what previously I had spoken; only I sang inwardly, and that for my Creator. But it was not suspected by those who saw me.[43]

As he explains in his vernacular epistles, this song in inarticulate. It does not involve 'bodily cryinge with þe mouth'.[44] It is impossible to describe, though he is confident (more confident than some of his commentators) that it comes from heaven. It transcends earthly language: 'who-so hath hit, hym thynke al þe songe and þe mynstralcie of erth nat bot sorowe and woo þerto. In souereyn rest shal þay be þat mow get hit' (*Form*, 582–4). *Canor* transcends all human utterance: 'How might I than writ hit' (*Ego Dormio*, 57–8), he asks, posing a question he struggled to answer throughout his writing career. Walter Hilton, who created a careful and cautious taxonomy of the experience of heightened language in his *Of Angel's Song*, agrees that true *canor* is ineffable : 'It may be feled and persayued in a saule, but it may noght be schewed'.[45] Most experiences of song, he argues, are merely heightened affective responses pouring out in the language of longing, by analogy with the songs of love longing in the psalms and the Song of Songs.

But Rolle felt his experience to have been different in kind, not just different in degree from the heightened discourses of earthly song. In *Melos Amoris* he is led to attempt to recreate something of the effect of his transfigured song by virtuosic rhetorical experiment:

> Amor utique audacem efficit animum, quem arripit ab imis dum eterni Auctoris incendium amicam inflammat et suscipit in sublimitatem supra sophiam secularem ut non senciat nisi sanctitatem. Urget igitur amoris habundancia ut audeam aperire eloquium ad informacionem aliorum, ostendens altitudinem amancium ardentissime iusticiamque iubilancium iocunde in Iesu ac charitatem canencium in conformitate celica, necnon et claritatem conscienciarum capacium increati caloris et delectationis indeficientis.[46]

[43] *Fire of Love*, cap. 15, p. 93. On the centrality of this experience to Rolle's mystical identity, see Watson, *Invention*, pp. 69–72; 113–41. On *canor* see Watson, pp. 171–91; Gillespie, 'Mystic's Foot', pp. 207–18.

[44] All references to Rolle's vernacular writings are to *Richard Rolle: Prose and Verse*, ed. S. J. Ogilvie-Thomson, EETS OS 293 (1988), this quote *Form of Living*, 575. (References are in the form of title and line number.)

[45] *Of Angel's Song*, ed. T. Takamiya in *Two Minor Works of Walter Hilton* (Tokyo, 1980), p. 11; J. P. H. Clark, 'The Problem of Walter Hilton's Authorship: *Bonum Est*, *Benedictus* and *Of Angel's Song*', *Downside Review* 101 (1983) 15–29. See also *Scale* 1.47 (p. 120), 2.29–30 (pp. 249–57).

[46] *The Melos Amoris of Richard Rolle of Hampole*, ed. E. J. F. Arnould (Oxford, 1957), p. 3; S. de Ford, 'Mystical Union in the *Melos Amoris* of Richard Rolle', in *The Medieval Mystical Tradition in England*, 1, ed. M. Glasscoe (Exeter, 1980), pp. 173–210. Watson, *Invention*, pp. 175–6, discusses and translates the same passage, and I

'The charity of those who chant in conformity with the celestial' leads him to dare to unveil eloquence for the edification of others. As Nicholas Watson has pointed out, the *Melos Amoris* is a highly self-referential text that is both about *canor* and aspires to be *canor*. It offers 'a rhetorical version or simulacrum of that experience'.[47] But even the *Melos Amoris*, as an exercise in quasi-*canor*, recognises that in flattening it into human language it is reducing and traducing the experience:

> Now a spirit sighing from the paternal piety swept over me and suddenly submerged me, so that I separated myself in solitude from secular solace. Then he changed my mind most miraculously from misery to melody, yet in such a way that I fear to declare the gift and to multiply magnificence lest loquacity lessen me.
>
> Deinde mentem tam mirifice mutavit a merore in melos, quod metuo monstrare munus et multiplicare magnificenciam, ne multiloquium me minuerit.[48]

The hyperbolic alliterative structure and the rhythmical pulse create a kind of rhetorical paradox of movement and stasis, the timeless mellifluosness of the sweeping alliteration and the temporal tug of the rhythmical prose:

> What is the nature of pleasure in such a situation? Nothing external to oneself and one's own proper existence, so long as this state lasts, one suffices to oneself, like God.[49]

The *Melos* chafes at the limits of language, offering prospects of neumatic bliss. Inevitably, the experiment fails. Difference in kind is provisionally transcribed as difference in degree.

In Rolle's works, the *Melos Amoris* stands at the head of a hierarchical repertoire of songs and lyrics that offers a linguistic ladder towards the ineffable. The rhapsodic prose of some passages of the epistles clearly signal a heightened order of signifying, while the imbedded and independent lyrics consistently draw attention to themselves as songs from the threshold. They combine prayer and praise in a euphoric and

have used his characterful translation; see also his 'Translation and Self-Canonization in Richard Rolle's *Melos Amoris*', in *The Medieval Translator: The Theory and Practice of Translation in the Middle Ages*, ed. R. Ellis (Cambridge, 1989), pp. 167–80.

47 *Invention*, p. 178.

48 Arnould, pp. 3–4; Watson, *Invention*, pp. 183–4.

49 Rousseau's *Essay*, as quoted by Derrida, 'Genesis and Structure', p. 250. Cf. Watson's comment ('Translation', p. 177): 'the fact that it is repetitive, endlessly self-reflexive, and remarkably lacking in intellectual content is entirely congruent with its status as a work of praise or celebration. Praise is always in a sense about itself as much as its ostensible subject'; S. de Ford, 'The Use and Function of Alliteration in the *Melos Amoris* of Richard Rolle', *Mystics Quarterly* 12 (1986) 59–66.

ecstatic reproduction of that longing and desire that signals the trace of the ineffable. In *The Form of Living*, for example, he offers a lyric which 'þou may in þi longynge synge. . .in þyn herte to thy lord Ihesu, when þou coueiteste his comynge and thy goynge' (*Form* 596–7). These songs of love longing are not meant to be *canor*, or even reproductions of it. They are instruments of affective focusing, like the songs of love described by Hilton, who may indeed have confused Rolle's claims to ineffable *canor* with these exercises in affective manipulation. Rolle's lyrics are steadfastly rooted in time and place, provisionally installed at the threshold of the ineffable through their focus on Christ:

> My songe is in sighynge, whils I dwel in þis waye;
> My lif is in langynge, þat byndeth me nyght and daye. . .
>
> I sit and synge of loue-langynge, þat in my brest is bredde;
> Ihesu, my kynge and my ioynge, why ne ware I til þe ledde?

In patrolling the liminal spaces of ineffability, they articulate for Rolle's readers the hope of transfiguration into *canor*:

> Thy songe and þi swetynge he wil be at þe laste.[50]

Rolle's vernacular lyrics define the space within which contact with the ineffable takes place, but they steadfastly and fastidiously deny themselves access to it, nor do they pretend to mimic *canor*. They embody and enact prayer and praise, love and longing, desire and delight, absence and expectation.

Liminality is marked by anxiety and uncertainty as much as by joy and bliss. The continuum between discursive and apophatic consciousness means that the experience of absence and presence is universal in mystical experience. The loss of old modes of perception, the abandonment of old devotional exercises, the gradual effacement of the means used in the process of affective noughting in preparation for oneing with God: these absences are not fully or consistently filled by a secure sense of the presence of God. Such tribulations, for the *Cloud*-author, are part of the training in humility and obedience: 'for he wil haue þee maad as pleying to his wille goostly as a roon gloue to þin honde bodely' (*BPC* 168.8–9). The loss of old certainties and comfortable practices is part of the rite of passage: 'For now arte þou in þe goostly see, to my licnes, schipping ouer fro bodelines into goostlines' (*BPC* 167.14–16).

[50] Ogilvie-Thomson, p. 44, ll. 21–2, 29–30; p.47, l.20. On Rolle's lyrics, see Gillespie, 'Mystic's Foot', pp.212–24; Watson, *Invention*, pp.232–6.

The threshold can be a lonely and stormy place, as Julian of Norwich discovers in her seventh showing, when she experiences the ebb and flow of God's presence more than twenty times. When securely beholding God, she is 'fulfillid of the everlesting sekirnes migtily susteinid withoute any peynful drede' (c.15; p.17), and she says with St Paul 'Nothing shal depart me fro the charite of Criste'. When this is withdrawn she is 'turnyd' away from the sight of God and 'left to myselfe in hevynes and werines of my life and irkenes of myself'. Her return to self-consciousness must be borne like a cross, and in the stormy sea of her passover she cries out with St Peter 'Lord, save me, I perish'. Yet she learns that 'peyne is passand', a function of time:

> And therefore it is not Godds will that we folow the felynge of peyne in sorow and mornyng for hem, but sodenly passing over and holden us in endless likyng. (c.15; p.18)

Although briefly turned back from the threshold into the world of pain, she places this temporal and temporary suffering into the enclosing and transfiguring eternal perspective of her loving God. Increasingly confident in the love that underpins her showings, she is prepared to suffer the play of absence and presence as part of the game of love.[51]

The sense of God's absence leaves the contemplative 'al cold and drie, swetnesse haue we noon ne sauoure in deuocioun'.[52] In return for their labours in earthly sciences, Suso's scholars were rewarded with a drink which, far from assuaging their thirst, enhanced it 'generynge a maner of drynesse'. They receive only partial relief because they 'hadden as hit were a manere veyle vpon here faces'. Dryness is a feature of mystical experience and of mystical writing, figuring a thirst for release from time and language into unmediated presence. Julian confronts this in her

[51] Hugo Rahner, *Man at Play*, trans. B. Battershaw and E. Quinn, London, 1965; Robert Neale, *In Praise of Play: Towards a Psychology of Religion*, New York, 1969; Marion Glasscoe, 'Means of Showing: An Approach to Reading Julian of Norwich', in *Spatmittelalterliche Geistliche Literatur in der Nationalsprache*, 1, Analecta Cartusiana, 106 (1983), pp. 155–77, esp. pp. 159–60; Gillespie, 'Strange Images', pp. 141–3; Tixier, '*Good gamesumli pley*'; Gillespie and Ross, 'The Apophatic Image'; cf. the interesting comments on textual play in W. Iser, 'The Play of the Text', in *Languages of the Unsayable*, pp. 325–39, p. 336: 'Negativity is therefore far from negative in its effects, for it lures absence into presence, but by continually subverting that presence, turns it into a carrier for absence of which we would otherwise not know anything. Through these constant shifts, the play of the text uses negativity in a manner that epitomizes the interrelation between absence and presence'.

[52] *The Chastising of God's Children and the Treatise of Perfection of the Sons of God*, ed. J. Bazire and E. Colledge (Oxford, 1957), p. 98. The *Chastising* borrows from Suso's *Orologium* the metaphor of the play of absence and presence as the play of love (pp. 98–100).

eighth showing of the Passion, which steadfastly refuses to blossom into the kinds of ghostly sight and understanding that she has enjoyed in her previous showings.

In the previous chapters, she has begun to develop a subtle and sophisticated technique for communicating to her audience the multidimensional discourses of her visions. In particular, she has evolved effective strategies for showing, in her role as *mean* or intermediary, how the pains of the passion are wrapped in a timeless and enfolding garment of love.[53] Sin, suffering and the passion of Christ are all fettered in time, but she experiences and communicates how her showings constantly change perspective, liberating her from the causality of time, the blindness of man's limited perspective and the linearity of his reason into the freedom and clarity of the divine perspective. Her text seeks to escape the structurality of linear narrative to enjoy the sense of ineffable freedom that is God:

> And after, or God shewid ony words, he sufferd me to beholden in him a conable tyme, and all that I had sene, and all intellecte that was therein as the simplicite of the soule migte take it. Than he, without voice and openyng of lippis, formys in my soule these words: 'Herewith is the fend overcome'. These words seyd our lord menening his blissid passion as he shewid aforn. (c.13; p.15)

The boundaries between time and eternity, between language and the ineffable are skilfully blurred here. The 'conable tyme' is simultaneously the linear time in which the showing happens, the timeless beholding that she experiences within it and the convenient or necessary time at which the passion took place; the fullness of time in which God sent his only beloved son to save the world. All that she has seen and understood is also grounded in this divine 'conable tyme' in which all meanings meet and are comprehended. God's words to her eschew physical *means*: He *means* (or speaks) without *means* (or intermediary) and his *meaning* (intention *and* signification) is resonant for the meaning of all the showings of the passion.[54] Christ as the figural passover offers metaphorical release from the perspective of sin and time.

[53] This discussion of Julian continues and develops aspects of Gillespie and Ross, 'The Apophatic Image'.

[54] Julian's lexical exploration of the word *mene*, as a noun, adjective and verb, is one of the most dazzling illustrations of her verbal dexterity in creating semantic clusters or 'word-knots'. The nominal senses of *mene* include: sexual intercourse; fellowship; a companion; a course of action, method or way; an intermediary or negotiator; an agent or instrument; an intermediate state; something uniting extremes; mediation or help; argument, reason or discussion. Adjectivally it can mean 'partaking of the qualities or characteristics of two extremes'. As a verb it has the senses of: to intend to convey something; to signify; to say or express something; to remember something; to advise, admonish or urge somebody to do something. It can also have the sense of: to

The eighth showing, however, denies her access to such fullness of unmediated showing. Instead she is subjected to a virtuosic and relentless piling up of physical torment that seems endlessly fettered in time and affords her no wider perspective or release. Poised in awful timelessness, yet afflicted with time passing with surreal slowness, she sees Christ on the verge of death, on the threshold of passing over. Yet he lingers in torment, racked with thirst, and in long paratactic accumulations of agony we share his suffering and come to thirst for release:

> This blissid bodye dreid alone long tyme, with wryngyng of the naylys and weyte of the bodye; for I understode that for tenderness of the swete hands and of the swete fete, be the gretnes, hardhede and grevoushed of the naylis, the wounds wexid wider and the body saggid for weyte be long tyme hanging, and peircing and wrangyng of the hede and byndyng of the crowne, al bakyn with drye blode, with the swete heire clyngand, and the drye flesh, to the thornys, and the thornys to the flesh deyand; and in the begynnyng while the flesh was fresh and bledand, the continuant sytyng of the thornys made the wounds wyde. (c. 17; p.19)

Time hangs in the air in incessant present participles as we and Christ dry out like a cloth hung in the wind. Dryness informs the showing, reverberating and resonating in the hollowness of the grief and sorrow it generates in her and in us. The text hangs on the edge of time, poised on the abyss of the death of God:

> This longe pynyng semyd to me as if he had bene seven night ded, deyand, at the poynt of out passyng away, sufferand the last peyne. . .the swete body was so discoloryd, so drye, so clongen, so dedely and so petevous as he had be seven night dede, continuly deyand.
> (c.16; pp.18–19)

There is nothing metaphorical about this Christ. She receives no spiritual meaning or ghostly sight to liberate her from physical suffering. She is brought to share the bodily thirst of Christ in her sense of abandonment at the foot of the cross. The interpretative virtuosity of her earlier showings is stunned by the sheer brutality of what she is shown. The cold wind of affective horror dries out the richness of her response. She seeks to recapture the 'beholdyng' of her apophatic joy by focusing on the crown of thorns, but finds the 'marvelling' of her discursive consciousness indivisibly coupled to it:

complain; to cry out for help; to pity, sympathize with or condole with somebody. A further adjectival set of senses coheres around notions of lowness, inferiority and smallness which resonates with Julian's sense of humble self-emptying. (*MED*, sv *mene*, n.; *menen*, v.) Julian's exploitation of the polysemousness of this word means that it becomes the meeting place for many of her key ideas, perceptions, responses and expressions.

> This continuid a while and sone it began to chongyn, and I beheld and merveled how it migt ben. (c.17; p.19)

If she hopes for release from this all too present absence into the absent presence of the apophatic, she is cruelly denied. The images loop around each other in concentric circles of suffering:

> And than I saw it was for it began to dreyen and stynte a party of the weyte and sette abute the garland. And thus it envyronyd al aboute, as it were garland upon garland. The garland of thornys was dyed with the blode, and the tother garland and the hede, al was on colour, as cloderyd blode whan it is drey.

Her relentlessly literal exegesis discerns four kinds of drying: bloodless; pain following after; hanging in the air as a cloth hung to dry; and 'that the bodily kind askyd licour and ther was no maner of comfort mynystid to hym in al his wo and disese'. Almost imperceptibly, Christ's bodily dryness becomes an image of her own thirst for some *licour* from this showing. Like Christ on the cross, Julian feels abandoned: Lord save me I perish. Her compassion with the thirst of Christ, her sense of desolation leads her to repent of her earlier request to have 'more trew minde in the passion of Christe' (c.2; p.2). Just as she shadows Mary in the annunciation in her conceiving of her showings and in her labour pains to understand and articulate them, now she shadows the compassionate Mary at the foot of the cross in the darkness of Golgotha by the sword of sorrow that pierces her:

> Here felt I sothfastly that I lovyd Criste so mech above myselfe that there was no payne that might be suffrid leke to the sorow that I had to se him in payne. (c.17; p.20)

The glib metaphoricity of dying to the world, bearing the cross of self-consciousness and acquiring the mind of Christ is transfigured in the crucible of her radical sense of sharing in Christ's *kenosis* of love:

> Her saw I a gret onyng betwyx Christe and us, to myn understondyng; for whan he was in payne, we were in peyne. . .Thus was our lord Iesus nawted for us, and we stond al in this maner nowtid with him; and shal done til we come to his blisse. (c.18; pp.20,21)

Christ is the way and he is the door. This humbling episode, and her obedient but grief-stricken response to it, added to her sense of her own partial responsibility for it, take her to the threshold of affective tolerance. She challenges the facile and superficial affectivity of most meditative engagement with the passion, taking us to the limits of language, deep within the metaphor of spiritual thirst.

When, much later, she returns to the thirst of Christ to explore its spiritual meanings, the difference is dramatic. Her showings have moved away from the details of the passion into the apophatic wound in the side of Christ. Increasingly her showings deal with words rather than images. Christ speaks to her in cryptic, performative utterances which Julian glosses and expounds:

> And with this our gode lord seyd ful blisfully 'Lo how that I lovid the', as if he had seid: 'My derling, behold and se thy lord, thy God, that is thy maker and thyn endles ioy. Se what likyng and bliss I have in thy salvation, and for my love enioy now with me'. (c.24; p.26)

Her glosses on Christ's words are confident because she believes herself to be at one in Christ's meaning. She places herself at the meeting place of the ineffable and the discursive: 'as if he had seid'. She tentatively transcribes into language – 'as it may be seid, that is to mene' – her own glosses or understandings of these liminal sayings:

> This is the understondyng simply as I can sey of this blissed word: 'Lo how I lovid the'.

Julian is increasingly loquacious on behalf of the ineffable, interpreting Christ's cryptic utterances at length and in detail, 'as be the menyng of these swete wordes, as if he seyd' (c.25; p.27).

Christ's invitation to Julian to see Mary ('Wilt the se hir?'(c.25; p.27)) receives lengthy exposition as 'the most likyng word that he might have gove me'. The *likyng word* is the word that likens Mary to Christ. Through her roles of obedient recipient, suffering mother and crowned Queen of Heaven, Mary offers a paradigm for all Christian lives. The word becomes flesh and dwells with her; she is transfigured and likened to Christ by the actions of her life and her bliss after death. Similarly, Julian's text suggests, we must conceive, give birth, suffer and die with and for the word, as Julian shows herself doing. She 'likens' herself to Mary and to Christ, becoming, like Mary, the bearer of the word for the benefit of mankind. *Likyng words* offer bliss and joy because they offer the route to oneing with Christ.

It is no surprise, therefore, that Julian engages with the keystone text of the ineffable tradition, God's words to Moses: 'I am that I am' (Exodus 3: 14), which in their refusal of referentiality and denial of the tyranny of grammar and syntax enact the ineradicable ineffability of the apophatic heart of God. She sees Christ 'more gloryfyed, as to my syte, than I saw him beforne', and in this state of transfiguration, she hears him repeatedly proclaim his ineffable essence and energies:

> I it am, I it am; I it am that is hyest; I it am that thou lovist; I it am that thou lykyst; I it am that thou servist; I it am that thou longyst; I it am that thou desyrist; I it am that thou menyst; I it am that is al; I it am that holy church prechyth and teachyth the; I it am that shewed me here to thee. (c.26; p.28)

In response to the ineffable, she effaces her own role as *mene* or intermediary, yielding the hermeneutical initiative to God:

> The nombre of the words passyth my witte and al my vnderstondyng and al my mights, and it arn the hyest, as to my syte; for therein is comprehendid – I cannot tellyn.[55]

Turning away from language and interpretation to face into the presence, she reports that

> the ioy I saw in the shewyng of them passyth al that herte may willen and soule may desire; and therefore the words be not declaryd here but every man after the grace that God gevyth him in vnderstondyng and lovyng receive hem in our lords menyng.

The reward for yielding up the hermeneutical initiative is the passover into transcendent joy.

Similarly, when, much earlier, she says of her ghostly sight that 'I cannot ne may not shew it as hopinly ne as fully as I wolde' (c.9; p.11), she is both affirming the limits of language and deferring to the initiative of the Almighty:

> But I truste in our lord God almightie that he shal of his godenes, and for yowr love, make yow to take it more gostly and more swetely than I can or may telle it.[56]

In chapter 31, 'the good lord answerid to al the question and doubts that I myte makyn, sayeing ful comfortably:

> I may makyn althing wele; I can make althing wele and I wil make althyng wele and I shall make althyng wele; and thou shal se thisself that al maner of thyng shal be wele. (p.31)

Julian understands these five utterances to refer to the persons of the trinity, their unity and the inevitable oneing of mankind into the trinity. Exploiting the tenses and moods of the verbs, she explores the immanent workings of God in time and eternity. God 'wil be onclosid in rest and pece' in these five 'words' and by this means the ghostly thirst of Christ will have an end. God's intention is to occupy the

[55] For similar strategies of effacement in the *Cloud*-author, see Tixier's discussions in '*Good gamesumli pley*' and '*This louely blinde werk*'.

[56] Cf. the similar gesture in the *Cloud*, c.26, 62. 17–21: 'þan schalt þou fele þin affeccion enflaumid wiþ þe fiire of his loue, fer more þen I kan telle þee, or may, or wile, at þis tyme. For of þat werke þat falliþ only to God dar I not take apon me to speke wiþ my blabryng fleschely tonge; and, schortly to say, al-þof I durst, I wolde not'. Hilton in *Scale* 2.40 (p. 280) voices similar doubts, but ventures on a description 'because I think Love asks and Love commands'.

ineffable space defined by the *perichoresis* of the Trinity and man's union with it in a oneing of love. God is not enclosed by the words, but he is enclosed in the words, like the Word enclosed in flesh in the incarnation and the mysteries enclosed in the Grail. God's will is for us to see for ourselves that all manner of thing shall be well. His promise is to make the wounded text of our understanding whole.[57] His longing for man is a mirror image of man's longing for God, and it meets in the incarnation of the word:

> Therefore this is his thirst: a love longyng to have us al togeder hole in him to his blis, as to my syte; for we be not now as fully hole in him as we shal be then. (p.32)

The bodily thirst of Christ was in time and torment. The ghostly thirst is eternal and generates a reciprocal thirst and longing in us. The bodily thirst generated 'in time of passion' was for escape from literal torment *into* metaphor. The ghostly thirst generated by the mystical text is for escape *from* metaphor into the paradise of the transcendental signified.

Julian ends her work with the comment that 'this booke is begunne be Gods gift and his grace, but it is not yet performid, as to my syte' (c.86; p.102).[58] The lesson of love showed in her book is grounded finally in the prayer of kenotic surrender in her very first showing:

> God, of thy goodnesse, give me thyselfe; for thou art enow to me and I may nothing aske that is less that may be full worshippe to thee. And if I aske anything that is lesse, ever me wantith, but only in thee I have all. And these words arn full lovesome to the soul and full nere touchen the will of God and his goodness; for his goodness comprehendith all his creatures and all his blissid works, and overpassith without end, for he is the endleshede. (c.5; p.6)

The words *touch* the will of God in that they both approximate to it in a performative utterance of intellectual *kenosis* and they gropingly gesture towards it. The words and images that God has given to us as *means* of approaching him are all functions of his goodness but cannot comprehend it: 'the goodness of God is the heyest prayer and it comith downe to the lowest party of our nede' (c.6; p.7).

57 The notion of wounded language derives from the work of Michel de Certeau. See A. Lion, 'Le Discours Blessé: Sur le Langage Mystique selon Michel de Certeau', *Révue des Sciences Philosophiques et Religieuses* 71 (1987) 405–20; McGinn, *Foundations*, pp. 310–13.

58 See the similar sentiment in *Cloud* c.73; 129.4–12; the orthodox glossator of *The Mirror of Simple Souls* comments: ' Lo, ȝe þat studien þis booke, þus ȝe moste wiþynne ȝoursilf glose suche derke wordis, and if ȝe may not come soone to þe vndirstondinge þerof, offriþ it mekeli up to God, and bi custom of ofte redynge þeron ȝe schulen come þerto' (Doiron, pp. 313–4).

The thirst for comprehension, the desire to pass over the threshold of language and the longing to escape from time into eternity: all are transfigured, circumscribed and definitively interpreted by the ineffable goodness of God, 'for we arn al on in Goddis menyng'. Although, through grace, we may begin to write the book of contemplation, we cannot hope to complete or perform it in this life:

> We may never blyn of willing ne of longing till we have him in fullhede of joy, and than may we no more willen; for he will that we be occupyed in knoweing and loveing til the tyme that we shall be fulfilled in hevyn. (c.6; p.7)

The fullness of presence will efface images and language, for 'the godenes of God is ever hole and more nere to us *withoute any likenes*'. Then, finally, Wisdom's scholars will quench their thirst for meaning without means:

> drinkynge þe watere of helefulle wisdam þat came out of his mowþe, þei were made so drunkyn þat þei forȝetene hemself and alle oþer worldely þingis, hauynge here hertis and here eyȝen euer vpwarde to þe mayster and feruently rauysched into his loue and heuenely þingis.[59]

[59] *The Seven Points of True Wisdom*, pp. 9–10.

UT PICTURA POESIS: A CRITIQUE OF ROBERT JORDAN'S *CHAUCER AND THE SHAPE OF CREATION*

JAMES SIMPSON

I have a problem, to which I'd like to confess. I can't help talking about authors. I know I shouldn't, but when I'm teaching Chaucer, say, I find myself irresistibly drawn to hypothesizing about authorial strategy. I find no other way of talking about Chaucer's poetry than to adduce the presence of an author behind the rhetorical surface of narratives, and behind the narrators of those poems. This is pretty bad, I know, but what's worse is that I attribute agency to narrators as well. Once one has accepted the idea of an author, after all, then it's only a short, slippery slope to narrators, since Chaucer's narrators themselves act like authors so often, crafting tales for an audience. I tend to do this even when Chaucer is debunking the very idea of authorship.

Some of my readers will be shaking their heads sadly already: here, they'll rightly say, is a chronic case of intentionalism, that critical sin which was supposed to have been eradicated in the nineteen forties by New Criticism, and which has been subject to ever more powerful remedies, most recently Deconstruction, for which presence and agency are a deceptive mirage.

If it offers any mitigation of my sorry case, might I say that I have tried to resist temptation: I still try to avoid use of the word 'character' in my teaching and writing; I readily acknowledge that just because tales are told *by* someone, that does not mean that those tales are *about* the teller; and I can see that literary institutions (genres) and social institutions both modify any simple notion we might have about free-floating agents. But for all this effort, there I am again in class, talking about the Pardoner's, or Chaucer's unspoken *strategy*, attributing agency and presence to speakers.

I think my troubles began when I read Robert Jordan's *Chaucer and the Shape of Creation*:[1] I found this book so persuasive in its account of the surface features of Chaucer's style – the constructed, delimited, inorganic quality of that style. This was extremely refreshing for a student wanting to escape from the dramatic principle of reading

[1] Robert M. Jordan, *Chaucer and the Shape of Creation, The Aesthetic Possibilities of Inorganic Form* (Cambridge, Mass., 1967).

Chaucer's works. Jordan, like Muscatine before him,[2] had decisively made the due distinctions between life and art by pointing to the crafted, multi-faceted, inconsistent surface of Chaucer's poetry. Accounting for meaning in Chaucer's works without at the same time taking full account of their broken rhetorical surface was, after these books, thankfully impossible. But with Jordan this gain brought an attendant prohibition, that we should no longer try to go beyond that broken, inconsistent surface.

For Jordan went further than Muscatine, by denying a unifying agency behind the inconsistent surface of Chaucer's poetry. Because the rhetorical surface could not be accounted for in any realist aesthetic, then neither should we seek the consistency of voice we look for in realist fiction. With regard to the *Merchant's Tale*, for example, he says that all attempts to characterize the Merchant as speaker 'are pursued on the assumption that there *is* a consistency which must be revealed',[3] and he concludes his discussion by saying this: 'Structural and stylistic evidence seems to indicate conclusively that there is no single viewpoint governing the narrative. The tale is less a unified presentation than a composite of several narrating attitudes and positions, often mutually contradictory'.[4] Jordan, who wrote this in 1967, must have felt like history had turned his way in the 1980s, with the arrival of postmodernism, which, like Jordan, reverses the standard relation between speaker and text, to the point where the speaker evaporates as a presence altogether. And in the last few years, a number of books have appeared in Jordan's tracks, all of which are concerned to attack ironic readings whose premise is a unified narratorial agent. This is true of Jordan's own, recent book, and of, say, the newer books by Lawton and Leicester.[5]

My confession of the sin of intentionalism might continue indefinitely; but I suspect you have already guessed at the as yet unstated intention of my confession: like all interesting penitents in medieval literature (Gower's Amans, Chaucer's Pardoner) I'm not really interested in absolution. I'd rather spread the contagion. I could do this in various ways – by analysing passages from Chaucer, and perceiving the moments at which reference outside the text to an authorizing agent is necessary; or I could step back to thirteenth-century literary theory of the kind

[2] Charles Muscatine, *Chaucer and the French Tradition, A Study in Style and Meaning* (Berkeley, Los Angeles and London, 1957).

[3] Jordan, *Chaucer and the Shape of Creation*, p. 146.

[4] Ibid., p. 150.

[5] Robert M. Jordan, *Chaucer's Poetics and the Modern Reader* (Berkeley, Los Angeles and London, 1987); David Lawton, *Chaucer's Narrators* (Cambridge, 1985); H. Marshall Leicester, *The Disenchanted Self: Representing the Subject in the 'Canterbury Tales'* (Berkeley, Los Angeles and Oxford, 1990).

elucidated by Alastair Minnis in the last volume of this Symposium – theory which justifies the use of ironic *personae*.[6] But I would like to step back even further, to twelfth century literary theory. Like Jordan (and, one should add in this context, like J. A. W.Bennett), I believe that the late twelfth century is a critical cultural horizon for late fourteenth-century poets. I want in particular to examine one aesthetic idea, that of *ut pictura poesis*, as it is found in Alan of Lille's *De planctu Naturae* (ca.1160–70) and *Anticlaudianus* (1182–3). In Alan's exploitation of this idea, we can see not only an extraordinary defence of poetry as a form of knowledge, but more importantly for my present purpose, we can see how the notion of agency is central to this aesthetic.

I

Marshall Leicester describes Jordan as 'the most thoroughgoing and principled opponent of the notion of consistent impersonation in Chaucer's work', and he says that Jordan's opposition is based on 'theoretical and historical grounds'.[7] The background to which Leicester refers is Neoplatonic cosmological theory, presented by Jordan in Chapter 1 of *The Shape of Creation*. Rightly perceiving that there is an intimate connection between cosmological and poetic theory, Jordan argues that the Platonic maker of the *Timaeus* is a 'master mathematician' – 'the universe is proportional; its unique structure is describable only in the quantitative and completely rational language of mathematics'.[8] The upshot of this cosmological theory for secular poetics was, according to Jordan, a concept of 'quantitative or "inorganic" art, that is, an art concerned with the management and disposition of the fixed elements constituting a preconceived whole'.[9] In this formulation, we might notice, Jordan does acknowledge the agency of a maker, with words like 'management', 'disposition' and 'preconceived whole'. But he wants to place the emphasis of his argument not on a controlling presence behind a work, but rather on the inorganic, prefabricated parts by which it is constituted.

We can observe Jordan's focus on the rhetorical surface at the expense of a controlling presence behind it in a variety of ways: he says, for example, that the 'quantitative mode of reasoning' is at the 'heart of

[6] A. J. Minnis, 'Theorizing the Rose: Commentary Tradition in the *Querelle de la Rose*', in *Poetics: Theory and Practice in Medieval English Literature*, Piero Boitani and Anna Torti, eds. (Cambridge, 1991), pp. 15–36.

[7] Leicester, *The Disenchanted Self*, p. 3, n. 1.

[8] Jordan, *Chaucer and the Shape of Creation*, p. 18.

[9] Ibid., p. 42.

medieval thinking about the nature of Creation'.[10] This points towards the formal rather than the efficient cause of creation – towards what creation looks like rather than how it was generated in the first place; as the chapter (and book) proceeds, the Platonic maker is quietly replaced by the parts of his creation. In talking about Neoplatonic poetics, Jordan speaks of how 'a strong sense of separation between the superficial veil and the true essence beneath it' produced Dante's formulation of poetry as a '*bella menzogna*';[11] at the end of the chapter, we are (historically) back with Geoffrey of Vinsauf, whose account of amplification is 'conceived in abstract, quantitative terms, exclusive of any consideration of content or substantive meaning'.[12] Here 'the strong sense of separation' between external shape and inner meaning has become a total rupture. By the time we get to the chapter on the *Merchant's Tale*, this rupture is taken for granted: 'Structural and stylistic evidence seems to indicate conclusively that there is no single viewpoint governing the narrative. The tale is less a unified presentation than a composite of several narrating attitudes and positions, often mutually contradictory'.[13]

In this last citation, we can see what we all knew already – that aesthetic ideas carry immediate interpretative consequences: in this case, Jordan would have it that the aesthetic idea of inorganic structure should constrain our interpretation of Chaucer's poetry by prohibiting reference to 'a single viewpoint'. I totally agree with Jordan on a number of points: that understanding of poetic theory should embrace scientific, especially cosmological, theory; and that aesthetic ideas have immediate interpretative consequences. Where I disagree with Jordan is in his account of 'Timaean' aesthetics. On the point of relating works back to a single maker, I think Jordan could not be more wrong. Whether or not his error about Timaean aesthetics makes him equally wrong about the interpretation of Chaucer's poetry is another question, which I will not have space to investigate here. Chaucer may be sensitive to a range of factors which displace authorial subjectivity in ways unconsidered by his twelfth-century predecessors. But let us focus on Jordan's chosen point of departure, 'Timaean' aesthetics.

II

The 'argument' of the *Timaeus* is built around, and itself designed to provoke, analogies between different discourses. The fundamental

10 Jordan, *Chaucer and the Shape of Creation*, p. 20.
11 Ibid., p. 34.
12 Ibid., pp. 42–3.
13 Ibid., p. 150.

analogy is that between the structure of the universe as macrocosm and that of man as microcosm. From this basic comparison, at once structural and ontological, analogies between many other discourses become possible. The set of comparisons which most concerns us now is that between divine, natural and human making. In his commentary on the *Timaeus*, Calcidius remarks that there are three kinds of 'work' (*opus*) – of God, of Nature, and of the human artificer. Calcidius himself does not discuss human making in his development of this point,[14] but his twelfth-century readers certainly did. Although they do not discuss *poets* as makers, twelfth-century thinkers associated with Chartres do bring the analogy between divine and human making into very sharp focus. In his gloss (1144–9) on the *Timaeus*, for example, William of Conches defines God's wisdom as the formal cause of the world, since God formed the world according to the pattern of his wisdom. William immediately goes on to make a comparison with a human maker:

> As, indeed, an artisan, if he wishes to make something, first disposes it in his mind; afterwards, having sought the material, he works according to his mental pattern; so too the creator, before he should create anything, first had it in his mind, and then fulfilled it in act. It is this which is called by Plato the world archetype: 'world' because it contains everything which is in the world; 'archetype' because it is the principle form (or model).
>
> Ut enim faber, volens aliquid fabricare, prius illud in mente disponit, postea, quesita materia, iuxta mentem suam operatur, sic Creator, antequam aliquid crearet, in mente illud habuit, deinde opere illud adimplevit. Hec eadem a Platone dicitur archetypus mundus: mundus quia omnia continet que in mundo sunt, archetypus id est principalis forma.[15]

We find this comparison between different makers in both the literary and discursive works of Alan of Lille.[16] Unlike his 'Chartrian' forebears, however, Alan consistently uses words associated with painting (and other visual arts) to describe the act by which the inner, mental form,

[14] Calcidius, *Timaeus a Calcidio Translatus Commentarioque Instructus*, edited by J. H. Waszink (London and Leiden, 1962), ch. 23, ll. 10–12, p. 73.

[15] William of Conches, *Glosae super Platonem*, edited by E. Jeauneau (Paris, 1965), 27d, cap.32, p. 99.

[16] See, for example, *Expositio Prosae de Angelis*, in *Alain de Lille, Textes Inédits*, edited by Marie-Therése d'Alverny, Etudes de Philosophie Mediévale, 52 (Paris, 1965), 194–217, pp. 199–200; the comparison between Nature and God as makers is essential to both the *De planctu Naturae* and the *Anticlaudianus*. See also Jean de Meun, *Roman de la Rose*, 16005–148 (though here the comparison is between Nature and the human artificer; God is omitted. It is significant that immediately after this account of how human makers imitate Nature, Jean himself seems to deny that by refusing to describe her (16165–248)). Dante also makes the comparison (central to his art as a whole), *Inferno* XI.97–105. See also Chaucer, *Physician's Tale*, 9–28.

produces a material product.[17] Take, for example, the way in which Alan addresses God in his prayer for inspiration in Book V of the *Anticlaudianus*. After describing God as 'enclosing all things by numbers', Alan goes on to win God's favour by describing to God God's own formation of the world:

> Qui rerum species et mundi sensilis umbram
> Ducis ab exemplo mundi mentalis, eumdem
> Exterius pingens terrestris ymagine forme. (V.288–90)[18]

> . . .who bring the species of things and the shadow of the sensible world from the exemplar of the conceptual world, painting it exteriorly in the image of an earthly form.

Or again, a few lines later, God is described as the formal cause of the world, '*dum pingis eam*' (V.295). And if God creates the world by painting his inner idea with the image of external form, so too, obviously, does he create the soul of man by a kind of painting. Fronesis explains her mission to ask for a newly created soul by saying that only God, not Nature, is capable of creating a soul:

> In superis nil iuris habens animamque creare
> Nescia, quam sola pictoris dextra superni
> Format . . . (V.217–19)

> Having no rights in the heavenly realm, and ignorant of how to create a soul, which only the right hand of the heavenly painter forms . . .

Like the 'divine painter', Nature, too, works by painting her works. In Book I she declares the inability of her art to produce a soul; she defines her art as especially one of painting:

> Ergo cum nostra genituram regula talem
> Nesciat et tantam stupeat pictura figuram
> Occasumque manus talem patiatur ad ortum . . . (I.388–90)[19]

[17] Two earlier studies have noted the frequency with which Alan uses the lexis of painting: J. Huizinga, *Uber die Verknüpfung des Poetischen mit dem Theologischen bei Alanus de Insulis*, in Mededeelingen der Koninklijke Akademie van Wetenschappen Afdeeling Letterkunde, 74, series B, 6 (Amsterdam, 1932), Section VI, pp. 59–65; and Edgar de Bruyne, *Etudes d'Esthetique Mediévale*, 2 vols (Brugges, 1946), II.296–8. de Bruyne goes no further than to remark on the lexis of painting; Huizinga's excellent study is, like mine, concerned with the philosophical sense of '*pictura*' in Alan's works; my study is more comprehensive and differently directed.

[18] All citations from the *Anticlaudianus* are from the edition by R. Bossuat (Paris, 1955). The translations are based on *Alan of Lille, Anticlaudianus, or the Good and Perfect Man*, translated by James J. Sheridan (Toronto, 1973). I freely diverge from this translation, however, without signalling the divergence.

[19] I emend Bossuat's reading '*nostram*' to '*nostra*' in I.388.

> Since, then, our rule knows no such birth, and our power to paint is staggered at so great a model, and our hand suffers failure at the very beginning of such a work. . .

In the *De planctu* the concept of Nature as painter is given greater force. After the description of the pictures on Nature's dress, we see Nature herself in the act of painting:

> In latericiis uero tabulis arundinei stili ministerio uirgo uarias rerum picturaliter suscitabat imagines. Pictura tamen, subiacenti materie familiariter non coherens, uelociter euanescendo moriens, nulla imaginum post se relinquebat uestigia. (IV.3–6, p. 821)[20]

> With the aid of a reed-pen, the maiden called up various images of things by drawing on clay tablets. The picture, however, did not cling closely to the underlying material but, quickly fading and dying, left no trace of the images behind.

The works of God and Nature, then, are seen as related by Alan, and as both acts of painting. What about the works of humans? Speech itself is represented by Alan as the act of painting an inner idea: when Fronesis speaks, she is said to 'paint her mind' ('*mentem . . . pingit*', I.324), or to 'paint her thoughts in speech' ('*tali pingit concepta loquela*', V.177).[21] But whereas the earlier reception of the *Timaeus* had not focused specifically on the art of poetry as an example of human making, Alan does. And, as with God and Nature, the human act of making poetry is presented as painterly. Comparison between poetry and painting is very frequent in both Alan's literary works, but especially so in the *Anticlaudianus*.

We might approach this set of examples of human making, and in particular of poetic making, by looking to the description of Rhetoric, in Book III. Rhetoric is said to be especially beautiful through her knowledge of painting:

> Cui magis arridet species et gracia forme,
> Quod comites multa pictoris preuenit arte,
> Totam pictoris artem sub pectore claudens. (III.148–50)

[20] All citations from the *De planctu Naturae* are from the edition by N. M. Häring, *Studi Medievali*, ser. 3, 19 (1978), 797–879. The translations are based on Alan of Lille, *Plaint of Nature*, translated by James J. Sheridan, Medieval Sources in Translation, 26 (Toronto, 1980). I freely diverge from this translation without signalling differences.

[21] I take Fronesis to represent the highest faculty of the human soul, the intellect. See James Simpson, 'The Information of Alan of Lille's *Anticlaudianus*: A Preposterous Interpretation', *Traditio* (forthcoming). Nature's speech in the *De planctu* is produced on a Timaean model: 'Que. . .mentales intellectus materialis vocis michi depinxit imagine, et quasi archetipa verba idealiter preconcepta vocaliter produxit in actum' (VI.11–13, p. 825). See also *Anticlaudianus*, III.340–358 for a description of the way in which a human idea is carried across into material form.

> On whom beauty and grace of form smile, since she outstrips her peers in many of the painter's skills and enfolds in her bosom the complete art of the painter.

And the emphasis of her skill as a painter is put, as we might expect, on the brilliance of her surface colour, a brilliance described by Alan in a passage which is itself exuberantly colourful rhetorically. Rhetoric's dress,

> . . . picturata colore
> Multiplici, gaudet uarios inducta colores.
> Hic pictoris ope splendet pictura coloris
> Retorici, sic picturam pictura colorat. (III.166–9)

> . . . painted in a variety of tints, it rejoices that it is overlaid with various colours. Here with the painter's aid gleams a picture of Rhetoric's colour, and thus a picture adds colour to a picture.

Here Alan's witty point is really that there are *three*, not two pictures: for just as the picture embroidered on Rhetoric's dress is a colourful picture of the pictures of rhetoric, so too, obviously enough, is Alan's own rhetoric a further (highly coloured) picture of the first two.

This description of rhetoric as a painter raises the most obvious level at which the phrase *ut pictura poesis* might apply: just as the painter uses colours, so too does the poet adorn his work with the colours of rhetoric. But in the context of all the other uses of the word '*pictor*' or '*pingere*' we have observed, we can see that the connection between the colour of poetry and painting is for Alan only the most superficial of connections between the two arts.[22] If the connection stays at the level of rhetorical schemes alone, of verbal embellishment, or 'colours', then it remains, literally, superficial. For in all the other examples we have observed, the

[22] As the title of my essay evokes Horace, it should be mentioned here that the topos '*ut pictura poesis*' of *De arte poetica* (l. 361) was not understood by late twelfth-century writers of poetic treatises to be restricted to the superficial level of verbal colouring by rhetorical schemes. See Geoffrey of Vinsauf, *Documentum de arte versificandi*: 'Superficies enim verborum ornata, nisi sana et commendabili nobilitetur sententia, similis est pictura vili quae placet longius stanti, sed displicet propius intuenti. Sic et ornatus verborum sine ornatu sententiarum audienti placet, diligenti intuenti displicet. Superficies autem verborum ornata cum ornatu sententiae similis est egregiae picturae, quae quidem, quando propius inspicitur, tanto commendabilior invenitur. Unde dicit Horatius: "Ut pictura poesis" '. Edited by E.Faral, *Les Arts Poétiques du xiie et du xiiie siècle*, Bibliothèque de l'Ecole des Hautes Etudes, 238 (Paris, 1924), III.2, p. 285. See also Geoffrey's *Poetria Nova*, ll. 737–55, in Faral, *Les Arts Poétiques*, p. 220. These texts are clearly drawing not only the connection of painting and poetry from Horace, but also elaborating the close up/long distance comparison made by Horace in the *De arte poetica* (ll. 361–5). Horace does not, however, himself dispraise the poem which pleases only from a distance; for the Horatian idea, see W.Trimpi, '*Ut Pictura Poesis*', *Traditio* 34 (1978) 29–73.

idea of painting is adduced to evoke not the idea of colour, but rather that of form, and especially the way in which the outer form of the painting is modelled on the form, or idea, within the mind of the painter. Three of the words most often associated with the lexis of painting in Alan's works are '*forma*', '*figura*', and '*imago*'. Alan is using each of these words in a philosophical sense, where each can designate both the outer shape of an artefact, or, in the case of '*forma*' and '*figura*', the inner, mental form upon which the artefact is modelled. The notion of painting is for Alan an active one, designating the action of drawing an inner exemplar out into material shape: God, we remember, 'draws' the material world 'from the exemplar of the world in the divine mind, painting it on the exterior with the image of an earthly form' (V.289–90). The act of painting is formative rather than merely colorative: it resides in the action of maintaining an inner form through the process of shaping a material image. To read a painting, then, involves appreciating not merely its colourful surface, but also penetrating its inner sense, or form.

I want to elaborate this philosophical conception of poetry as painting in a moment, because we can see in it a powerful defence of poetry as a form of knowledge. By way of ending this set of examples about poetic makers as painters, however, let me adduce a few of the many points in the *Anticlaudianus* at which Alan makes a connection between poetry and painting. Classical rhetorical treatises recommended the practice of bringing action before the eyes of listeners, using technical terms like '*demonstratio*', '*enargeia*', '*illustratio*', and '*evidentia*' to describe the techniques by which an orator might do this. What they generally mean is simply to speak in such a way as to make the audience believe that they are present at the scene being described, by bringing the events 'before the eyes' of an audience.[23] The treatises do not mention a more specific case of '*illustratio*', that of describing an actual artefact in poetry. Like many other late medieval poets, Alan includes description of such visual artefacts in his poetry.[24] When we look to these we can see how, even at a

23 See *Rhetorica Ad Herennium*, edited by Harry Caplan (Cambridge, Mass., 1954), IV.55.68: 'Demonstratio est cum ita verbis res exprimitur ut geri negotium et res ante oculos esse videatur' (p. 404); Quintilian, *Institutio Oratoria*, 4 vols, edited by H. E. Butler (Cambridge, Mass., 1939), VI.ii.32: 'Insequitur enargeia, quae a Cicerone illustratio et evidentia nominatur, quae non tam dicere videtur quam ostendere; et adfectus non aliter, quam si rebus intersimus, sequentur' (II, pp. 434–6) (though the term '*illustratio*' does not appear in Latin before Quintilian).

24 Take, for example, Chrétien de Troyes, *Erec et Enide* 6651–6728 (descriptions of faldstools and embroidered cloak); Dante, *Purgatorio* X.28–102; XII.16–69 (bas-reliefs of humility and pride respectively); Guillaume de Lorris, *Roman de la Rose*, 139–462 (paintings on the outer side of the walls enclosing the garden of Love); Chaucer, *Knight's Tale* 1914–2088 (descriptions of the temples of Venus, Mars and Diana respectively, which contain both paintings and sculptures); *House of Fame* 140–475 should be mentioned here, where writing and painting are deliberately confused in

first glance, they provide models of visual art by which we might understand the making of poetry.

In Nature's palace, we find two murals, one depicting ideal natural models, the other images of natural deformity. A brief look at the words used to describe these and other pictures in the poem reveals how the lexis of writing and painting are inextricably intertwined: '*picture gracia scribit*' (I.119); Virgil is depicted 'colouring' (I.142); Walter of Chatillon is said to fail as he tries to 'paint' (I.169) (both these last being paintings of poets 'painting'); what Nature gives is shown by the fable of the painting, '. . . *inscriptum calamis picture fabula monstrat*' (I.186). Or on the dresses of the Arts are embroidered further pictures; these images are described as '*scriptura*' (II.509); reading them is like reading a book ('*velud in libro legitur*'); in another, although the picture is silent, it 'speaks through writing' ('*pictura loquens scripto*', III.299); 'the letter' of a further picture proclaims the original masters of Geometry: '*Illic artifices pictoris littera clamat*' (III.522); and, finally, one 'reads' the images on the dress of the *puella poli* ('*Hic legitur*. . .', V.147).

III

For Alan, then, the arts of writing and painting are equivalents. And, as we have already seen, the comparison between poetry and painting does not reside essentially in the surface colouring processes common to each. The principal connection is, rather, formal – to do with the way in which a visual image carries a mental form across into matter. When we read a painting, we are implicitly being asked to read back into this process of translation. So looking at visual images involves a dynamic relationship between three elements: the image itself, the mind of the viewer, and the mind of the maker implied in the image. The image pleases the senses, but once we apprehend it mentally, it activates a sense of its maker's presence in our mind. We can see this dynamic relationship between image, mind and maker in the description of the images embroidered on Grammar's dress:

> Hec artis series seriatim picta propinat
> Delicias oculis et menti fercula donat,
> Nam pictor predoctus eam descripserat, immo
> Plus pictore potens, picturaque clamitat illum. (II.472–5)
>
> This painted series of pictures serially sets pleasures before the eyes

the abbreviation (and distortion) of Virgil's *Aeneid*; *Parlement of Foules* 284–94 (lovers painted on the walls of Venus's temple).

> and offers feasts to the mind; for an extremely learned painter had painted it, or rather one more powerful than any painter, and the painting declares him.

The image appeals both to the senses and to the mind of its recipient; and this experience itself produces a sharp sense of the '*pictor predoctus*' behind the image.

'*Pictor predoctus*': this could easily be a covert reference to Alan himself, a '*predoctus*' philosopher at the forefront of various disciplines in the late twelfth century, including the newly defined discipline of theology.[25] But once we look at Alan's kind of theology, we might initially be surprised to find him praising the power of images. For one of the key texts behind Alan's theology is the *De trinitate* of Boethius.[26] And in Book II of that work Boethius defines the methods of the speculative disciplines: physics, mathematics and theology. For Boethius (and for Alan) theology is not that wide ranging discipline it was to become in the thirteenth century, but rather an intensely philosophical study of pure form. In it, says Boethius, we should procede 'intellectually', by which he means *without* recourse to images. Alan cites the relevant text many times in his works of speculative theology:

> . . .in theology we should procede intellectually, and we will not be diverted to play with imaginations, but will simply apprehend that form which is pure form and no image.
>
> . . .in divinis intellectualiter versari oportebit neque deduci ad imaginationes, sed potius ipsam inspicere formam quae vere forma neque imago est.[27]

The key distinction here is between 'form' and 'image', where 'form' designates the pure idea, and 'image' its realization in matter. But given

[25] For the emergence of theology as an academic discipline in the twelfth century, see G. R. Evans, *Old Arts and New Theology, The Beginnings of Theology as an Academic Discipline* (Oxford, 1980); for Alan's place within that, see Marie-Therése d'Alverny, 'Alain de Lille et la Theologia', in *L'homme devant Dieu. Mélanges offerts au Père Henri de Lubac*, 3 vols (Paris, 1964), II, pp. 111–28, and G. R. Evans, *Alan of Lille. The Frontiers of Theology in the Later Twelfth Century* (Cambridge, 1983).

[26] I present the evidence for this in 'The Information of Alan of Lille's *Anticlaudianus*: a Preposterous Interpretation', *Traditio* (forthcoming); for Alan's dependence on Boethius's *De trinitate* and *De hebdomadibus* see d'Alverny, *Textes Inédits*, p. 66, and Evans, *Alan of Lille*, pp. 45, 67.

[27] Boethius, *De trinitate*, in *Boethius, The Theological Tractates*, edited and translated by H. F. Stewart and E. K. Rand (Cambridge, Mass., 1918), II.17–20, p. 8. I emend '*diduci*' to '*deduci*'. For references in Alan's works of speculative theology to this text, see, for example, *Liber in distinctionibus dictionum theologicalium*, *PL* 210, cols 685–1012 (col. 796); *Quoniam homines*, edited by P.Glorieux, *AHDLMA*, 20 (1953), 113–369, Bk.II, ch. 144, p. 282.

that the material product takes its outer form from the pure form, this distinction opens the way for a certain fuzziness in the use of the word 'form'. Boethius recognizes this at the end of Book II, and is very firm about the proper distinctions between 'form' and 'image'. He says that the forms which are in matter and produce bodies derive from those forms which are outside matter; so, he says, we should not use the word 'form' for material bodies at all:

> For we misname the entities which reside in bodies when we call them forms; they are mere images. They only resemble those forms which are not incorporate in matter.
>
> Nam ceteras quae in corporibus sunt abutimur formas uocantes, dum imagines sint. Adsimulantur enim formis his quae non sunt in materia constitutae.[28]

Boethius's rejection of images might seem like an unpromising basis for the theological poet Alan to praise the art of painting above all, and for a defence of poetry via its connections with the visual arts. But unlike Boethius in the *De trinitate*, Alan is passionately concerned with the ways in which the mind can pass from material images back into the pure forms which produced them. And the single path of this passage back into pure form is that of metaphor. In his work of speculative theology known as the *Quoniam homines*, for example, he says that words have no literal purchase on the nature of God, who is pure form; only, he says, can metaphor hope to designate the immateriality of pure form:

> With regard to God literal designation has no place, because God is 'god-ness' itself . . . only metaphorical, not literal reference has any purchase in divine matters.
>
> In Deo vero non habet locum denominatio quia Deus est ipsa deitas . . . Transnominatio locum habet in divinis, sed non denominatio.[29]

Alan's Neoplatonic defence of metaphor here is essential for his literary works: it is precisely this notion of metaphor which justifies the role of poetry in treating the pure ideas of God; by the same token, it is the notion of metaphor which equally justifies Alan's readers in looking back into his literary works for Alan's own 'pure idea' as a literary artist. But in the context of our discussion of pictures, I think we are now in a position to define Alan's concept of the pictorial image as essentially 'metaphor', a translation from pure form into image. When we turn back to earlier examples of making, we can see how the idea of metaphor, or

[28] Boethius, *De trinitate* II.53–56, p. 12.
[29] *Quoniam homines* Bk.I, Part I, 9b, p. 143.

'carrying across' is implicit in the description of painting; we can also read the words 'image' and 'form' with a sharper idea of their philosophical sense. God, we remember, is addressed as a maker of the world:

> Ducis ab exemplo mundi mentalis, eumdem
> Exterius pingens terrestris ymagine forme. (V.289–90)[30]

Alan plays with the double sense of 'form' here, though reserving the word 'image' for its role as defined by Boethius. But the especial point we might now notice here is the verb '*ducis*': the art of painting involves a leading, or carrying across; it is essentially metaphorical.

Painting, then, is code in Alan's usage for metaphor. The image of painting is not static, but has the movement implied in the spatial metaphor behind the word 'metaphor' itself. And the space in which the image as metaphor works is between the reader, the image itself, and the mind of its creator. As for fifteenth-century Italian Neoplatonists, so too for Alan it is the function of metaphor which justifies (even necessitates) the lies of poetic or visual fiction.[31] We can see the root of this in the way in which God himself is said to think metaphorically. About the picture embroidered on the dress of the '*puella poli*' in Book V, we read this:

> Hic archana Dei, divine mentis abyssum
> Subtilis describit acus formaque figurat
> Informem, locat immensum monstratque latentem.
> Incirconscriptum describit, visibus offert
> Invisum, quod lingua nequit pictura fatetur. (V.114–18)
>
> Here a fine needle has traced the secrets of God and the depths of the divine mind; a form informs the formless, localises the boundless and reveals the hidden; it describes the uncircumscribed, and brings the invisible into view. What the tongue cannot tell the picture does.

This set of paradoxes suggests how, through metaphor (or '*pictura*'), painting can do more than words. This is a representation of an artefact, but its procedures are themselves modelled on God's own way of thinking; for, a few lines further on, we see how the picture reveals that God contains the names of all things, and

30 This formulation is, of course, indebted to Boethius, *De consolatione Philosophiae* III, m.ix, 7–9, where Boethius, however, does not use the word '*pingens*': '. . . tu cuncta superno / Ducis ab exemplo, pulchrum pulcherrimus ipse / Mundum mente gerens similique in imagine formans'.

31 For the later, Neoplatonic defence of poetry, see, for example, Pico della Mirandola, *De hominis dignitate*, edited by Eugenio Garin (Florence, 1942), p. 162, and E. H. Gombrich, '*Icones Symbolicae*', in his *Symbolic Images, Studies in the Art of the Renaissance* (London, 1972), pp. 123–95.

> Cuncta tamen, mediante tropo, dictante figura
> Concipit et voces puras sine rebus adoptat. (V.126–7)
>
> However he conceives everything by means of a trope and by way of a figure, and assumes the unadulterated name without the object.

God himself, then, thinks poetically, by unravelling literal names into their pure form by means of metaphor.[32]

And if the pictures of theological discourse work in this way, we can also see how, on this model, human artefacts might also be pictured as a kind of miracle, bringing a sharper sense of reality through a fictive, metaphorical play. The murals in Nature's palace are described in ways which might apply to the human making of Alan's own poetry:

> Hic hominum mores picture gracia scribit:
> Sic operi proprio pictura fideliter heret,
> Ut res picta minus a vero deviet esse.
> O nova picture miracula! Transit ad esse
> Quod nichil esse potest picturaque simia ueri,
> Arte nova ludens, in res umbracula rerum
> Vertit et in verum mendacia singula mutat. (I.119–25)
>
> Here the beauty of the picture inscribes the characters of men. The painting faithfully fastens its attention on its special project, so that the representation may the less depart from reality. Oh new wonders of painting! What can have no real existence comes into being, and painting, aping reality and diverting itself with a new art, turns the shadows of things into things and changes every lie into truth.

In keeping with his Boethian background, Alan recognizes the falsity of images here: the picture produces something which could not really exist; it is the 'ape of reality'; its materials are mere 'shadows' and 'lies'. As Jordan would have it, Alan is not describing a realistic art. But that is not to say that we should rest, as Jordan would have us do, on the rhetorical surface. For, despite the accent on the surface falsity of the fictive picture's image, it is said to act 'faithfully'; not to deviate from the truth; to turn lies into reality. These paradoxes of lies being truthful are possible through the playful, even miraculous, *movement* of the picture, where the verbs '*transit*' '*vertit*' and '*mutat*' all designate the movement of metaphor between the pure idea in the mind of the artist and the image itself.

This is a remarkable defence of poetic fiction, which declares at once the truth of lying fiction and playful originality of such a poetry (*arte*

[32] This passage has been discussed by Peter Dronke, *Dante and Medieval Latin Traditions* (Cambridge, 1986), p. 12.

nova ludens).[33] Like God who thinks through the trope of metaphor, so too does the human maker. But the truth of these images only appears if we mentally enter into the movement implied by metaphor, the movement between the image on the one hand and the idea of the picture's maker on the other.

And, before we leave this defence of fiction, we should observe how Alan distinguishes poetry from, and prizes it above, other forms of deceptive discourse. Immediately following the passage cited immediately above, Alan goes on to praise the powers of poetry above those of sophistic logic:

> Sic logice vires artis subtiliter huius
> Argumenta premunt logiceque sophismata vincunt:
> Hec probat, ista facit; hec disputat, impetrat illa
> Omne quod esse potest: sic utraque vera videri
> Falsa cupit, sed ad hoc pictura fidelius instat. (I.126–30)
>
> Thus this art's power subtly checks logic's arguments and triumphs over the sophisms of logic. Logic gives proof, painting enacts; logic argues, painting brings to pass everything that can exist. Thus, both wish the false to appear true, but painting pursues this end more faithfully.

Poetry and sophistic logic are comparable because both deal in lies, and both seek to pass lies off as truth. But, the argument of the passage implies, the picture lies (paradoxically) 'more faithfully' because it *enacts*, by 'doing' and 'accomplishing' ('*facit*', '*impetrat*') while sophistic logic remains in the realm of words alone. Painting, and therefore poetry, do more than merely designate the truth through their 'lies' – they somehow enact that truth. It is only with this defence of

[33] I have not been able to elaborate on the idea of *novelty* in Alan's pictures, or his poetry more generally. Alan describes his poem as itself new: *'Scribendi novitate vetus iuvenescere carta / Gaudet'* (Prol. 4–5), just as he often refers to the newness of paintings: *'O nova picture miracula'* (I.122); *'Illic arte nova pictor novus'* (III.33). The simplest sense in which painting renews is through recollection, or re-presentation: thus the embroidery on the dress of Fides is said to renovate the models of faith: 'Hic renovat veteres vivens pictura magistros' (VI.35). But there is a more profound sense in which the recuperation of ideal form renovates. Thus words themselves are painted as wanting to return to their old senses in the empyrean, where they are renewed through metaphor: the embroidery on the dress of the *puella poli* shows

> Quomodo Nature subiectus sermo stupescit,
> Dum temptat divina loqui, viresque loquendi
> Perdit et ad veterem cupit ille recurrere sensum. (V.119–21)

Humans and things are renewed through contact with the divine form on which they are modelled; it is in this sense that we should understand the formation of the 'new man' in the poem, just as we should understand the newness of Alan's own poem by perceiving its inner form, or idea.

fiction in mind that we can see how what might seem a dismissive description of Virgil, among the portraits painted on the walls of Nature's palace, is in fact high praise:

> Virgilii musa mendacia multa colorat
> Et facie veri contexit pallia falsi. (I.142–3)[34]
>
> Thus Virgil's muse colours many lies and weaves cloaks of falsehood with the appearance of truth.

Likewise in the description of logic's rules in Book III we can see how painting might measure up with different kinds of logic. Logic itself is presented as a ferociously aggressive discipline armed with a sword, cutting back the false, and disallowing what is false to hide under the shade of truth ('*recidit/ Falsa, negans falsum veri latitare sub umbra*', III.37); beside this logician is placed the pseudo-, sophistic logician, who tries to sell the false as truth ('*temptat pro vero vendere falsum*', III.41). In this opposition between different kinds of logic Alan's might seem like a straightforward presentation of how truth is arrived at; but the logicians are themselves presented in a painting, made by a 'new painter' who mimics the truth: '*Illic arte nova pictor novus, histrio veri, / Monstrat elenchorum pugnam*' (III.33–4). The ideas used to describe the sophistic logician negatively (lying, wishing to present falsehood as truth) are presented as positive and powerful virtues in relation to the painter, that *histrio veri*, and, by implication, to the poet.[35]

IV

Everything I have said so far about Alan's 'Timaean' poetics would suggest to my mind that Jordan has badly misunderstood that area of thought: whereas he would have us rest with the broken rhetorical surface of late medieval poetry, I have been arguing that the theory works in precisely the reverse direction, by inviting us to see the coherent, inner sense behind the poetic surface, a sense which can only be located in the mind of a poetic maker. My spatial metaphor of 'behind' here ('behind the poetic surface') could, however, lead to misunderstandings. I seem to be suggesting that we should read the images of Alan's poetry by moving

[34] I emend Bossuat's reading '*falso*' to '*falsi*' in l. 143.

[35] See also the description of the pictures embroidered on Concord's dress, where the (normally negative) language of sophistic logic is used positively:

> Hec pictura suis loquitur misteria signis;
> Non res ipsa magis, non lingua fidelius unquam
> Talia depingit talique sophismate visum
> Decipiens oculis, rerum concludit in umbra. (II.200–203)

to the idea behind individual images. The concept of movement backwards from the image into the mind of a maker is one that I want to hold on to, but it would be a mistake to think of moving back simply from individual images to the sense behind them.

Because the meaning of the cosmos, according to the *Timaeus*, is inherently bound up with its wholeness, the inter-relation of all its parts, the kind of thinking invited by the dialogue is ecological and structuralist rather than focused on individual species in isolation. In this last section of my article, I would like briefly to suggest one further, crucial aspect of the picture/poetry comparison, which is the *wholeness* of the picture. We can only start moving back from the images of Alan's literary works once we see the image of the *whole* work. Poems are sequential, whereas we see pictures all at once.

In what could have served as an apt description of Alan's *Anticlaudianus* before its composition, John of Salisbury describes how the combination of a poet's knowledge, rhetorical skill, along with the matter of a story, all combine to produce an 'image':

> For when the *auctores*, by way of *diacrisis* (which we may call *illustratio* or *picturatio*) took up the unformed matter either of a history or a verisimilar story, or of a fable, or any other narrative whatever, they refined it with such plenitude of learning, and with such grace of composition and taste, that the completed work seemed to be in some way an image of all the arts.
>
> Illi (the *auctores*) enim per diacrisim, quam nos illustrationem siue picturationem possumus appellare, cum rudem materiam historie aut argumenti aut fabule aliamve quamlibet suscepissent, eam tanta disciplinarum copia et tanta compositionis et condimenti gratia excolebant, ut opus consummatum omnium artium quodammodo uideretur imago.[36]

This passage uses cosmological, Timaean language to describe poetic making: the 'rude material' of the narrative is shaped and adorned by the poet's knowledge and rhetorical skill, to produce an image (John is using

[36] *Ioannis Saresberiensis episcopi Carnotensis metalogicon*, edited by Clemens C.I. Webb, 2 vols (Oxford, 1909), I.853a–b, 19–25, p. 54) (date 1159). Hugh of St Victor (ca.1096–1141) also describes what I take to be contemporary poems as pictures, even as he dismisses them. In saying that the songs of the poets are only 'appendages to the arts', he gives examples of fictive writing, including, he says, 'Illorum etiam scripta quos nunc philosophos appellare solemus, qui et brevem materiam longis verborum ambagibus extendere consueverunt, et facilem sensum perplexis sermonibus obscurare. vel etiam diversa simul compilantes, quasi de multis coloribus et formis, unam picturam facere'. *Hugonis de Sancto Victore didascalicon de studio legendi*, edited by Charles H. Buttimer, Studies in Medieval and Renaissance Latin, 10 (Washington, 1939), III.iv.16–21, p. 54.

the word carefully) of all the arts. I adduce this citation here because the Timaean language highlights the fact that the image produced in the '*opus cosummatum*' refers to the *whole* work, rather than any one of its parts.

When we look to Alan's own explicit defence of poetry in the *De planctu*, we see the same language of 'picture', and the same concentration on the wholeness of the poetic picture. The narrator of the *De planctu* asks Nature about homosexuality as it is represented in classical poetry. This reference to poetry elicits Nature's anger, which she vents in a dismissal of poetry as, interestingly, a false, shadowy, picture: 'should you', she says to the narrator, pay any credence to '*umbratilibus poetarum figmentis, que artis poetice depinxit industria . . .?*' (VIII.125–6, p. 837). Nature's angry dismissal of poetry is pitched in terms of its deceptive falsity – poets, she says, prostitute 'naked falsity', or else they cover falsity with the mantle of hypocritical probability. These dismissals of poetry seem to be unpromising for any defence of fiction, but suddenly, without apparently changing tack, Nature does acknowledge that some poets hide an inner truth:

> Aut in superficiali littere cortice falsum resonat lira poetica, interius uero auditoribus secretum intelligentie altioris eloquitur, ut exteriori falsitatis abiecto putamine dulciorem nucleum ueritatis secrete intus lector inueniat. (VIII.133–6, p. 837)
>
> Or, how the poetic lyre gives a false note on the outer bark of the composition but within tells the listeners a secret of deeper significance so that when the outer shell of falsehood has been discarded, the reader finds the sweeter kernel of truth hidden within?

This is a very succinct statement of the three way dynamic I have described above, involving image, reader and maker: by throwing aside the false poetic exterior, the intelligence of the reader is satisfied by discovering the sweeter nucleus of truth within. But this sweeter, inner truth is discovered only through approaching the outer image, or picture of the poem as a *whole*. For Nature goes on, in the way I read this rather choppy passage, to elaborate the kind of fiction she admires, in this way:

> Poete tamen aliquando hystoriales euentus ioculationibus fabulosis quadam eleganti sutura confederant, ut ex diuersorum conpetenti iunctura ipsius narrationis elegantior pictura resultet. (VIII.137–9, p. 837)
>
> However, at times poets combine accounts of historical events and entertaining fables by a kind of elegant stitch-work, so that, from a fit construction of diverse elements in their narrative, a more elegant picture may emerge.

Jordan is certainly right to stress the importance of 'fixity, divisibility, and juxtaposition' as against 'limitlessness, continuousness and coalescence' in Timaean poetics.[37] And he is right, too, in his discussion of this very passage, to say that poetry is 'primarily a manipulative art, consisting in the conscious, deliberate disposition of clearly delimited parts'.[38] But he is wrong to go on from there to point to the 'strong sense of separation between the superficial veil and the true essence beneath'. For in Alan it is, as it is in Chrétien's use of the word '*conjointure*', precisely the 'construction' of a whole artefact, its '*iunctura*', which should provoke the reader to construct the idea behind the poem.[39] Alan always stresses not the radical disjunctions between image and idea, but rather the way in which the image 'faithfully', or 'familiarly' adheres to its idea; but the image, as we can see from this discussion, is the picture of the whole poem.[40] If we do not move beyond the surface, and beyond the *whole* surface, then we are left with 'fragments' only, as Alan says about the 'grammarians' (by which term he means what we would call

[37] Jordan, *Chaucer and the Shape of Creation*, p. 14.

[38] Ibid., p. 34.

[39] For Chrétien's use of the word '*conjointure*', see *Erec et Enide*, l. 14. For discussion of this word as meaning 'the arrangement of different elements found in the poet's *matiere*', see Douglas Kelly, 'The Source and Meaning of "*Conjointure*" in Chrétien's *Erec*', *Viator* 1 (1970) 179–200. Kelly agrees with, but extends, the definition given to '*conjointure*' by D. W. Robertson, 'Some Medieval Literary Terminology, With Special Reference to Chrétien de Troyes', *SP* 48 (1951) 669–92. Alan's sense of the '*iunctura*' of artefacts revealing the idea of their maker extends beyond verbal artefacts. Thus in the *Anticlaudianus* the chariot constructed by the arts individually is joined by Concord. The finished product is described in this way:

> Apponensque manum supremam, fine beato
> Concludens operam, sparsas Concordia partes
> Ordine, lege, loco confederat, unit, adequat.
> Ergo iunctura, clavis gumfisque ligate
> Partes effigiant, currum qui luce decoris
> Preradians, facie propria demonstrat in ipso
> Divinam sudasse manum superumque Minervam. (IV.76–82)

The word '*iunctura*' is also given prominence in the description of Concord's person (see II.165–77).

[40] Unlike the practice of much allegoresis in the later medieval period, Alan insists on an intimate connection between outer (artificial) and inner (natural) form. Take, for example, the description of Nature's boots and their decoration: 'Calcei vero, ex alutea pelle traducentes materiam, ita familiariter pedum sequebantur ideas, ut in ipsis pedibus nati ipsisque mirabiliter viderentur inscripti. In quibus vix a vera degenerantes essentia sub picture ingenio flores amenabantur umbratiles' (II.288–92, p. 819). Here there are two examples of the outer form sticking close to the inner – both the boots (to the feet, significantly described as 'ydeas') and the flowers (to the true form of flowers). In the prose immediately following, we hear of how Nature's pictures fade quickly, because they do not 'cohere familiarly' to the material: 'pictura tamen, subiacenti materie familiariter non coherens . . .' (IV.4–5, p. 821). The model of a perfect picture for Alan is one whose outer form coheres closely to its inner form, and therefore to the material it shapes. For the (same) idea of the picture doing its work '*fideliter*', see *Anticlaudianus* I.120, 130; II.201.

'literary critics') who are not embroidered on Grammar's dress.[41] These are the readers who

> . . . sola cortice gaudent,
> Quos non dimittit intus pinguedo medulle:
> Si foris exposcunt framenta, putamine solo
> Contenti, nequeunt nuclei libare saporem. (II.510–13)[42]
>
> . . .who rejoice in mere husks, whom the richness of the marrow within does not set apart: if they seek fragments from the outside, content with mere shells, they cannot taste the flavour of the nut.

As I said in my introduction, I have not necessarily demonstrated anything about Chaucer's poetry: even if I am right and Jordan is wrong about Timaean poetics, it may well remain the case that Chaucer is, as I said, sensitive to a variety of ways in which authorial subjectivity is displaced, and how it may not be possible to retrieve the 'o sentence' of his works. Indeed, I think Chaucer is, more than any late medieval English poet I know (except Hoccleve) sensitive to the ways in which poetic and political institutions displace authors. One need only think of the 'pictures' of Virgil's *Aeneid* in Book I of the *House of Fame*, for example, where the presentation of the *Aeneid* as writing is deliberately blurred with its presentation as visual images. Geoffrey's affective

[41] It should be mentioned here that Alan's structuralist conception of meaning is quite different from the principles of Victorine exegesis, and quite different from the ideas expressed by Alan's own lyric (so often cited as typical of the late medieval view of nature):

> Omnis mundi creatura,
> Quasi liber, et pictura
> Nobis est et speculum,
> Nostrae vitae, nostrae mortis,
> Nostri status, nostrae sortis
> Fidele signaculum
>
> Nostrum statum pingit rosa,
> Nostri status decens glosa,
> Nostrae vitae lectio. . .

PL 210, col.579. See d'Alverny, *Textes Inédits*, pp. 39–40 for the attribution to Alan. For the profound differences between 'Chartrian' and Victorine principles of interpretation, see Winthrop Wetherbee, 'The Function of Poetry in the *De planctu Naturae* of Alain de Lille', *Traditio* 25 (1969) 87–125. Wetherbee defines the essential difference in this way, describing the 'Chartrian' and Victorine positions respectively: 'It is the difference between seeing in nature as a whole the copy of a higher world – analogous to, and so metaphorically accessible in terms of, the world of nature – and seeing the natural world as a cluster of individual natures, any one of which is fully comprehensible only as it is seen to embody the divine' (p. 96).

[42] Alan's concept of wholeness in poetry is often expressed in terms of cloth-making; a good poem will, as we have seen, be 'sewn' (*De planctu Naturae* VIII.138, p. 837). Poems which are bad in Alan's view are described as 'patchwork' affairs: Joseph of Exeter is mocked as popularizing 'pannoso. . .carmine' (I.165).

response as reader there certainly displaces Virgil as *auctor* altogether – the images provoke Geoffrey to reimagine the poem rather than to look for the strategy of their maker.[43] That being said, this discussion of poetry and the visual arts in twelfth-century poetic theory and practice should give us pause before we accept Jordan's badly skewed account of the poetics implicit in the Timaean model. So too should it give us pause before we accept Jordan's account of the formal poetics to which Chaucer certainly did have access, that of, for example, Geoffrey of Vinsauf's *Poetria Nova*.[44] And given that these traditions were one obvious source of poetic theory for Chaucer, perhaps we should also pause before we dismiss the idea of the architect or painter behind the inconsistent, 'prefabricated' surface of Chaucer's poetry. If we understand 'peynture' in this passage in the way Alan would have us do, as referring to works of poetry, then maybe Hoccleve is more than moving – maybe he's *right* to re-present to us a maker's 'person' (the stanza is set beside the famous portrait of Chaucer in British Library MS Harley 4866, f.88):

> Althogh his lyfe be queynt, the resemblaunce
> Of him hath in me so fressh lyflynesse,
> That, to putte othir men in remembraunce
> Of his persone, I have heere his lyknesse
> Do make, to this ende in sothfastnesse,
> That thei that have of him lest thought and mynde
> By this peynture may ageyn him fynde.
>
> (*Regement of Princes*, 4992–98)[45]

[43] For the way in which Geoffrey's reading of these images produces an interpretation 'rooted in the authority of the reader', see Jill Mann, 'The Authority of the Audience in Chaucer', in *Poetics: Theory and Practice in Medieval English Literature*, edited by Piero Boitani and Anna Torti (Cambridge, 1991), pp. 1–12 (pp. 8–10).

[44] Jordan's discussion of Geoffrey of Vinsauf's treatment of amplification in 'abstract, quantitative terms, exclusive of any consideration of content or substantive meaning' neglects the opening sequence of Geoffrey's treatise, whose precepts are concerned with the way in which outer form should be constrained by an inner meaning. Geoffrey's treatise, itself imbued with Timaean concepts of formation and embellishment, begins by teaching the aspiring poet to think through the poem before writing it; the shape of the work should be '*prius archetypus quam sensilis*' (*Poetria Nova*, l. 48, Faral, *Les Arts Poétiques*, p. 198). The date of the *Poetria Nova* is ca. 1200–1202. Chaucer's indebtedness to Geoffrey of Vinsauf, which I believe to be deep, needs yet another look, after the overly sceptical article by James J.Murphy, 'A New Look at Chaucer and the Rhetoricians', *RES*, 15 (1964), 1–20.

[45] *Hoccleve's Works*, edited by Frederick J.Furnivall, EETS, ES 72 (1897), p. 180.

THE *FIDUS INTERPRES*, OR FROM HORACE TO PANDARUS

JOHN V. FLEMING

Among the defining roles of Geoffrey Chaucer's authorial career is his role as a translator. Indeed his twin achievements of original and intermediary composition were strikingly similar to those of the vernacular poet who was among the first and most enduring influences upon his poetic career, Jean de Meun, the principal author of the *Roman de la Rose*. Jean had translated numerous texts, works of striking tonal variety, ranging from Cistercian spirituality in Aelred's *De amicitia spirituali* to fabulous history in Gerald of Wales to the ancient Roman textbook of military fundamentals written by Vegetius. But his most famous translation was, and is, that of the *Consolation of Philosophy* of Boethius.

This work, we might say, Jean translated twice: once straight, and once decidedly crooked. What I mean by his 'straight' translation is of course obvious: the medieval French vernacular version undertaken for Philip the Fair that has survived integrally with its brief but important introductory essay touching upon, among other subjects, the options and difficulties facing the linguistic translator.[1] What I mean by his 'crooked translation' is not so easily defined. I refer to the way in which he brought cardinal parts of the *Consolatio* of Boethius into the indeterminate love fiction undertaken by his predecessor Guillaume de Lorris to make of it something altogether different from what that author appears originally to have intended; that is, Jean pursued a philosophical and moral as opposed perhaps to a sentimental or a psychological examination of the erotic. The complex processes by which Jean achieved his poem were denoted by various technical terms in the vocabulary of antique Latin literary criticism. One was *imitatio*, another *aemulatio*; but as the German classicist Arno Reiff has shown in a careful study, the most common term was *interpretatio*, or what we usually call 'translation'.[2] As I shall go on to explore in this paper, there is a notorious slipperiness in the medieval vocabulary of 'interpretation' both

[1] Ed. V. L. Dedeck-Héry, *Mediaeval Studies* 14 (1952) 165–275.

[2] Arno Reiff, *Interpretatio, imitatio, aemulatio: Begriff und Vorstellung literarischer Abhängigkeit der Römern* (Würzburg, 1959).

as regards the process (*interpretatio*) and as regards the person executing the process (*interpres*). It is a slipperiness that served poets well.

Perhaps what we often call the tradition of 'medieval classicism' would in some respects better be called the tradition of 'medieval interpretation'. If we search among early Christian humanists we see that Boethius himself was primarily a *translator*, whose own original works betray on nearly every page the strategies of classical imitation. In his own time Geoffrey Chaucer would become the imitator, the emulator, and indeed the interpreter in English of Jean de Meun. He, too, translated the *Consolation of Philosophy* into the vernacular (not to mention the *Romance of the Rose* itself) and he, too, gave us straight and crooked versions of the works translated. That is, he has given us, in addition to the integral text of *Boece* and the partial text of the *Romaunt*, repeated creative imitations or interpretations of those works throughout the course of his original poetic career. Who can imagine the *Canterbury Tales* without the Wife of Bath or the Pardoner? But who, once having studied Chaucer's textual filiations with the *Roman de la Rose*, can imagine that the Wife of Bath or the Pardoner could possibly be as they are without Jean de Meun?

Vernacular poets who were also textual translators were constantly confronted by the challenges of interpretive responsibility whether in their creative or in their intermediary roles, insofar as it is actually licit to draw a distinction between the two, and there are many examples in medieval poetry of the thematization or dramatization of interpretive dilemmas. There are several examples, in my opinion, in the *Consolation of Philosophy* itself. The famous image of a human sensibility so dulled by sublunar immersion that it is like the ass standing incomprehendingly before the harp is very frequently used by later medieval writers to underscore a crucial distinction between a literal and a spiritual understanding of a text, often but by no means exclusively the sacred text. Jean de Meun's own *imitatio* of this Boethian passage in the *Roman de la Rose* is the episode in which Lady Reason exposes the vapid Lover's incapacity to understand the allegorical significance of the story of the castration of Saturn as mediated by Virgil in the *Georgics* and by Ovid in the first book of the *Metamorphoses*.[3]

Geoffrey Chaucer, who learned so much from Boethius, Jean de Meun, Dante, Boccaccio, and several other writers whose works are replete with classical *imitatio* and *interpretatio*, repeatedly turns to interpretive themes in his major poetry; yet in no poem are such themes more conspicuous than in his greatest masterpiece, *Troilus and Criseyde*,

[3] *Roman de la Rose*, ed. Lecoy, lines 6949ff. (I. 213f.).

a poem which is both a translation and about translation.[4] We can perhaps grasp the centrality of the medieval idea of 'interpretation' to the *Troilus* by thinking for a moment about the poem's narrator, whose perennial fascination is unchanged by the several cubic yards of explicatory prose surrounding him in the burgeoning Chaucer criticism. My claim is that we can know one fact, and one fact only, about this mysterious narrator: the fact that he is an interpreter. We do not know *as fact* that he is an unsuccessful lover, or that he is donnish, or that his is a 'bumbleninny' (Barry Windeatt's term), or that he likes Criseyde or any other of numerous propositions that he makes about himself or that others have plausibly drawn on his behalf. We do know that he is a translator, and we know this not because he tells us so, though of course he does, but because we have independent, reliable, verifiable access to the texts he has translated. The same texts whose anterior existence proves the truth of his claim to be a translator prove also the radical untruth of the specific terms in which the claim to be a translator are couched. He says that he is translating the Latin of Lollius while we know as fact that he is translating the Italian of Boccaccio. Thus it is that the one fact that we know about the narrator must necessarily encourage the fear that we can know no others.

In a recent book I had the temerity, or the foolishness, to join the not inconsiderable number of scholars who have proposed 'solutions' to the problem of 'Lollius', the phantom Roman poet whose work Chaucer pretends to be translating in the *Troilus* when he is actually translating Boccaccio.[5] I believe that the figure of Lollius is connected textually and contextually to the dramatized theme of interpretation within Chaucer's poem. My theory is that Lollius is an actual, historical author of similar substantiality with Dares, Dictys, and Homer, other ancient writers cited as authorities in the text of the *Troilus*. Specifically he is the 'Lollius' addressed in two of Horace's verse epistles (numbers two and eighteen of the first book). The incipit of the second epistle is particularly important:

> Troiani belli scriptorem, Maxime Lolli,
> dum tu declamas Romae, Praeneste relegi;
> qui, quid sit pulcrum, quid turpe, quid utile, quid non,
> planius ac melius Chrysippo et Crantore dicit.[6]

[4] I pursue the question of Chaucerian imitation in a recent book, *Classical Imitation and Interpretation in Chaucer's Troilus* (Lincoln, 1990), which amplifies some of the points made in the present essay.

[5] *Classical Imitation and Interpretation*, pp. 179–200.

[6] *Epistolae* I, ii, 1–4. Latin citations of Horace are from *Le opere*, ed. Enrico Turolla (Torino, 1963). English translations are based on those of E. C. Wickham, *Horace for English Readers* (Oxford, 1903).

> (While you have been practising declamation at Rome, Lollius Maximus, I have been reading again at Praeneste the story-teller of the war of Troy; who shows us what is fair, what is foul, what is profitable, what not, more plainly and better than a Chrysippus or a Crantor.)

I am not the first to suggest the Horatian ancestry of Chaucer's Lollius. The suggestion was first made by Latham in 1873, elaborated in a famous article by Kittredge in 1917, and elaborated further by Pratt in 1950. All these scholars maintained, however, that Chaucer read a seriously corrupted text of Horace, or read a genuine text incompetently, constructing the accusative singular *scriptorem* as a genitive plural so as to believe that an actual Roman poet named Lollius was a 'great', perhaps even the 'greatest' poetic authority on the subject of the Trojan war.

My own conclusion is that Chaucer could read Latin and that, in consequence, he knew that Horace's claim in this epistle is that Homer's two great poems were moral allegories designed to teach, rather more effectively indeed than the great philosophers of the Stoa had been able to do, that men should pursue virtue and flee vice. Thus what he has given us in the *Troilus*, in my understanding, is an English 'interpretation' of the epic poem that the young Roman poet Lollius *would* have written had he followed Horace's advice. I believe that Chaucer, in common with other intelligent readers of poetry before and since his time, connected in his mind the concerns of Horace's epistle to the Pisones – more familiarly known as the *Ars poetica* – and of this first epistle to Lollius. In both of them the authoritative teacher of poetry gave advice to younger men, in the first instance on the art of poetry and in the second on the moral utility of poetry. In the one Horace maintained that the poet should follow Homer both in the selection of poetic subject and in the prosecution of the poetic theme; in the other he argued that the chief business of epic poetry was moral instruction, and he sketched brief allegorical interpretations of the *Iliad* and the *Odyssey* in support of his claim. To be the 'interpreter' of Lollius – which is the claim put forward by the narrator of the *Troilus* – would mean to be the modern renovator of ancient moral allegory.

The scholarly attempt to establish the certain presence of Horace in Chaucer met with stiff resistance in the nineteenth century, but as long ago as 1923 C. L. Wrenn definitively identified three specific passages from the *Ars poetica* in Chaucer's poetry.[7] Two of them are in the *Troilus*, and both of them deal with self-consciously literary themes. The well-known lines concerning linguistic change in the proemium to book two derive from Horace. Much more obviously Chaucer clearly imitates

[7] C. L. Wrenn, 'Chaucer's Knowledge of Horace', *MLR* 18 (1923) 286–92.

the famous opening image of the *Ars poetica* in the comic passage in which Pandarus is teaching Troilus how to write a love letter.

Horace writes:

> Humano capiti ceruicem pictor equinam
> iungere si uelit et uarias inducere plumas
> undique collatis membris ut turpiter atrum
> desinat in piscem mulier formosa superne:
> spectatum admissi risum teneatis, amici? (1–5)
>
> (If a painter chose to set a human head on the neck and shoulders of a horse, to gather limbs from every animal and clothe them with feathers from every kind of bird, and make what at the top was a beautiful woman have ugly ending in a black fish's tale–when you were admitted to view his picture should you refrain from laughing, my good friends?)

Pandarus's version is this:

> Ne jompre ek no discordaunt thyng yfeere. . .
> For if a peyntour wolde peynte a pyk
> With asses feet, and hedde it as an ape,
> It cordeth naught; so nere it but a jape. (II.1037–43)

The textual connection with the *Ars poetica* is certain, but that is not to say that it is certain that Chaucer wrote with a copy of Horace's poem on his writing-stand. Do we have actual firsthand quotations or merely vague reminiscences taken from a florilegium or some intermediary author? The question is eventually a vain one, but I find that the dramatic nature of the narrative moment – a moment in which an older expert offers instruction to a younger, fledgling author – strongly argues for Horace's conscious contextual, as well as textual, presence. I believe that Chaucer knows what he is doing – and that is to raise some sharp questions about the nature of poetic 'interpretation'. For that purpose no text could be apter than Horace's *Ars poetica*.

From the point of view of an important strand of medieval literary theory, the epistle to the Pisones was less an art of 'poetry' than it was an art of 'translation'. The Latin poetry that has come down to us from classical Antiquity is, viewed from one perspective, perhaps the most derivative and unoriginal body of literature the world has ever known. It is all, or nearly all, derived from Greek models according to varying processes I have already identified, in the Latin technical vocabulary, as *aemulatio*, *interpretatio*, *imitatio*, or *translatio*, processes which by their very nature assure the traditionality as well as the originality of the major Latin poets. The specific counsel of Horace in the *Ars poetica* is that the poet must be at once imitative and original, at once an intermediary interpreter and an active creator. The poet must 'follow Homer'; yet in pursuing his traditional Trojan subject he must be original.

> publica materies priuati iuris erit, si
> non circa uilem patulumque moraberis orbem
> nece uerbo uerbum curabis reddere fidus
> interpres nec desilies imitator in artum,
> unde pedem proferre pudor uetet aut operis lex,
> nec sic incipies, ut scriptor cyclicus olim:
> 'fortunam Priami cantabo et nobile bellum'. (131–7)
>
> (It is a hard task to treat what is common in a way of your own; and you are doing more rightly in breaking the tale of Troy into acts than in giving the world a new story of your own telling. You may acquire private rights in common ground, provided you will neither linger in the one hackneyed and easy round; nor, a faithful interpreter, trouble to render word for word; nor by your mode of imitating take the 'leap into the pit' out of which very shame, if not the law of your work, will forbid you to stir hand or foot to escape; nor so begin as the old Cyclic writer: 'Of Priam's fate and glorious war I'll sing'.)

The phrase in this passage to which I have drawn attention in my title is this:

> Nec verbo verbum curabis reddere fidus
> Interpres. . .
>
> (Nor, a faithful interpreter, trouble to render word for word)

Context in this passage makes it certain that to be a faithful interpreter or translator, a *fidus interpres*, is to commit a literary sin. The phrase which seems benign is in fact pejorative. Brink, from whose elaborate exegesis of *Horace on Poetry* all students of classical literary theory have so much to learn, explains that the fault of the 'faithful interpreter' is to have put his faith in another person rather than in himself. It is important to appreciate that the *interpres* is a poet. Indeed the terms are synonymous. Brink writes: 'The poet in question, unlike the Horatian poet, has "trusted" another person, not himself. . . Use of a traditional theme must be original'.[8]

Late antique Christians were no less aware than their Augustan ancestors that they embraced what might be called a 'translated' culture, especially Christians like Jerome and Boethius, men who took as a principal part of the intellectual enterprise the actual translation of texts – in the case of Jerome the Holy Scriptures, in that of Boethius the dialectical works of the Aristotelian *Organon*. Thanks to Bartelinck's

[8] C. O. Brink, *Horace on Poetry: The 'Ars Poetica'* (Cambridge, 1971), p. 211.

recent brilliant edition of Jerome's fifty-seventh letter, sometimes entitled the *Liber de optimo genere interpretandi*, or the 'Book Concerning the Best Mode of Translating',[9] we are in a position to understand the intellectual context of Jerome's defence of 'free translation' – that is, translation according to authorially mediated sense rather than the slavish transposition of the foreign idiom and syntax. Jerome defends his precept, naturally, by citing Horace:

> sed et Horatius, uir acutus et doctus, hoc idem in Arte poetic erudito interpreti pracipt:
>
> Nec uerbum uerbo curabis reddere fidus
> Interpres. . .[10]

We may count ourselves lucky, perhaps, that it was the Hieronymite theory of interpretation, which might be described as a Christian adaptation of Horace, that directed the enterprise of the Vulgate Bible. One can only imagine what Boethius would have made of the job. It was Boethius above all who did in fact establish for the Middle Ages the norms of translation practice as opposed to those of theory; and the unidiomatic and at times nearly unreadable nature of his word-for-word translation will be only too well known to anyone who has tried to work with his adaptations of Greek originals. Even so, Boethius was clearly aware of the opprobrium of the *fidus interpres*, and he alludes to it explicitly in his version of Porphyry's *Isagoge*:

> in qua [serie translationis] quidem uereor ne subierim fidi interpretis culpam cum uerbum uerbo expressum comparatumque reddiderim.

This is a confession of sorts. Boethius is pleading guilty to the fault of the faithful interpreter. He has been driven to his life of literary crime, he asserts, by the extraordinary exasperations of philosophical Greek.

Of course Boethius had to deal only with simple authors like Aristotle or Porphyry. Consider poor John the Scot, who undertook to translation the *Celestial Hierarchies* of pseudo-Dionysius. In a preface he insists that he is the translator (*interpres*) of the word only, not its interpreter (*expositor*). And he adds: 'Ubi valde pertimesco, ne forte culpam fidi interpretis incurram'. W. Schwarz, the only scholar known to me who has explored the specific linguistic history of our curious phrase, demonstrates the clear dependence of John the Scot on Boethius. We already have a traditional topos, the translator's confession of the

[9] G. J. M. Bartelink, *Liber de optimo genere interpretandi (Epistula 57): ein Kommentar* (Leiden, 1980).

[10] This text, and the related texts that follow, are conveniently gathered together by W. Schwarz, 'The Meaning of Fidus Interpres in Medieval Translation', *Journal of Theological Studies* 45 (1944) 73–78.

Horatian vice of the faithful interpreter. We have as well clear signals of increasing confusion on the part of the scribes. All manuscripts of Horace read **fidus interpres**; so do all manuscripts of Jerome quoting Horace. But in one tenth- and one eleventh-century copy of Boethius *In Isagogen* we find the reading **infidi**; and in John the Scot's Dionysius all but a single surviving manuscript have the faithless reading **infidi**. The Horatian doctrine of the *fidus interpres* could not survive the dubious improvements of the *infidus scriptor*. Since it made more superficial sense to talk about the 'vice of the **un**faithful translator' than of the 'vice of the **faith**ful translator', that is what he did.

Though the Boethian mode of translating painful word by painful word became the academic norm for translations from the Greek, Horace's ideas, and his image, nonetheless have an important afterlife in medieval literary culture, especially among those translators, like Jean de Meun and Geoffrey Chaucer, who are also poets. Let us return to the textually ambiguous *fidus interpres* as he exists in Chaucer's *Troilus*. I have so far in this paper been concerned with only half of Horace's phrase *fidus interpres*, with the adjective *fidus*, and with the paradox of 'faithful' translation. What of the word *interpres*? It is a particularly rich word, deriving from the ancient vocabulary of commercial intermediation on the one hand and of religious rite on the other. As its etymons suggest, the *interpres* is the broker, whether of things or of people. In the religious vocabulary of Cicero and Seneca its common meaning is priest, augur, or diviner. For example, in the *Agamemnon* of Seneca, from which Chaucer may have gleaned certain details of the *Troilus*, Calchas is *interpres divum*, the 'mouthpiece of the gods'. In the *De divinatione* of Cicero the *interpres* is precisely what John the Scot denied he was, the interpreter in the usual modern sense, that is the explainer, the exegete, the literary critic. One specialized kind of intermediation is of particular interest. In the *Pamphilus*, the twelfth-century Ovidian closet drama that is the mediate source, direct or indirect, of the most interesting vernacular Ovidiana of the thirteenth and fourteenth centuries, the lover, in search of a go-between, explains why he must seek out the traditional old crone, why a brother or a nephew would not do:

> Non meus interpres fuerit fraterque nepos que
> Nam nullus leuiter inuenit inde fidem. . . (275–6)

Thus an *interpres* may be a pimp. It may also be a text itself, as the following example will demonstrate. In the twelfth century Baudri of Borgeuil wrote a pair of splendid heroids – imaginary letters from Paris to Helen and from Helen to Paris – in imitations of the most celebrated of the paired epistles in Ovid's *Heroides*. Paris's letter ends with a traditional conceit of the Ovidian lover, the wish that he might enjoy the physical fate of the parchment that will be held against Helen's presumably bountiful bosom. Baudri complicates the Ovidian humour with an evocation of Horace:

> Essem legatus pro me bonus atque fidelis
> Interpres Paridis Paridisque vicarius essem. . . .

I cannot prove that Chaucer knew and used this text, but it is obvious to me that the *Troilus* shares its cultural tradition. For he, too, makes dramatic as well as thematic use of the concept of the *fidus interpres*. The two real power brokers of his poem – the narrator and Pandarus – are both conspicuous *interpretes* whose infidelity is to be judged in nearly exactly inverse ratio to their self-proclaimed rhetoric of fidelity.

Of the two the more interesting by far is Pandarus, an *interpres* in an astonishing number of senses. We have already seen him in one interpretative role, that of the leader of a poetry workshop teaching his young student Troilus how to write a verse epistle. Here he is a rhetorician or teacher of composition, a surrogate for Horace himself who points his lesson with an obvious allusion to the opening lines of the *Ars poetica*. Once the letter has been written, his pimping changes from passive to active mode, and he becomes a sexual go-between of an explicitly textual sort, as in the passage in which he crams the letter into Criseyde's bodice in a kinky variation on the venerable game of 'Post Office'. His erotic sacerdotalism has been recognized by numerous scholars, and in his formal act of oneirocriticism he specifically imitates the typical action of the vatic *interpres* of classical epic and tragedy. He himself is also a translator, a trickily faithless one. His amusing version of a passage in the fifth letter of the *Heroides* will not soon be forgotten by those who – unlike Troilus himself – have actually read the text.

Yet the very richness and complexity of the interpretive theme in Chaucer's conception of Pandarus would make it impossible to do justice to it in a paper of this length, and I return to the slightly more tractable problem of his interpreter-narrator. I earlier made the claim that the one certain fact we know concerning the narrator is that he is an *interpres*, or translator. Yet the claim to be an *interpres*, while true, is advanced in the terms of an untruth, namely that he is the *interpres* of a Latin poem by Lollius. Repeatedly throughout the text of the *Troilus* the narrator defends himself with the plea of textual necessity. He must say certain unflattering things about his central characters, things he is loathe to report and perhaps even loathe to believe, because he is constrained by the code of faithful translation to do so. Near the end of the poem, palpably pained by the way his own story is turning out, the narrator implies that he would be happier producing a different poem altogether, a poem about Troilus's feats of arms, rather than a poem about his double sorrow in love. Yet loyal to the letter of the master-text of Lollius, he must persevere to the last salt tear of his tragedy. The duly complex and paradoxical situation may be summarized thus. Chaucer's narrator's claim to be a *fidus interpres*, part of the inventive fiction of a genuine Horatian *interpres*, makes him a marvellously *infidus interpres*.

These matters are, I suggest, much on Chaucer's mind precisely at those moments when his narrator most explicitly claims the title of *fidus interpres*. The most conspicuous of these is the so-called 'Cantus Troili':

> And on a song anon right to bygynne,
> And gan loude on his sorwe for to wynne;
> For with good hope he gan fully assente
> Criseyde for to love, and nought repente.
>
> And of his song nat only the sentence,
> As writ myn auctour called Lollius,
> But pleinly, save our tonges difference,
> I dar wel seyn, in al, that Troilus
> Seyd in his song, loo, every word right thus
> As I shal seyn. (I. 389–98)

These lines, among the most disingenuous in the poem, have been much discussed in the context of the Lollius problem. The narrator says that he will provide the reader not merely with the gist of Troilus's song as found in Lollius but with every word of the song's text, fully and accurately. He explicitly promises, that is, to be a *fidus interpres*. Of the three ways in which this is misleading, only the first and most obvious has been fully appreciated: that the text translated is not that of Lollius (either as an ancient Latin author or a stable proxy for Boccaccio) but that of Francis Petrarch. The second point is that there is no way in which the text translated actually accords with the *sentence* as reported, or at least implied, in the *Filostrato*, or with the motive ascribed in the Middle English. According to Boccaccio, Troilo

> si diede a cantare,
> bene sperando, e tutto si dispose
> di voler sola Criseida amore,
> nulla pregiando ogni altra che veduta
> ne gli venisse, o fosse mai piaciuta.

With his English song Troilus

> gan loude on his sorwe forto wynne;
> For with good hope he gan fully assente
> Criseyde for to love, and nought repente.

I suggest that any reader who thinks that Petrarch's 132nd sonnet is an ejaculation of 'good hope' or that its tune is one a lover might well whistle to keep his pecker up, has no very profound understanding of poetry. Such a stricture, alas, does consistently apply to Troilus in this poem. The 'Cantus Troili' is deeply subversive of the superficial erotic optimism that defines the ethos of the early sections of the *Filostrato* and that reappears in the more jovially immoral behaviour of Chaucer's Pandarus. What Chaucer has in effect done – wicked and faithless *interpres*! – is to have invoked the profounder Petrarch to redress the amatory puerilities of Boccaccio, just as in a larger sense he invokes throughout the poem the mature Latin Boccaccio to balance the superficialities of the young vernacular Boccaccio.

The claim to have translated the song 'pleinly, save our tonges difference. . .every word right thus' likewise turns out to be false, or at the very least misleading. Chaucer has transformed Petrarch's fourteen lines to twenty-one, giving a full stanza to each of the quatrains and to the sestet. To increase the size of the text by half required an effort of emulative invention as well as of expansive translation, and Chaucer's version of the 'Cantus Troili', while indeed true to the 'sentence' of the original, is no monument of a *fidus interpres*. One of the remarkable achievements of the *Canzoniere* as a whole is its distinctive humanistic syncretism. Petrarch builds an erotic fiction based on Ovidian myth on the one hand and on the Augustinian doctrine of the two loves on the other. Chaucer honours this achievement in his own competitive addition in line 406, 'For ay thurst I, the more that ich it drynke'. The idea brings together Ovid's frequently quoted line about Narcissus in the third book of the *Metamorphoses* with Jesus's riddling remarks to the Samaritan woman about 'living water' – a collation already established in a courtly and amatory literary context in the speech of Genius in the *Roman de la Rose* of Jean de Meun.[11] Chaucer's addition here is very much in the spirit of the initial line of Petrarch's next sonnet (133), 'Amor m'a posto come segno a strale', where an Ovidian cliché is formulated in the language of a Bible text (Lamentations 3: 12).

A second passage in which the narrator speaks explicitly about his function as an interpreter (III.501ff.) likewise disingenuously suggests that he is a *fidus interpres*. He claims to be unable to give the contents of a long letter that passed between the lovers:

> For ther was some epistel hem bitwene,
> That wolde, as seyth myn autour, wel contene
> Neigh half this book, of which hym liste nought write;
> How sholde I thanne a lyne of it endite? (III.501–4)

[11] See John V. Fleming, 'The Garden of the *Roman de la Rose*: Vision of Landscape or Landscape of Vision?', in *Medieval Gardens*, ed. Elisabeth B. MacDougall (Washington, 1986), p. 223n.

Since there is no mention of a letter at this point in the auctorial text and consequently no possibility that it is the auctor rather than the narrator/translator who controls its simultaneous presence and absence, the lines are of course the purest fiction. Yet when it becomes a possibly significant critical act to discover that Chaucer's fiction is fiction, we may be reminded how powerfully and perversely his text manages to suggest otherwise. Here we discover that the two passages in his poem that most clearly imply on the surface that the narrator has adopted for himself the role of the *fidus interpres* actually distance him from that office, furtively but decisively.

The thematization and dramatization of the interpretive moments within Chaucer's *Troilus* are, in my opinion, not without their own interpretive drift. Yet there are nearly as many interpretations of it as there are *interpretes* who approach its text, and it would surely be intellectually impertinent to attempt to impose any particular view on this group of experts in *Interpretation: Medieval and Modern*. Thus I shall impose no further than I have already imposed in suggesting the outlines of my own interpretation. It is probably safer to end, instead, with a certain gesture of hermeneutical whimsy. Everyone knows that the narrator of the *Troilus* is more than a little like Pandarus; but he is also more than a little like Troilus himself. Both the diffident narrator and his frequently supine hero seek self-exculpation on the grounds of powerful duress – textual fidelity on the part of the narrator, fatal necessity on that of the lover. It is of some historical interest perhaps that Boethius, who was the first medieval author to confess the crime of the former, was also the most authoritative refuter of the latter. May we call this the hermeneutical circle?

Index